C000027354

The Which? Book of
HOME
MAINTENANCE

The Which? Book of
HOME MAINTENANCE

John Reynolds

Published by
Consumers' Association
and Hodder & Stoughton

Which? Books are commissioned and researched by
The Association for Consumer Research
and published by Consumers' Association,
2 Marylebone Road, London NW1 4DX, and
Hodder & Stoughton, 47 Bedford Square, London WC1B 3DP

Cover artwork and text illustrations by Peter Harper
Cover design by Philip Mann (ACE Ltd)
Typographic design by Dick Vine

Acknowledgements to Sara Checkley and Paul Gurowich

First edition March 1991

Copyright © 1991 Consumers' Association

British Library Cataloguing in Publication Data
   Reynolds, John
      The Which? book of home maintenance
      1. Residences. Maintenance
      I. Title
      643.7

ISBN 0 340 52799 4

No part of this publication may be reproduced or transmitted
in any form or by any means, electronically or mechanically,
including photocopying, recording or any information storage
or retrieval system, without prior permission in writing
from the publisher. The publication is not included under
licences issued by the Copyright Agency.

Photoset by Tradespools Ltd., Frome, Somerset
Printed and bound in Great Britain by Bath Press,
Lower Bristol Road, Bath

Contents

Introduction

Houses don't look after themselves. Maintenance is essential to keep our homes in good condition and thereby preserve their value and ensure that they're comfortable to live in.

A substantial part of home maintenance can be planned: there's little doubt that external paintwork will need to be renewed every two or three years, for example, or that gutters will benefit from an annual clear-out. Where planning is a practical proposition, it's almost always worthwhile because it avoids more costly and time-consuming repair work in the long run. Planned maintenance includes jobs which need to be done every year (clearing the gutters, flushing the drains, servicing the boiler and so on), jobs which need doing every three years or so (painting, for example), and jobs which roll around on a longer-term cycle (such as having your wiring inspected).

Not all home maintenance can be planned, though. There's no point in digging up the drains every few years to check whether they're in good condition, for instance, or in heaving up floorboards just to inspect the joists. For things like these, a running repair approach is more appropriate. Nevertheless, it's a good idea to inspect your home at least once a year to try to spot the early signs of potential trouble and deal with them before problems turn into disasters.

This book covers a wide range of topics involving both routine preventive maintenance and running repairs. It assumes neither that you're an avowed d-i-yer nor that you will choose to entrust maintenance or repair work to a professional; whatever your preference it will be useful to know what's involved so you can compare alternative courses of action, have a clear idea of what you're being asked to pay for, and assess whether the work has been done satisfactorily.

Part One deals with maintaining the fabric of the house: the walls, roof, doors, windows, floors, ceilings, stairs, fences, garden walls, gates and paintwork. Part Two deals with household services: electricity, plumbing, central heating, gas, rainwater removal and drains. Part Three is intended to help you preserve your assets; it deals with your legal rights and responsibilities as a householder and evaluates common home improvements you might be considering, including information on funding and permission.

Hire a professional or do-it-yourself?

Whether you choose to hire a professional or tackle home maintenance and repair yourself depends on a number of factors:

- the nature and extent of the task in hand
- the cost
- your competence as a d-i-yer
- the time and degree of committment you can devote to it

In some aspects of home maintenance there are legal restraints which also have a bearing on whether or not to d-i-y.

The Building Regulations

The Building Regulations set out the principles to which all new buildings must conform. They also apply to significant additions and extensions to existing buildings. They have the full force of law, and all new building work must be approved under the Building Regulations and inspected at intervals during construction.

There are separate Building Regulations for Inner London, the rest of England and Wales, Scotland and Northern Ireland, although in many respects they are similar.

Repairs to houses constructed in accord with the Building Regulations must maintain at least the original standards. But there is no requirement for repairs to meet current standards, only those which were in force when the house was built.

The Gas Safety Regulations

The Gas Safety (Installation and Use) Regulations are also legally binding, and make it illegal for anyone who is 'not competent' to carry out any work on gas installations or fittings. In practice, this means that all work on gas supplies and appliances should be entrusted to professional gas fitters – see Using Professionals.

The potential hazards of gas in the home should not be underestimated. Although many of the techniques and fittings used with gas are similar

A home maintenance schedule

The spring offensive

Spring is an important time for home maintenance. It's a time to see how well the house has survived the winter months, and to plan jobs which you need to do over the summer.

Walls
- inside and out, look for signs of damp, cracks, crumbling masonry and plaster
- make sure airbricks are clear

Roofs
- outside, use binoculars to check for loose and missing slates or tiles
- inside, check for damp, rot and woodworm
- check flat roofs for bulges and puddles
- check flashings and chimneys

Doors and windows
- outside: look for flaking or blistering paint; check for rot
- inside and out: check for sticking doors and windows, warps and twists, broken sash cords, broken glazing

Floors, ceilings and stairs
- check for damp, rot and woodworm
- look for uneven, springy or creaking floorboards
- look for sagging or discoloured ceilings
- check stairs for creaks and groans and for broken handrails and balusters

Fences, outside walls and gates
- check fences for rot, wind damage and fixings which have broken or rusted away
- check chain link fences for damage and for slackness in the supporting wires
- check walls for frost damage and for bulges and cracks
- check gates for rot or damage; make sure hinges and catches work efficiently

Electricity
- ask yourself when your wiring was last checked
- look for damaged, discoloured or over-heating fittings
- brittle or crumbling insulation on wiring

Plumbing
- clear debris around the outside stopcock
- give all stopcocks and valves a few turns to make sure that they move freely
- look for dripping taps
- check for jammed or noisy ballvalves and dripping overflows
- flush through sinks and wastepipes with hot water and washing soda
- check supply and waste pipes for leaks

Heating
- arrange to have the boiler and other appliances serviced
- if you have solid fuel fires or appliances, arrange to have the chimneys swept

Gutters and downpipes
- check for cracks and leaky joints
- check iron gutters and downpipes for rust

Drains
- remove any debris which might block drains
- check masonry inside inspection chambers
- check inspection covers for rust
- check water runs efficiently through drains

to those for plumbing, you would be very unwise to embark on d-i-y gas work.

The Wiring Regulations

Electrical installations in all types of buildings, including private homes, are covered by the IEE Regulations for Electrical Installations – the Wiring Regulations, for short. These have the force of law only in Scotland, where they are incorporated in the Building Regulations. Elsewhere in the UK there are no legal restrictions on anyone carrying out his or her own electrical repairs and alterations.

Nevertheless, you should not embark on repairs to household electrics unless you fully understand what's involved and are familiar

The summer season

Your spring inspection should generate a list of jobs which need to be done before the next winter. Most external maintenance jobs and repairs are a good deal easier to carry out in summer.

For painting, choose a time when the weather's been warm and dry for a while, if you can: the lower the moisture content of the wood, the better the result you'll get.

The Autumn review

Walls	• check that the damp-proof course is clear all round the house – soil piled against the wall can 'bridge' the dpc and cause rising damp. • check that airbricks are clear
Roofs	• outside: check for loose or missing slates or tiles • inside: check loft insulation and lagging on pipes; ensure sufficient ventilation in roof space
Fences	• check for wind damage
Heating	• check fittings for leaks

- check that ballvalve in feed and expansion cistern is working properly
- check radiators for cold spots which indicate trapped air
- check that thermostats are working and set correctly
- for warm air systems, clean the filters

Gutters and downpipes
- rake out debris and silt from gutters
- check for cracks and leaky joints
- check brackets supporting gutters and downpipes

---

with the relevant parts of the Wiring Regulations. Electricity can be very dangerous. If there's any doubt, call in a professional electrician – see Using Professionals, below.

If you need to consult any of these regulations, copies should be available in the reference sections of major public libraries. The regulations themselves aren't designed for 'lay' readers and can be difficult to follow, so it's worth asking the library whether they also have any explanatory notes or manuals.

In matters of interpretation of the Building Regulations, you should always ask your local authority Department of Planning and Building Control for advice.

Using professionals

Finding the right professional help can be difficult. Professional associations can go some way to ensuring that the people you are dealing with are properly qualified, and providing a means for settling disputes if the need should arise.

Builders

Choosing the right builder is notoriously difficult. There are two builders' trade associations who offer guarantee schemes for their members' work. Builders who are members of the Building Employers' Confederation (BEC) can take advantage of the BEC Building Trust guarantee scheme, which guards against structural defects and the builder going out of business. The Federation of Master Builders also offers a warrantee scheme for selected members who are on their register of 'warranted' builders. In either case, you have to pay an additional premium on top of the contract price, though.

Otherwise, ask friends and neighbours whether they know of builders who they would recommend. Ask prospective builders for examples of their work, and go to see them before you commit yourself.

Electricians

Qualified electricians will be members of the Electrical Contractors' As-

sociation (ECA) or on the roll of the National Inspection Council for Electrical Installation Contracting (NICEIC). All the electricity companies are on the NICEIC roll.

The ECA (and the ECA of Scotland) have a contract completion guarantee scheme and will advise on on the design and layout of household wiring, but they won't get involved in disputes over prices.

NICEIC contractors must issue a completion certificate for every job, confirming that the work has been done in accordance with the appropriate regulations. NICEIC will investigate complaints about approved contractors' work, and in some circumstances will arrange for another contractor to make good work which is incomplete or not up to scratch.

Plumbers

Horror stories of 'cowboy' plumbers are commonplace. The best way to avoid being a victim yourself is to look after your plumbing, taking care to inspect it regularly, and putting faults right before disasters can develop.

The Institute of Plumbing is a professional association (registered as a charity) rather than a trade association. It keeps a register of plumbers which is monitored by the British Standards Institution. They publish an annual Business Directory of Registered Plumbers which you should be able to find in the reference section of major public libraries.

The Institution offers no formal guarantee scheme, and cannot mediate in disputes over the cost of work or the time taken.

Roofing contractors

Prospective members of the The National Federation of Roofing Contractors have to satisfy the Federation's standards before being allowed to join. These include a responsible trading record over at least two years, and inspections of their work and premises.

They offer an insurance-backed guarantee scheme covering defects in their members' work for ten years, though you have to specify that you want this insurance at the outset and there is a premium to pay.

Central heating contractors

Members of the Heating and Ventilating Contractors' Association (HVCA) are obliged to offer the association's one year guarantee on all new central heating installations. For repair and maintenance work, the HVCA has a code of practice, a copy of which should be provided by HVCA members with their quotations.

Glazing contractors

The Glass and Glazing Federation (GGF) has drawn up a code of practice, in consultation with the Office of Fair Trading, which all its members are expected to stick to. The GGF has a scheme to protect your deposit if a glazing firm goes bust before they finish the job, and offer an arbi-

tration procedure to deal with disputes between member firms and their customers.

Surveyors

For serious problems with buildings you may need the advice of a chartered surveyor – someone with ARICS or FRICS after his or her name, showing that they are a member of the Royal Institution of Chartered Surveyors (RICS). However, the term surveyor covers a wide range of professional skills from auctioneering through estate management to technical and legal aspects of buildings. It's likely that you'll want a surveyor in the RICS Building Surveyors Division.

The RICS has an information centre which can put you in touch with a number of appropriate surveyors in your area – see Useful Addresses, p. 136.

Structural engineers

Structural engineers specialise in particular aspects of buildings, including foundations. If you suspect that your foundations have failed, or a wall is buckling or bulging, a member of the Institution of Structural Engineers would probably be the best choice to consult. They can put the letters C.Eng.MIStructE or C.Eng.FIStructE after their names.

Maintenance contracts

For fittings and appliances which need to be serviced regularly by qualified professionals, you may be tempted to take out a long-term maintenance contract. *Which?* has found that on average you'd be better off paying for repairs as you go along: the cost of maintenance contracts can be ten times the cost of the repairs likely to be needed during the contract period.

If you decide that a maintenance contract or service agreement would be worthwhile for peace of mind, however, it pays to shop around. Ask neighbours and friends with similar appliances what arrangements they

use, and whether they're happy with them. Check the small print of any contract before you sign it, to be sure you know what's included in the basic service charge. Does it cover the cost of spare parts, for example, and the labour costs for fitting them? And make sure you know whether you'll be charged if you have to call out the engineer for an unscheduled emergency visit.

For oil and solid fuel boilers, you may be offered an agreement combining servicing of the boiler and arrangements for supplying the fuel. Always compare these carefully with separate service and supply arrangements. With heating oil in particular, the cost can swing sharply up or down over short time spans, and it may not be in your interests to be tied to a particular supplier. When you need oil, it doesn't take long to contact several local suppliers to find the best price.

Extended guarantees

Extended guarantees are now widely available on all sorts of domestic appliances, typically covering the first three to five years of use. Like maintenance contracts, *Which?* has found that extended guarantees are likely to cost you more on average than paying for repairs if and when they're needed.

If you're offered an extended guarantee by the retailer of a new appliance, check whether you might also be able to get one from the manufacturer. Manufacturers' guarantees are often on more favourable terms.

A house log book

To keep track of maintenance and repairs to your home, a log book can be very helpful. The most convenient format is a loose-leaf folder of A4 or foolscap size, so you can file away manufacturer's brochures and the instructions supplied with appliances, along with your own notes.

Divide the book into sections for structural repairs, painting and decorating, electrics, plumbing and so on. Keep notes not only of the dates when work was carried out, but of where you bought the materials and how much they cost. For painting and decorating in particular, being sure of how much paint or wallpaper you needed last time can save you making calculations afresh, and will prevent you buying too much or too little.

The scope of the notes you make in the book is up to you, of course, but a typical log book entry might include the following:

- date
- a brief description of the work
- the names and addresses of any professionals or tradesmen who were involved
- a list of materials
- where you bought them and how much they cost
- the tools required, including any which were hired
- difficulties which arose during the work, and how you overcame them
- any other information which would be useful when doing the same job again, or a similar job elsewhere.

Tools and materials

A home maintenance tool kit

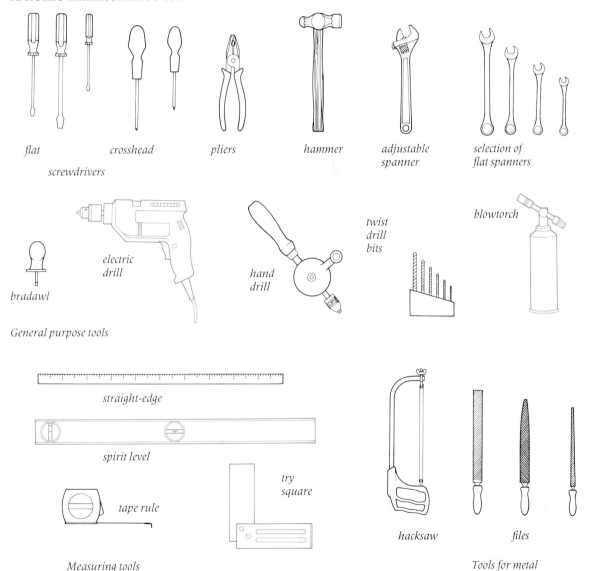

flat   crosshead   pliers   hammer   adjustable spanner   selection of flat spanners

screwdrivers

bradawl   electric drill   hand drill   twist drill bits   blowtorch

General purpose tools

straight-edge

spirit level

tape rule   try square

Measuring tools

hacksaw   files

Tools for metal

11

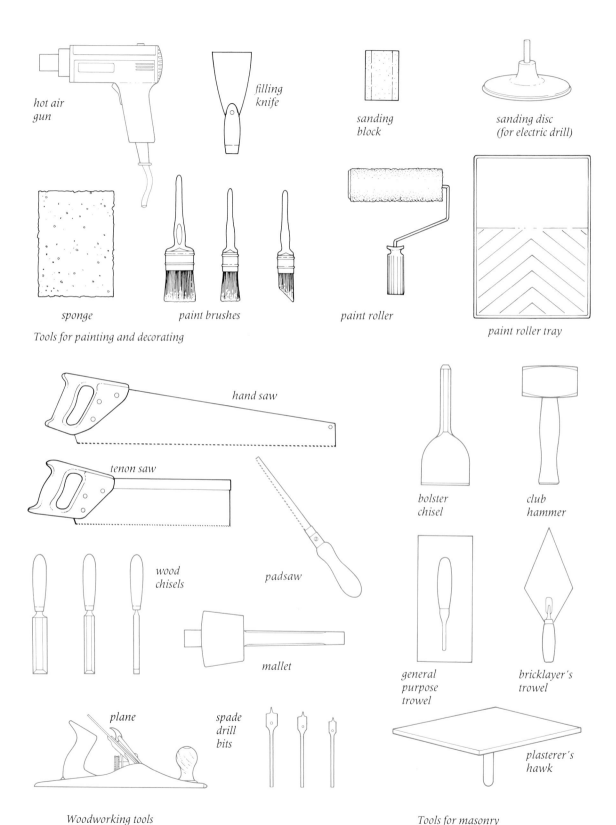

hot air
gun

filling
knife

sanding
block

sanding disc
(for electric drill)

sponge

paint brushes

paint roller

paint roller tray

Tools for painting and decorating

hand saw

tenon saw

padsaw

bolster
chisel

club
hammer

wood
chisels

mallet

general
purpose
trowel

bricklayer's
trowel

plane

spade
drill
bits

plasterer's
hawk

Woodworking tools

Tools for masonry

goggles

gloves

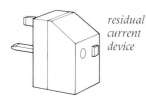

*residual
current
device*

Safety equipment

ear defenders

The tools shown in black form a basic home maintenance tool kit. This doesn't mean you must have them all before you begin, but rather that they are worth buying when you first need them. Tools shown in colour are ones you will need less often, which you might prefer to borrow or hire. Other tools for very specialised tasks, such as a frenchman or a slate ripper, are described and illustrated where relevant throughout the book.

Hiring special purpose tools

A large selection of tools and equipment for home maintenance and repair can be hired. For tool hire in your area, look in Yellow Pages under Hire Services – Tools and Equipment.

Hire charges are usually on a steep sliding scale, so that hiring for a day can cost almost as much as hiring for a week. If you can get the job done quickly, you can sometimes save a little by returning the equipment in less than a day: within four or eight

---

Tools and equipment you can hire

Access	• platforms, to enable you to work more safely above ground • ladders, including roofing ladders, and ladder accessories such as stand-offs • trestles and scaffold boards
Breakers and drills	• demolition hammers, for breaking up masonry • hammer drills, for drilling holes in masonry
Building	• concrete mixers • compactors, for tamping downs paths and foundations • ceiling props, to support the structure of the house while building work is in progress • stone cutters, for paving slabs and facings • wheelbarrows • building dryers
Cleaning	• carpet cleaners • floor polishers • vacuum cleaners • chimney sweep's brush set • pressure washers (high pressure water jet)
Decorating	• steam strippers for removing wallpaper • hot air guns for stripping paint • tile cutters • rough applicators, for applying render to masonry • paint spray guns and compressors
Plumbing	• pipe freezing kits, to isolate a length of pipe during plumbing work • copper tube benders • tap re-seating kits, to cure dripping taps • drain rods, to clear blockages • pressure drain cleaners, similar to pressure washers above • copper tube soldering pliers, for heating capillary-type plumbing joints
Sanders, planes and routers	• belt sanders, power planes and routers – for woodwork • angle grinders, for smoothing and cutting masonry and metal
Saws	• chainsaws • circular saws • jigsaws

hours, for example. To minimise the hire charges, plan the work in advance to ensure that everything else you'll need will be ready for use as soon as the equipment arrives.

Where to buy materials

Most of the big d-i-y superstores stock good selections of decorating materials, tools, electrical and plumbing fittings, and more limited ranges of building materials. When they have what you need, they're usually cheaper than specialist suppliers, though it always pays to check. The disadvantage with large items is that you usually have to transport them yourself or pay for delivery.

For bulky and awkward items – plasterboard, for example – builders' merchants may be a better source of supply because they will generally deliver free within the local area.

You'll need to go to specialist builders' and plumbers' merchants anyway for items which aren't 'run of the mill'. Specialist suppliers can also be useful sources of advice. They're listed in Yellow Pages.

Don't be afraid to go to wholesale or trade suppliers if necessary: they're usually happy to make cash sales, but bear in mind that they're unlikely to be open at weekends.

Part One
THE FABRIC OF THE HOUSE

1 Walls

The walls of our homes have a lot to do. They must keep the weather out, the heat in, hold up the roof and the floors, and allow space for doors and windows.

The walls of most houses are constructed from masonry, usually bricks or blocks, either solid or as a cavity wall with two 'leaves' and a gap between them. In timber-framed homes, the main wall structure is of wood, though there may be a 'skin' of masonry on the outside.

The walls of all but the oldest houses should incorporate a horizontal barrier called a damp-proof course to prevent moisture seeping up the wall from the foundations.

Inspecting walls

Once a year, make a methodical inspection of your walls, outside and in.

Outside the house, look for:
- loose or flaking masonry, particularly the pointing between courses of bricks
- fresh cracks, or any changes in older cracks
- cracked or crumbly exterior render
- 'bridging' of the DPC by soil piled up against the walls or by ground levels which have been raised when paths or patios have been constructed
- blocked airbricks – poke them out with a screwdriver or a wire coathanger.

Inside the house, look for:
- any signs of rising or penetrating damp
- damage or discoloration of interior decorations caused by condensation
- loose or flaky plaster.

How walls are built

Cavity walls

Modern homes – those built in the last 50 years or so – have cavity walls. This means that all the outer walls of the house consist of two layers, or 'leaves', with a gap or cavity of at least 50mm between them. The cavity prevents water soaking through from the outside and helps to insulate the house. The outer leaf is usually of brickwork; the inner leaf is more likely to be built from blocks. The two leaves are connected by wall ties: pieces of steel embedded in the mortar between the bricks or blocks as the wall is built, which prevent the two leaves from bulging or bowing away from each other. Except where they meet at the foundations, and around doors and windows, the two leaves of a normal cavity wall are independent of one another. The inner leaf normally does the work of supporting the roof and intermediate floors.

A variation on the standard cavity wall is timber-framed construction. In this, the inner leaf is replaced by a load-bearing timber framework.

When designed and constructed properly, timber-framed buildings can be strong and durable, and this method of construction readily

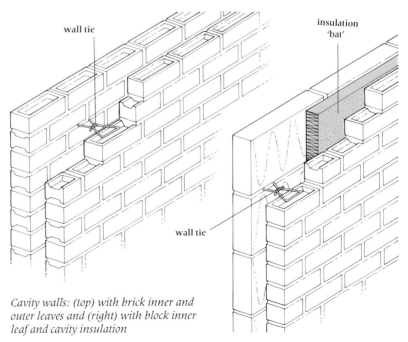

Cavity walls: (top) with brick inner and outer leaves and (right) with block inner leaf and cavity insulation

Walls – symptoms, faults and remedies

Symptom	Fault	Remedy	*see page*
Rising damp	• DPC bridged • DPC failed • No DPC	• Eliminate bridge • Repair or replace • Have a DPC installed	20
Penetrating damp	• Blocked or leaking gutters • Dripping window sills • Loose or crumbling pointing • Cracked or missing render	• Clean and repair – see Chapter 11 • Clean out drip channel on underside of sill • Repoint brickwork • Repair or replace render	111 22 22
Condensation	• Cold spots on inside walls	• Improve ventilation	21
Damp cellar or basement	• Inadequate damp-proofing	• Dry-line walls with plasterboard or polyethylene lathing	24
Cracked plaster	• Wear and tear	• Repair or replace	25
Serious cracks in masonry	• Settlement • Subsidence • Heave	• Get professional advice	27

allows for a high standard of insulation. The outer skin may be a cladding of timber, tiles or lightweight render, or it can be a heavier construction of bricks or blocks standing on its own foundations. If the outer wall is built from brick, the external appearance is identical to a conventionally constructed house.

Bricks and brickwork

Most bricks are made from clay, though calcium silicate and concrete are also used. Bricks come in a wide variety of types, differentiated by colour, texture, weather-resistance and load-bearing capability. All bricks are porous; engineering bricks are less water-absorbent than most, and less likely to be damaged by frost, and are used in conditions that demand these qualities – house foundations, for instance.

The normal size of brick is 215 by 102.5 by 65mm, which has replaced the traditional size of 9 by 4$\frac{1}{2}$ by 3in, while allowing new bricks to bond with older ones in most applications. Bricks may have a 'frog' – a v-shaped indentation in the top – or a series of holes, depending on how they're made.

Bricks are laid in courses on beds of mortar – a mixture of sand and cement. The courses are arranged so that vertical joints between the bricks are staggered. The way the bricks are arranged is called the bonding pattern, and can help you determine, if there's any doubt,

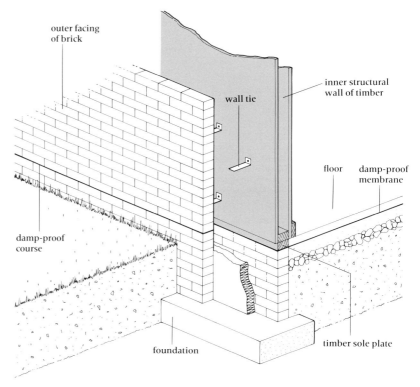

Timber-framed construction with brick outer skin

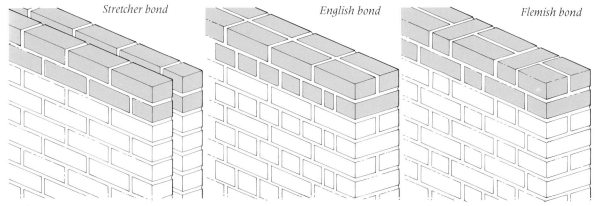

Stretcher bond *English bond* *Flemish bond*

Methods of bonding for cavity and solid walls.

Below: styles of pointing

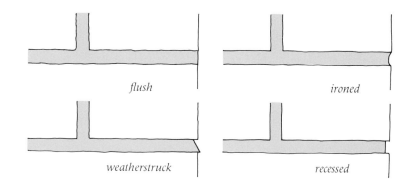

flush *ironed*

weatherstruck *recessed*

whether your house has cavity or solid walls – bricks seen end-on indicate a solid wall.

The spaces between courses of bricks must be completely filled with mortar and neatly finished to encourage water to run off the wall. Pointing, as this is called, can take several forms, and is very important to a wall's weather-resistance.

Flush pointing is produced by rubbing the 'green' mortar – mortar before it's fully set – with a piece of wood or sacking, leaving it level with the surface of the bricks.

Weather-struck pointing is formed with a trowel held at an angle. This is the most weather-resistant method of pointing.

Tooled or **ironed pointing** is produced by running a suitable tool – an old bucket handle or a piece of hose, say – along the mortar to give a concave finish.

Recessed pointing is produced by raking out the green mortar with a steel or hardwood tool. It is rarely suitable for external walls.

Foundations and damp-proof courses

Masonry walls are heavy in themselves, and also have to bear the weight of the rest of the house. They must therefore rest on secure foundations. The depth and width required for foundations varies around the country, since it depends on the type of soil and the local water

table. The main principles are that the depth should be such that the moisture content of the soil under the foundations will be constant and unaffected by frost, and that the width should be sufficient to support the weight without subsiding. For most purposes a depth of 1m and a

width of $1^1/_2$ to 2 times the thickness of the wall will be adequate.

To prevent moisture from the ground rising up the walls of the house by capillary action, the walls should incorporate a damp-proof course (DPC) just above ground-level. The provision of a DPC in new

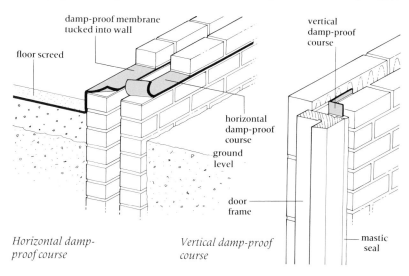

damp-proof membrane tucked into wall

floor screed

horizontal damp-proof course

ground level

door frame

vertical damp-proof course

mastic seal

Horizontal damp-proof course

Vertical damp-proof course

homes has been compulsory for over 100 years. Modern homes with solid concrete floors also must include a damp-proof membrane (DPM) under the ground floor.

Where the inner and outer leaves of the wall come together around door and window openings, there should be vertical DPCs to prevent moisture seeping through to the inside.

Wall finishes

External brick walls normally need no additional protection. But brick walls which are exposed to very severe weather, or walls built of blocks, will need a weather-resistant external finish.

Claddings can be of timber, or plastic designed to look like timber but requiring less maintenance. Cladding usually takes the form of tongued and grooved planks which can be applied vertically or horizontally.

Tiles of clay, concrete or asbestos cement may be hung on horizontal battens fixed to the wall.

Traditional **render** is a mixture of sand and cement applied direct to the masonry. It has good weather-resistance but needs to be applied with care and skill. Modern lightweight renders are also available and are usually applied to mesh fixed to the walls.

Interior walls are usually finished with plaster. This may be applied direct to the masonry, or over an intermediate layer of sand/cement mixture, or as plasterboard.

Cavity-wall insulation

A good deal of the energy we use to heat our homes is lost through the walls. Although cavity walls allow less heat to escape than do solid walls, extra insulation within the cavity is almost certain to be cost-effective. The Building Regulations in most of England, Wales and Scotland have required conventional brick/block cavity walls to include extra insulation since 1982.

Cavity-wall insulation incorporated in new buildings generally takes the form of a mineral fibre blanket or sheets of expanded polystyrene. Insulation can also be installed in existing walls by drilling holes in the outer skin, pumping in the insulation material and making good the holes. Three types of material are used for this:

- polystyrene beads or granules,
- blown mineral fibre, or
- ureaformaldehyde (UF) foam.

Maintaining outside walls

There's not a lot of scope for routine preventive maintenance of masonry walls beyond keeping painted and rendered surfaces in sound condition, ensuring that the DPC is not bridged and that airbricks are kept clear. In the longer term, pointing must be maintained in good condition and renewed when necessary.

The most common problems with walls are concerned with damp: penetrating damp, rising damp and condensation. All require urgent treatment because they can suggest or lead to structural problems. Although the evidence is on the inside of the house, the root of the problem is more often than not on the outside.

More serious structural problems with walls, when bulges or cracks appear, betraying subsidence or heave, are mercifully less frequent.

Dealing with damp

Walls are not impermeable barriers to moisture. Most building materials are porous to some degree, which allows houses to 'breathe'. But problems arise when the degree of moisture inside the house is excessive, and the house then suffers from persistent damp.

Rising damp

The tell-tale sign of rising damp is moisture creeping up the interior walls from behind the skirting boards. It tends to leave a 'tide-mark' about 60 to 90cm above floor-level, and the degree of damp will usually vary with the seasons.

Rising damp is almost always caused by inadequacies in the damp-proof course. Either the house does not have a DPC, or it has become ineffective with age, or it has been bridged so that moisture from the ground can bypass it.

Older DPCs may be made of slate, lead or copper. Over the years they can crumble or embrittle and become less effective. More modern DPCs are generally made of bituminised felt or plastic. It is possible to remove an old DPC by sawing it out with a tungsten-carbide-tipped chainsaw (a job best entrusted to professionals). Only a short length is taken out at a time to prevent the wall collapsing under its own weight. A new DPC is installed in the gap, which is closed with mortar.

As an alternative to a physical DPC, there are chemical treatments available. The most common of these is to inject the walls with a silicone-based liquid which is intended to soak into the masonry and form an impermeable barrier to moisture. Other techniques include electro-osmosis, where the rising damp is repelled by earthing electrical charges in the wall, and the insertion of porous clay pipes in the wall to carry away excess moisture, although the effectiveness of these two methods is open to question.

In newer houses the cause of rising damp is more likely to be that the DPC has been bridged, so that water can bypass the DPC. Bridging can occur when earth is piled up against an exterior wall, or when paths and patios raise the ground-level, or when rendering on the outside or plaster on the inside are carried down too far.

On the outside, there should be a clear minimum of 150mm between ground-level and the DPC. It's worth checking this regularly. You may be able to see the edge of the DPC or be

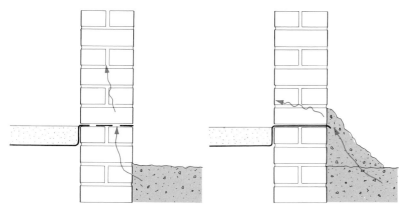

DPC faulty or deteriorating with age

DPC bridged by soil piled up on the outside

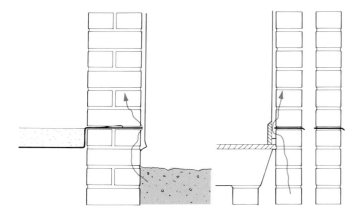

DPC bridged by external render carried down too far

DPC bridged by internal plaster carried down too far

able to recognise it as a thicker layer of mortar between courses of bricks. Make sure that any air bricks are clear at the same time. External rendering should stop above the DPC, and the same is true of internal plastering: the gap between the plaster and the floor is concealed by the skirting board.

Penetrating damp

Penetrating damp is moisture which gets through from the outside of the wall to the inside. There's a wide variety of possible causes, and it can sometimes be difficult to distinguish penetrating from rising damp and from condensation.

The signs of penetrating damp are

that it is restricted to a particular area, and that it is more severe when the weather is wet; it may disappear altogether during dry spells.

The first place to look for the cause of penetrating damp on the inside is the corresponding area of wall on the outside. Look for:

- leaking or blocked gutters or downpipes which allow water to cascade down the brickwork
- windowsills where the drip channel beneath the sill has been blocked with paint and become ineffective
- gaps around door and window frames
- loose, cracked or missing roof

slates or tiles, and leaking flashings and valleys
- crumbling mortar in the pointing between bricks
- cracks or crumbly patches in render.

Some of these problems are dealt with in other chapters: see Roofs, p. 29, and Doors and Windows, p. 37. Penetrating damp may also be caused by leaking water pipes: see Plumbing, p.82.

Condensation

Condensation is caused by the temperature of part of the inside of the house being markedly lower than the general air temperature. Then some of the water vapour in the air – the inevitable result of cooking, washing and simply breathing – condenses on the cold surface. Condensation often gives rise to the growth of unsightly mould.

Condensation tends to be more of a problem in winter, when there's the greatest contrast between inside and outside temperatures, and in steamy rooms like kitchens and bathrooms. The cure lies in improved heating and ventilation. Increasing the temperature by just a degree or two can sometimes eliminate the problem. Try to avoid putting furniture against cold walls, and ensure that cupboards are well ventilated.

Over-zealous draughtproofing around windows and doors tend to make matters worse, so fit ventilation you can control, such as extractor fans and trickle ventilators in the tops of window frames.

Drying out

If you've had a problem with damp, or a serious leak – from a washing machine, for example – you may need to dry out the house once the cause of the damp has been eliminated. Often this means nothing more than turning up the heating a bit, but for more serious problems you can buy or hire a de-humidifier.

Repointing brickwork

1. Rake out the old mortar

2. Dampen the brickwork

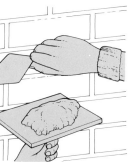

3. Press the mortar into the joints with a small trowel

4. For an 'ironed' finish, use a piece of metal or hose

5. Brush off any loose mortar

Repointing brickwork

Unless only a small area of wall near ground-level needs attention, you would be well advised to use a scaffold tower for repointing brickwork. Working on a ladder doesn't give you the freedom to use both hands which you'll need.

Work on about 1 sq m at a time, progressing from top to bottom and left to right if you're right-handed, right to left if you're left-handed. Rake out the old mortar to a depth of 10 to 20mm with a plugging chisel and brush away the debris carefully. If the brickwork is dry, dampen (but don't drench) the surface with a broad brush dipped in water.

You can buy ready-mixed mortar or make your own. For old brickwork a suitable mixture is 1:1:6 of cement, lime and sand. With newer walls a mixture of 1:3 cement and sand will probably be more suitable. You can get coloured cements to help you match the existing mortar. Add the water slowly: the mixture should be just wet enough to be worked. You'll need a hawk to carry the mortar to the wall (a piece of plywood or chipboard with a simple handle will suffice) and a 'dotter' or pointing trowel. For weather-struck joints, you'll also need a 'frenchman' (an old kitchen knife or a strip of thin metal with the end bent over at right angles) and a straight-edge.

Press the mortar into the joints – vertical joints first, then horizontal – using the trowel. Remove surplus mortar by drawing the trowel across the surface at right-angles. Finish the joints to match those elsewhere on the house, using the trowel and 'frenchman' to produce weather-struck joints or a suitable piece of wood or metal for other types of joint. Take care not to smear mortar on to the face of the wall.

Finally, brush the surface gently to remove any surplus mortar. Stubborn patches can be removed by rubbing with a piece of brick.

Rendering

Rendering is a traditional way to waterproof an exterior wall. Render is a mixture of sand and cement which is applied direct to the masonry. To keep it in good condition, inspect it regularly – at least once a year – and deal without delay with any cracks that appear. If water gets behind it, the render will soon come away from the wall. To check for this, tap the area around – and especially below – the crack. If it sounds hollow, then you may have to remove and patch the affected area of render.

Ideally, cracks should be filled with the same material as the original render. This is usually 1:4 cement and sand. For small cracks, however, filling with a proprietary exterior filler is better than not filling at all. Remove any loose material, then press the filler firmly into the crack and smooth off flush with the original surface.

To patch render, start by removing *all* the suspect old material. This may simply pull away from the wall, or have to be chipped away with a hammer and chisel. Brush away debris and wet the exposed masonry and the edges of the original render. Apply the patching render using a steel float or general-purpose trowel, starting at the bottom and pressing it on to the wall with an upward

Forming weatherstruck joints

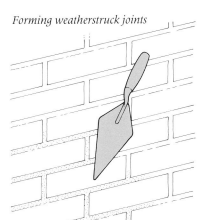

1. Press in mortar: level off using trowel at right angles to wall

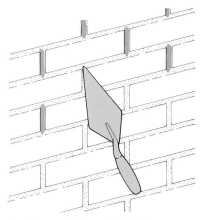

2. Form vertical angled joints

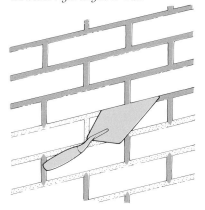

3. Form horizontal joints

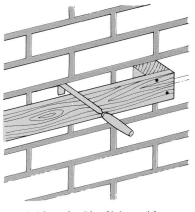

4. Finish underside of joints with frenchman and straight-edge

Patching mortar

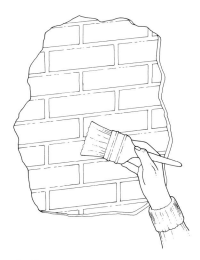

1. Dampen brickwork

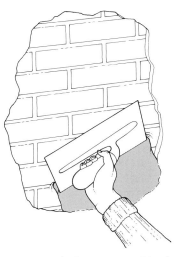

2. Press on fresh mortar, working from bottom to top

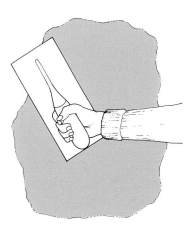

3. Smooth off and level to finish

motion. Smooth the surface level with the original render. If the rendering needs to be more than about 15mm thick, it should be applied in two or more coats. Score the undercoats before they've cured to provide a key for the next coat.

To match an existing pebble-dash finish, put plastic sheet or sacking under the wall to catch the excess, then fling pebbles on to the wet render with a small shovel. Gently press the pebbles in with the float.

Leave new rendering for at least a week before painting over it.

Maintaining inside walls

As with outside walls, the main problems with inside walls are associated with damp. If the cause can be identified and dealt with, then you can remove and replace any damaged plaster and renew interior decorations which have been damaged or stained. But sometimes – in basements and cellars, for example – there's little opportunity to deal with the problem at source. Then, the treatment, known as dry-lining, has to be applied to the inside walls.

Before embarking on dry-lining, however, you should seek professional guidance. Dry-lining does

Dry-lining with plasterboard

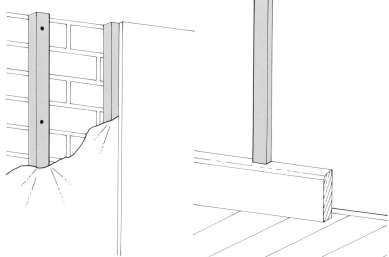

1. Fix battens to the walls using non-rusting nails

2. Fix the plasterboard to the battens, with a layer of polyethylene between

3. Hide the joints with strips of wood

little more than conceal damp, and you need to be assured that you are not risking serious structural damage by not dealing with the problem at source.

Dry-lining interior walls
Plasterboard
This method creates a new interior wall surface which is separated from the original, damp walls, leaving a gap for ventilation.

Start by giving the original walls a thorough treatment with fungicide. Then fix vertical wooden battens, treated with a wood preservative and at least 20mm thick, to the walls. Use masonry nails or stainless steel screws. Then nail plasterboard to the battens, using galvanised plasterboard nails, leaving gaps at the top and bottom for ventilation. The plasterboard must be of the vapour-check type, with a layer of foil or plastic on the back; alternatively polythene sheeting can be stapled to the battens before the plasterboard is installed. Fill the joints between the boards and the depressions around the nail heads, or use wooden fillets to conceal them, and fit skirting boards at the bottom and coving at the top to cover the ventilation gaps.

Polyethylene lathing
This method involves fixing waterproof sheets of ribbed or dimpled polyethylene to the original damp wall, and plastering over. The ribs or dimples allow for ventilation between the original wall and the polyethylene sheet. On the side facing into the room, the lathing may have

mesh to act as a key for the plaster.

Fix the polyethylene lathing to the original wall. Special plastic plugs are available for this. The lathing must be secure, since it has to carry the weight of the new plaster: place the fixings not more than 300mm apart both vertically and horizontally. Overlap sheets of lathing by at least

Attach to the wall with special fixings

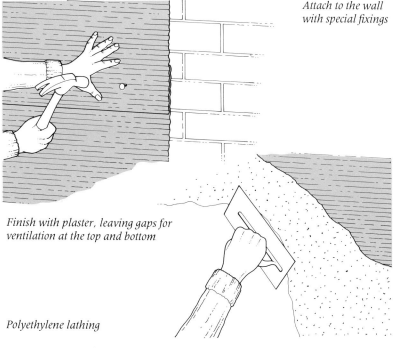

Finish with plaster, leaving gaps for ventilation at the top and bottom

Polyethylene lathing

Types of plaster

		maximum thickness
Thistle browning	Traditional, non-lightweight gypsum undercoat plaster – may be mixed with sharp sand (1:3) for use on brickwork	10mm
Thistle finish	Finishing coat for use on Thistle browning or sand/cement	3mm
Thistle board finish	Thistle finish specially formulated for use on plasterboard	5mm
Carlite browning	Lightweight gypsum-based plaster	10mm
Carlite finish	Finishing plaster for use on Carlite browning	3mm
Sirapite finish	Non-lightweight plaster for use on sand/cement undercoats and for repairs. Sets in two stages, but slowly, so very smooth finish possible	3mm
One-coat general purpose	D-i-y repair plaster	50mm

100mm. Where the lathing meets window and door frames, or has to be cut around pipes, seal the gaps with mastic.

Finally, finish the new 'wall' with plaster, leaving gaps at top and bottom for ventilation, and conceal the gaps with skirting boards and coving.

Plaster

Plaster is a very durable finish as long as it remains dry. Water softens it, but it hardens again when it dries out, so occasional spills should cause no permanent damage. But plaster will need attention from time to time as a result of everyday knocks, electrical or plumbing work, or the effects of persistent damp.

The principal constituent of plaster for interior use is gypsum. It's a dense material, and has acquired a reputation for being hard to handle. Unless the surface to be plastered is prepared adequately, the mixture is correctly made up and your plastering technique is up to scratch, the plaster is likely to fall off the wall as you try to apply it. Lightweight plasters, which include aggregates like perlite or vermiculite, are easier to apply, however. Repairs to plaster

are well within the scope of a competent d-i-yer.

Some d-i-y plasters are available ready mixed in tubs. This is convenient for small repairs, but a very expensive way to plaster larger areas. Most plaster is supplied dry, in bags of up to 50kg. Plaster doesn't keep well – it may deteriorate in storage in as little as two months – so don't buy more than you need. You can test plaster by mixing a little in a cup or bowl. If it goes too stiff to work in less 30 minutes (10 minutes or less for Sirapite), you may need to buy fresh plaster.

As a rough guide to quantities, to replaster 1 sq m of wall to a thickness of 15mm, you'll need about 5kg of undercoat and 2.5kg of topcoat plaster.

Repairs to plaster

Minor repairs and small cracks are best dealt with using a proprietary filler. For larger areas, remove all suspect old plaster and brush away dust and debris. Just before replastering, dampen the area to prevent water being absorbed too quickly from the new plaster.

The undercoat must be applied evenly. If the area is large, fix tem-

porary battens or screeds to the wall. The screeds should be about 5mm thinner than the depth of the original plaster, and about 15mm wide. You'll need a plasterer's or general-purpose trowel and a hawk to carry the plaster to the wall. You can make your own hawk by screwing a simple handle to a piece of plywood or chipboard about 300mm square. If you're making good the plaster over electrical wiring, make sure it's covered by a suitable protective channel – don't embed the cables in the plaster (see Electricity, p. 75).

Mix the undercoat plaster in a bucket (or a bowl for smaller quantities). Fill the bucket about one-third full with fresh tap water and add the plaster to the water until you get a mixture with the consistency of whipped cream – just thick enough to not fall off the mixing stick. Tip the plaster on to a 'spot board' – any flat surface is suitable – and scoop some plaster on to the hawk with the trowel.

Place the hawk against the wall below the area you want to plaster, tip it towards you and in one movement push the plaster off the hawk and on to the wall with the face of the trowel. Move the trowel

Repairing plaster

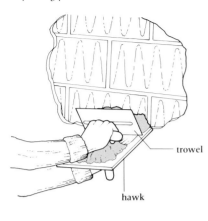

1. *Push the plaster off the hawk and on to the wall*

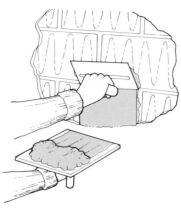

2. *With a steady upward movement, smooth the plaster on to the wall*

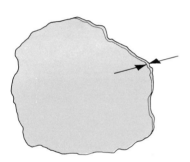

3. *Leave about 3–5mm for the finishing coat*

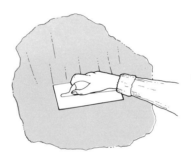

4. *Smooth on the finishing plaster*

upwards steadily, keeping it at about 45 degrees to the wall. As you come to the end of the stroke, flatten the trowel off slightly, but keep the top edge clear of the wall – don't let it flatten out completely. Don't try to work right up to the edge of the original plaster with the trowel – it will be much easier to fill in details with a filling knife. Aim to get the undercoat levelled off about 3 to 5mm below the surface of the original plaster.

If you've used screeds, remove them after about two hours and fill in the gaps. When the undercoat has become stiff, scratch it with a nail to provide a key for the finishing plaster. Leave it overnight before applying the finishing coat.

The finishing plaster is mixed and applied in the same way as the undercoat. If the repair is small, the trowel can be used to make sure that the new plaster is level with the old. Check larger areas with a straight-edge. Don't press too hard with the trowel when the plaster is wet or you'll tend to get a rippled effect. As the plaster begins to set, you can press more firmly and smooth the surface with the trowel at an angle of about 20 degrees. If the plaster dries too quickly, dampen it slightly with a large brush, but don't get it too wet or it won't set properly.

Lath-and-plaster walls

In older homes at least some of the inside walls may be of lath-and-plaster construction. If lath-and-plaster walls develop bulges, or give when pressed, it's likely that the laths have parted company with the supporting timbers. Provided that the bulging is not too severe, it should be possible to re-attach the laths using galvanised screws, covering the heads with proprietary filler. If you can't locate the timbers by tapping on the wall, it will be necessary to drill a series of small holes which can be filled when the repairs are complete.

To repair small areas of damage, lath-and-plaster walls can be patched with plasterboard. Strip the damaged area back to the centre of the supporting timbers on either side, cutting through the laths. Then cut a piece of plasterboard to fit the hole, and fix it – grey side outwards – to the joists with galvanised screws. Don't use nails: the hammering could make the damage worse.

Finally, bring the patch level with the rest of the wall by smoothing on board finish plaster; you'll need more than one coat if the difference in levels is greater than about 3mm.

Plastering an entire wall

The basic techniques described for repairs to plaster can be extended to plastering an entire wall. To get a consistent thickness of undercoat, fix vertical battens 10mm thick and about 15mm wide, 400mm apart, across the wall. Start in the top left-hand corner of each section (top right for left-handers), working down and then across. Level off using a straight-edge laid across the battens. A couple of hours later remove the battens and fill in the gaps.

External corners can be awkward. You could use temporary battens and then make good the plaster after they're removed. But the best way is to use corner beading. This is a galvanised metal strip with mesh at each side, held in place with blobs of plaster and plastered over permanently.

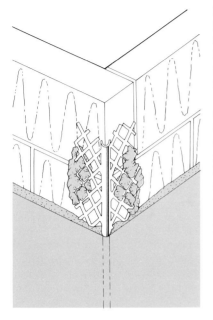

Corner beading for supporting plaster

Structural failure in walls

Cracks in interior walls may be the result of nothing more than the normal expansion and contraction of the house. Cracks between walls and ceilings are often caused by this, and tend to open up again even though you fill them repeatedly: there's nothing you can do about this except hiding the cracks by installing coving at the top of the walls.

Cracks and bulges in outside walls are likely to be more serious, however, and could be evidence of subsidence or heave. Other tell-tale signs are gaps opening up between floors and skirting boards and doors which become difficult to open and close.

Subsidence occurs when the foundations of the house sink into the soil beneath them. This may be because the foundations are too small to spread the load sufficiently, or because the nature of the soil wasn't assessed accurately. Subsidence can be the result of building on land which hadn't stabilised after

being used for another purpose – for the disposal of refuse, for example – or when old mine-workings collapse. It can also be caused by sustained dry weather or tree roots taking moisture from the soil.

Heave is the result of movements of the soil beneath the house which tend to push the foundations up out of the ground. The usual cause is frost, which can be a particular problem with clay soils. Foundations should be carried down to a depth where frost will not penetrate. The roots of large trees can also cause heave as they continue to grow. By contrast, the remnants of roots of large trees which have been cut down can cause subsidence as they rot away.

The first thing you'll want to know is whether the movement has stopped. There can be some settlement in the early life of a new house, for example, but once it has bedded down the trouble will cease. To test for continuing movement, bridge the crack with a piece of glass glued to the masonry with epoxy resin adhesive, or with plaster of paris. If the crack continues to move, the 'bridge' will break, though you should allow several months before you assume that the movement has stopped.

To combat subsidence and heave, the foundations can be underpinned. This involves excavating around and beneath the existing foundations to create a new, more secure sub-foundation. Once the house is stable, other problems can be dealt with. Cracks can be filled, out-of-true frames can be reset and floors raised.

Whatever the cause, these structural problems demand a professional approach both in identifying and dealing with them. If you suspect that there may be shortcomings in the foundations of your home, consult a surveyor without delay. If you're worried about trees close to your home, your local authority Building Inspector may be able to help.

Fireplaces

Maintaining the outside of chimneys is covered in Roofs, p. 29. Here we deal with the maintenance of fireplaces and chimneys on the inside of the house.

Inspecting your fireplaces

The obvious time to look at working fireplaces is the autumn, before you light any fires in them. Check for:

- falling soot or debris
- cracks in the cement lining of the fireplace
- loose grates
- insecure, cracked or broken tiles.

You also need to check that there's sufficient up-draught to 'draw' the fire and to make sure that all the smoke and fumes go up the chimney and not into the room. Loosely roll up a sheet of newspaper, hold it in the fireplace and light it. The flames and all the charred fragments should go straight up the chimney. If they don't, the problem could be with the chimney itself, or it could be that there's not enough ventilation getting into the room. To check, open a door or window a little and see if that makes the chimney work more effectively. If it does, then the problem is lack of ventilation rather than any shortcomings in the chimney itself.

How often chimneys need to be swept depends on how often they're used and on what's being burned in the grate. Chimneys used regularly with any sort of solid fuel generally need sweeping at least once a year: twice if they're used intensively. If you light only an occasional fire, on the other hand, the chimney should need sweeping less often.

The chimneys of fireplaces which are no longer used and have been blocked off can suffer from condensation, causing staining of the chimney breast in cold weather. Once again, ventilation is the key to both the problem and its solution.

Maintenance of solid fuel room heaters and boilers

Solid fuel appliances tend to make relatively heavy maintenance demands. As well as regularly raking out the ash, it's important to prevent soot and fly ash building up in flue-ways where they might hinder the smoke and flue gases; the flueways should be brushed out every month. If your appliance also has a throat plate, this must be removed and cleaned at least once a month.

Fireplace repairs

Fill cracks in the fireplace lining with special fireproof cement, following the manufacturer's instructions. Replace any cracked fire bricks.

If the grate is loose, rake and brush out any loose debris and repair any damage to the hearth before pushing the grate back into place and fixing it down firmly. Some grates have a fireproof cord which acts as a seal between the grate and the sides of the fireplace: check whether this needs to be replaced at the same time.

Improving a chimney's up-draught

Chimneys can be affected by wind eddies caused by high buildings or large trees, or even by the shape of your own house when the wind is in a certain direction. This can restrict the chimney's up-draught or even drive the air – and the smoke – back down into the room.

The normal solution is to fit a cowl to the chimneypot. Various types of cowl are available, and it's rarely easy to say which is likely to be effective in a particular case. Your builders' merchant may be able to advise you, but if possible get them to agree that you can exchange the cowl if it doesn't work. Take all the precautions necessary when working on the roof.

Ventilation for working fireplaces

A room with an open fire or any solid fuel appliance must be ventilated,

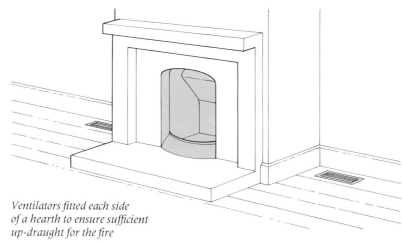

Ventilators fitted each side of a hearth to ensure sufficient up-draught for the fire

both to provide oxygen for the fire and to ensure a proper up-draught in the chimney. If you need extra ventilation, the best place to provide it is near the fireplace. If the room has a suspended wooden floor, you could fit ventilators in the floorboards on either side of the hearth.

If you have cavity walls, an alternative would be vents in the inner walls on either side of the hearth.

If vents aren't possible, you will have to let air in through the doors or windows. You can avoid cold draughts by fitting trickle ventilators into the upper parts of window frames, or by allowing air into the room above the doors.

Ventilation for blocked-off chimneys

There are a number of ways of blocking off a chimney for a fireplace which is no longer used. In all cases, however, ventilation must be provided to prevent condensation forming inside the old chimney.

The top of the chimney can either be left open – though it may be worthwhile installing a hood to prevent rainwater getting in – or be capped, in which case airbricks should be incorporated for ventilation. The chimney must be vented at the bottom, either into the room or through the wall to the outside.

If the old fireplace has been bricked up, at least one airbrick should be included or some of the vertical joints between the bricks be left open. If the old fireplace recess remains, but the chimney has been blocked off above it, the 'roof' of the fireplace should incorporate a vent.

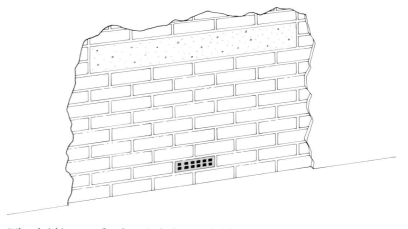

When bricking up a fireplace, include an airbrick

2 Roofs

The expression 'to keep a roof over your head' is used to mean looking after the whole house, and it illustrates how important roofs are. House roofs may be flat or pitched, and weatherproofed by a combination of slates, tiles, shingles, thatch, felt, lead and zinc. Roofs need regularly looking after to maintain their weather-resistance, and occasional repairs to put right damage after high winds and stormy weather. Dealing with problems as they arise can prevent a roof having to be replaced, which is inevitably a very costly and disruptive undertaking.

Inspecting the roof

It's worthwhile inspecting the roof twice a year – in spring and autumn – and whenever it's been buffeted by severe weather. This doesn't necessarily mean shinning up a ladder, though. Many roofs can be inspected from the outside using binoculars, and from the inside by taking a look in the loft.

If you have to climb on to the roof itself, take care. Don't walk about on the roof covering. On flat roofs use boards to spread your weight; on pitched roofs use a proper roofing ladder which hooks over the apex of the roof. See Working Safely on Your Roof, p. 33.

Outside the house:

- on pitched roofs check for missing, damaged or misplaced slates or tiles – pay special attention to the edges and to the ridge tiles at the apex of the roof
- on flat roofs check for blisters and bumps, and for puddles which show that water isn't draining away as it should
- check that flashings – the strips of felt or metal which seal the joints between roofs and walls – haven't lifted or worked loose
- on chimneys check that chimney-pots and the mortar 'flaunching' around their bases are sound. Look for crumbling pointing between the bricks and damaged or misplaced flashings where the chimney meets the roof.

Inside the house:

- look for chinks of daylight which may indicate potential leaks
- look for signs of damp. If you suspect a leak, make your inspection while it's raining if you can. Otherwise, look for water stains on the inside of the roof and on the roof timbers. Check for any signs of rot or woodworm – see Floors, Ceilings and Stairs, p. 58.
- check the ventilation – in most pitched roofs you should be able to see daylight all around the eaves of the roof. If you can't, the chances are that you need better ventilation
- check the loft insulation – make sure it's spread evenly and that it doesn't cover electric cables.

How roofs are built

The roofs of houses are built on timber frames. These frames are themselves supported on lengths of timber known as **wallplates**, which are bedded down on mortar at the tops of the walls. For extra security they may be retained by metal **straps**. On cavity walls the wallplates are usually fitted to the inside 'leaf' of brick or blockwork. On timber-framed houses the wallplates are attached to the inner structural frame. Where a roof over a lower storey meets a vertical wall, the wallplate will be bolted to wall anchors embedded in the masonry.

Pitched roofs

The simplest form of pitched roof is the **lean-to** or monopitched roof. It's widely used for porches, garages and single-storey extensions built on to two-storey houses. The **rafters**, the main timbers which support the slates or tiles and define the slope of the roof, are attached to wallplates at each end. Horizontal **joists** to support the ceiling will rest on a third wallplate. Struts may be used to stiffen the rafters.

Most houses have double-pitched roofs. Traditionally, these were constructed on-site. The rafters rest on wallplates at the tops of the walls and meet at the apex of the roof at the **ridgeboard**. The rafters are firmly attached to the **ceiling joists**, which act as ties, resisting the tendency of the weight of the roof to push the walls apart. Further stiffening is provided by **purlins**, **hangers**, **struts** and **binders**.

In more modern homes, roofs are often built from factory-made **trussed rafters**. The prefabricated sections are designed as a series of triangles, which maximises the strength of the structure while minimising the amount of timber used. Roofs built from trussed rafters do not usually have a ridgeboard, but do require some stiffening in the form of purlins and binders.

Roofs – symptoms, faults and remedies

Symptom	Fault	Remedy	*see page*
Leaking pitched roof	• Missing, broken or displaced slates or tiles	• Replace slates or tiles	34
	• Faulty flashings or valleys	• Repair or replace flashings or valleys	34
Leaking flat roof	• Split, punctured or decayed roofing felt	• Repair or replace felt	35
	• Faulty flashings or valleys	• Repair or replace flashings or valleys	34
Chimney problems	• Cracked chimneypot	• Replace	35
	• Faulty flaunching	• Replace	35
	• Crumbling pointing	• Repoint brickwork	34
Sagging roof	• Faulty roof timbers	• Get professional advice	36
Condensation in loft	• Inadequate ventilation	• Drill holes in soffits	36
		• Fit soffit ventilators	36
		• Fit ventilated ridge tiles	36

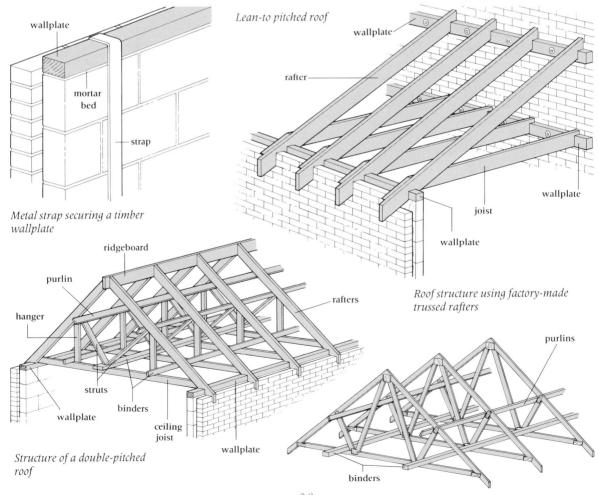

Metal strap securing a timber wallplate

Lean-to pitched roof

Roof structure using factory-made trussed rafters

Structure of a double-pitched roof

Variations on pitched roofs

A common variation for pitched roofs is for the ends to be 'hipped'. This means that the ends of the roof slope down at the same angle as the sides. Other variations include L-shaped and T-shaped roofs and the addition of dormer windows, which involve 'internal' corners where valleys must be provided to drain off rainwater.

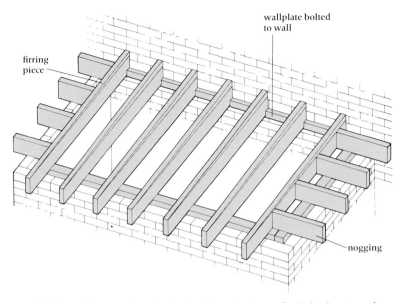

Typical flat roof construction; the firring pieces give the roof a slight slope to make water run off

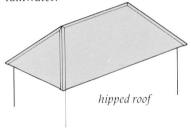

hipped roof

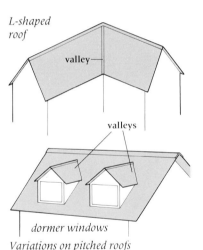

L-shaped roof

Variations on pitched roofs

Flat roofs

Flat roofs are a good deal simpler in construction than pitched roofs. They're often used for garages and single-storey extensions.

Most flat roofs consist of rafters which also act as ceiling joists, attached to the wallplates and covered by boards or man-made sheeting such as chipboard. To allow the roof to overlap the walls, which both looks better and provides better protection for the masonry against the worst effects of the weather, the rafters usually extend beyond the walls, and **noggings** may be added at right-angles to the rafters.

A flat roof must be inclined at a slight angle to make sure that rainwater will run off. Where an interior ceiling is not required, the rafters can be laid at the required angle – up to 10 degrees from the horizontal. But where a ceiling is to be fitted, it's normal to install the rafters level, and then add **firrings** – long wedges of timber – to the tops of the rafters to achieve the drainage 'fall'.

The boarding laid over the rafters must be moisture-resistant: either exterior-grade plywood or chipboard of type 2/3 as defined in BS5669 (1979).

Slates and tiles

Pitched roofs are usually covered by slates or tiles, fixed to battens laid across the rafters at right-angles. In older homes the battens will have been attached direct to the rafters, so that from inside the loft you can see the battens and the undersides of the tiles or slates. In more modern homes a layer of roofing felt will have been placed between the rafters and the battens, so that only the felt is visible from inside.

Tiles come in a variety of materials, shapes and sizes. Traditional clay tiles have been largely replaced – for new houses at least – by tiles made from coloured concrete. Traditional shapes continue to be reproduced in modern tiles, however, including plain tiles, pantiles, Roman tiles and large tiles which look like slates. Most modern tiles are interlocking: they have special channels moulded into their edges so that each tile fits accurately against its neighbour to form a weather-resistant joint.

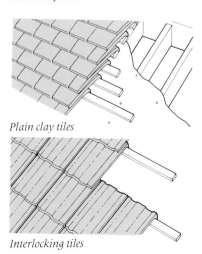

Plain clay tiles

Interlocking tiles

All tiles have projections called **nibs** under their top edges to enable them to be hooked over the battens. For extra security, the top and bottom rows of tiles, every fifth row in between, and tiles at the edge of a roof should be nailed or clipped. Edge tiles should also be laid on a bed of mortar to provide a weatherproof seal. The gap between successive rows of tiles is called the **gauge**; the size of the gap depends on the type of tile.

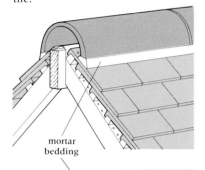

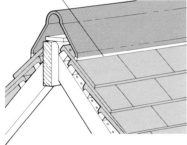

Types of ridge tiles

Ridge tiles are laid on a bed of mortar, with strips of roofing felt beneath the joints. The joints should also be pointed. Special tiles are available for the ridges of hipped roofs and for valleys. Alternatively, valleys may be lined with sheet lead.

Slates are also attached to rows of battens, but, because slates do not have nibs, each one must be nailed. Two methods are used. Head nailing is used for roofs which have a relatively shallow pitch – with head nailing the gauge is less than half the length of the slate. Centre nailing is used on steeper roofs and allows a greater gauge so that fewer slates are needed for a given area.

Shingles are thin pieces of weather-resistant wood, usually red cedar. They're used in much the same way as slates.

Roofing felt, for flat roofs and pitched roofs on buildings like garden sheds, is made from bitumenised or mineral fibre. On flat roofs, two or three layers are normally applied; these are coated with a reflective paint or topped off with granite chips or gravel to protect the felt from the sun. The first layer of felt is nailed in place, and subsequent layers are bonded to it using a bitumen-based compound. Hot and cold bonding compounds are available. Builders and professional roof repairers generally use hot bonding methods – for d-i-y, cold bonding is more practical.

To make sure water runs off the roof only into the gutters, some of the edges of a flat roof must be built up with wooden battens and fillets.

Flashings

Flashings seal the joints between roofs and the vertical faces of walls and chimneys. Flashings may be bitumenised felt, with or without a coating of metal foil, zinc, lead or copper. Flashings are tucked into raked-out joints in the masonry, and fit over or under the slates or tiles depending on the direction of flow of water on the roof. Gutter flashings

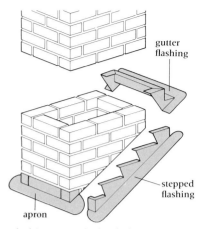

Flashing around a brick chimney

and valleys are normally fitted under the slates or tiles, apron flashings over them. Stepped flashings are used where vertical brickwork meets a sloping roof surface.

The finishing touches

At the eaves of the roof, a **fascia board** is attached to the ends of the rafters to carry the guttering. If the roof is felted beneath the tiles of slates, the felt should overhang the upper edge of the fascia. Behind the fascia, the **soffit** fills the gap between the fascia and the wall.

The Building Regulations now require lofts to be well ventilated, since loft insulation tends to make roof spaces prone to condensation. Modern homes therefore usually

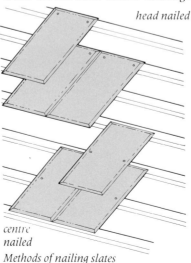

head nailed

centre nailed

Methods of nailing slates

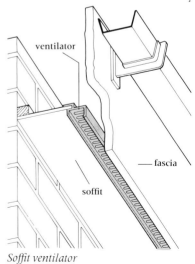

Soffit ventilator

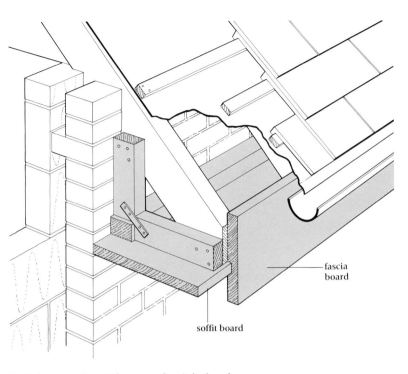

Typical construction at the eaves of a pitched roof

have soffit ventilators. If you don't have these, ventilation can be provided by drilling holes in the soffit boards, by special ventilated ridge tiles or by fitting air bricks in gable end walls. See Ventilating Your Loft, p. 36.

To finish the gable ends of roofs, **barge boards** may be fitted to protect the ends of the wall plates and tiling battens.

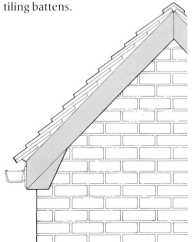

Barge boards

Maintaining your roof
Working safely on your roof

Don't attempt d-i-y roof repairs if you're nervous about heights. Even if heights don't bother you, don't compromise on safety.

Before you start, move or protect anything that could be damaged by something falling from the roof: cars and conservatories are especially vulnerable. Mark out a danger zone at ground level and discourage other people, especially children, from straying into it.

A platform tower is much safer to work on than a ladder. Towers can be hired. If you have to use a ladder, make sure it's long enough to extend by at least three rungs above the edge of the roof, and tie it to a large hook screwed into the fascia board.

If you need to climb on to the roof itself, don't walk on the roof covering. On flat roofs, use boards to spread your weight, and try not to press on areas which look as though

they could be in need of repair – you're almost certain to make matters worse if you do. On felted roofs with a coating of chippings try to pick cool weather – when the felt is hot sharp edges on the chippings can easily puncture it.

On pitched roofs use a special roof ladder. These have wheels, so they can be rolled up the roof, and a large hook which fits over the ridge. A roof ladder can also be hired. It is much safer for both you and the roof than walking on the tiles or slates.

Temporary roof repairs

If your roof has been badly damaged by storms or high winds, the only effective emergency treatment is to cover it with a waterproof tarpaulin. Even if you have one, putting it in place – especially if the wind is still fairly strong – is a tricky job and best left to professionals. See Getting Professional Help, p.36.

A d-i-y approach may be appropriate for smaller leaks, however. In modern homes, where the tiles or slates are fitted over a backing of roofing felt, the roof shouldn't leak even if one or two tiles or slates come adrift. If it does, because the felt has also been damaged, you may be able to repair the felt from inside the loft. Try working a piece of waterproof material – thick polythene sheet, for example – through the split, and apply adhesive tape on the inside. You should be able to buy suitable tapes from builders' merchants; camping shops sell similar products for repairing tents.

On older roofs without a felt backing, use a larger patch and work it under the tiles above the missing one and over the tiles below it. Be gentle when lifting tiles: don't let the projecting nibs slip off the battens.

Tiles or slates may leak because they've cracked or split. A temporary repair can usually be made by sealing the gap with mastic or silicone sealant. For a permanent repair, however, it is necessary to replace the broken tile or slate.

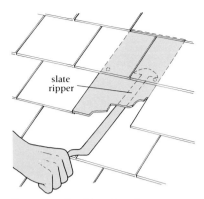

Remove nails with a slate ripper

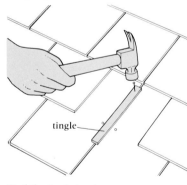

Carefully slide out the slate

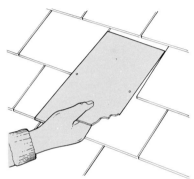

Nail the tingle in place

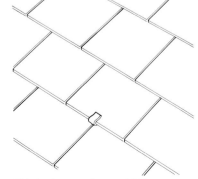

Slide in the new slate and fold over the tingle to secure it

Replacing slates and tiles

Before you can replace slates or tiles, you clearly need new ones which match the existing ones. This can prove difficult, particularly for older homes. Look in Yellow Pages for builders' mechants who specialise in second-hand or 'reclaimed' materials. Even modern types of roofing tiles can be hard to get following stormy weather, since demand often outstrips supply.

Slates are generally more difficult to replace than tiles, since every slate is attached to the battens by nails. The best way to remove a broken slate is to use a **slate ripper**, a thin steel blade with a hooked end which you slip under the slate and around the nail. A sharp pull will break the nail and free the slate.

Unless you remove a whole series of slates, however, you still won't be able to nail the new slate in place in the same way as the old. Instead, fit a **tingle** – a strip of lead, zinc or copper – between the slates, push in the new slate and bend up the end of the tingle to hold the slate in position.

A tile which is undamaged but has simply been displaced by the wind can usually be worked back into place – gently lift the adjacent tiles if necessary. If the projecting nibs are broken, the tile must be replaced. If the tile is at the edge of the roof, chip away the old pointing and bed down the new tile on fresh mortar.

Repairs to flashings

Replacing a complete flashing – especially a complex one around a chimney, say – calls for fair degree of skill and may be better left to a professional. But smaller repairs are possible using self-adhesive aluminium-faced tapes or mastic. The life of old flashings which have begun to deteriorate may also be extended by painting them with bitumen paint.

Flashings can leak because they've worked loose from joints in the masonry. Secure them by wedging in pieces of lead and repoint.

Zinc flashings are more springy than lead or roofing felt, and can become distorted if high winds get under them. Pressing them back into place does no good because they simply spring out again. One cure is to rake out the joint in the masonry, remove the flashing, reshape it and replace it. But if the joint with the masonry is in good condition, an alternative is to glue the flashing down with silicone sealing compound. Inject the compound under the flashing and hold it down with bricks while it sets. You shouldn't need a continuous bead of sealant – simply enough to hold the flashing in place. Don't try to use a mastic for this: because mastic never sets hard the flashing will come away again before long.

Chimney problems

Because the masonry of a chimney is completely exposed to the elements, it tends to deteriorate more rapidly than the house walls. Such deterioration cannot be ignored – if part of the chimney comes away it is likely to do serious damage to the roof.

If the **pointing** on brick chimneys shows any signs of decay, it should be replaced promptly. If the deterioration has reached the point where large cracks are visible or the chimney has started to lean to one side, *act*

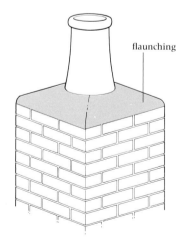

Cement flaunching around a chimney pot

immediately. Unless the chimney is easy to get at, repointing is a job best left to professionals – see Getting Professional Help, p. 36. It is usually necesssary to erect scaffolding. The pointing on chimneys should always be weather-struck for maximum weather-resistance – see Walls: Repointing Brickwork, p. 22.

Chimneypots which are cracked or broken should be replaced or, if the chimney is no longer in use, removed and the chimney capped (see below).

Chimney pots are held in place by flaunching – cement formed into a wedge around the pot to secure it and to encourage water to run off. If you have to remove defective flaunching, collect the pieces in a bucket hooked to the ladder – don't let them fall on to the surface of the roof. If you have to remove an old chimneypot, first cover up the fireplace below to keep dust and debris out of the room. Lift the pot with care: it will probably be heavier than it looks.

To renew flaunching, use a dry-mixed mortar or make your own from one part of cement to three parts of sharp sand. Use a trowel to achieve a smooth surface which slopes away from the pot all the way around.

Use a suitably sized paving slab, bedded down on mortar to cap an unused chimney. To prevent condensation, replace a couple of the old bricks in the chimney stack with air-bricks. See also Fireplaces, p.27.

Repairing flat roofs

Small leaks in flat roofs can be difficult to locate. The water tends to run along the timbers of the roof for some distance before it appears as a damp patch on the inside. However, moisture which has got under a flat roof covering usually causes it to blister. If the covering is in good condition, an isolated leak can be cured by removing the granite chippings in the area of the blister, cutting through it and opening out the edges

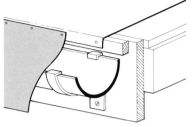

Nail the edging strip to the fascia

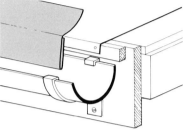

Fold it over and (below) stick it down

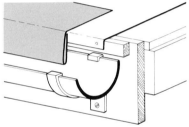

Applying the gutter edging on a felted roof

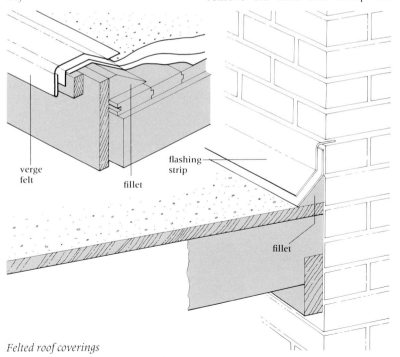

verge felt

fillet

flashing strip

fillet

Felted roof coverings

of the felt. If the boards underneath are moist, allow them to dry out. Then apply a generous layer of cold bitumastic to the boards, fold the felt back and press it into the bitumastic. Spread a sealing layer of bitumastic over the surface and replace the chippings.

If the surface is in poor condition overall, the felt should be stripped off and replaced. Don't be tempted simply to cover old felt with new.

Replacing a felt roof

Before you start, check which grade and type of roofing felt you need. The types of felt which can be used on flat roofs are defined in the Building Regulations. Builders' merchants should be able to offer advice, but it will pay you to consult your local authority Department of Building Control. When you're working out how much new felt you'll need, allow for overlaps between the sheets of felt and around the edges.

Carefully lift flashings where the roof meets vertical walls. If the flashings are in good condition they can be reused. Strip off the old felt, remove old nails and sweep the boards clean. Repair or replace any defective boards.

Start the first layer of felt at the centre of the gutter edge. Nail from the centre of the felt outwards at about 150mm intervals. Overlap the strips of felt by about 50mm. At the gutter edge, allow the felt to overlap the corner of the fascia and turn it down. At built-up edges, trim the felt just inside the corner of the verge batten. Where the felt meets a vertical wall, trim the felt just short of the top of the fillet.

Now cut a strip of felt about 250mm wide for the gutter edge. Nail it to the fascia (or to the verge batten if there is one) then fold it back on itself so that it hangs into the gutter. Apply bitumastic along the edge of the top of the roof and press the strip down on to it.

Spread bitumastic over the rest of the top of the roof and apply the second layer of felt, butting up to the strip on the gutter edge and overlapping the other edges. Make sure that the joints in the first and second layers of felt do not coincide – they should be at least 50mm apart. Bond the third layer of felt to the second, once again ensuring that the joints don't coincide. Trim the third layer inside the edge of the roof all round.

Cut verge felts for the built-up edges of the roof about 350mm wide. Apply them in the same way as the strip on the gutter edge. Fold down existing flashings or make new ones. Felt flashings should be about 300mm wide and tucked into a groove raked out of the brickwork at least two courses above the main level of the roof. Repoint the brickwork – see Walls: Repointing Brickwork, p. 22.

Finally, spread another coat of bitumastic and sprinkle granite chippings evenly over the roof.

Ventilating the roof space

Without loft insulation, a good deal of expensive heat will escape through the loft space. Up to 150mm of loft insulation will easily pay for itself by the savings you make on your fuel bills. However, loft insulation means that the roof space is likely to be cold at night but will heat up more rapidly when the sun shines on the tiles or slates by day. Without improved ventilation, this will probably cause condensation.

Recognising this, the Building Regulations now set standards for loft insulation. Thus usually means that the soffits around the eaves of newer homes will be fitted with ventilators. In older homes, ventilation must be provided to match the degree of insulation installed. As a rule of thumb, for loft insulation up to 150mm thick, you need ventilation equivalent to a gap of 10mm all along the eaves.

If you need to replace the soffit boards – because of rot, for example – it is relatively simple to install strip-type ventilators – see the drawing on p. 32. Alternatively, you could simply bore a series of holes – 12mm in diameter, say – or install circular soffit ventilators with plastic grills which fit into larger holes. The easiest way to make the holes is with a hole saw and an electric drill.

If it's not practical to improve ventilation at the eaves, fit ventilated ridge tiles on the apex of the roof.

Getting professional help

Finding a reliable professional roofing contractor can be difficult, particularly when they're in great demand following stormy weather.

As with many aspects of building and home maintenance, a personal recommendation from friends, colleagues or other tradesmen who have proved to be reliable is a good starting-point. Qualified professional roofers are likely to be members of the **National Federation of Roofing Contractors**, the **Federation of Master Builders** or the **Building Employers Confederation**. All these bodies operate warranty schemes in addition to a conciliation service. The **Thatching Advisory Service** maintains a register of qualified thatchers around the country. They do not have a warranty scheme, but will arbitrate in cases of disagreement. For addresses and telephone numbers, see Useful Addresses, p. 136.

Once you have a shortlist of suitable tradesmen:

- Always contact trade associations to check claims of membership
- Get three estimates for any substantial roofing work so you can compare prices and technical details
- Make sure that estimates are clear about whether or not VAT has been included
- Ask for references and examples of other work the contractor has carried out – and follow them up
- Don't pay anything in advance
- Draw up a specification of what you want done, including a timetable.

Whole roof treatments

If you are having problems with an unfelted slate or tile roof – the sort where you can see the underside of the slates or tiles from inside the loft – you may be tempted to go for one of the 'whole roof treatments' which are advertised. These are designed to combat 'nail-sickness' – when all the nails in the roof are reaching the end of their useful life.

Whole roof treatments seal off the roof from inside the loft space and consist of polyurethane blocks which are glued in place, PVA adhesive mixed with a bulking agent and sprayed on to the backs of the slates or tiles, or quick-hardening chemical foam which is sprayed on to the backs of the slates or tiles.

Use only treatments and contractors which have been approved by the **British Board of Agrément** (BBA). Before proceeding with a whole roof treatment, compare the cost with having the tiles or slates lifted temporarily so felt can be added over the rafters. After treatment, make sure there is plenty of ventilation in the loft space.

3 Doors and windows

Doors and windows can be made of many materials. Wood is still the most common, and the most demanding in terms of maintenance. Modern alternatives which make much lower maintenance demands include aluminium, upvc and fibreglass.

The style of exterior doors and windows has an important bearing on the overall appearance of a house, and they must be well protected against the rigours of the weather in order to maintain that appearance and keep the house properly weather-sealed.

All doors and windows should be easy to open and close, and should sit straight in their frames.

Inspecting doors and windows

Inspect your doors and windows annually.

On the outside, look for:
• flaking or blistered paint

• rot in door and window frames – especially in the lower parts of the frame and in the sills
• gaps in the mastic seal around door and window frames
• cracked glazing

On the inside, look for:
• doors and windows that stick
• doors and windows that droop or sag
• warps
• broken sash cords in sash windows.

Types of doors

Panel doors

Panel doors consist of a framework of stiles – the vertical sections – and rails – the horizontal sections. Traditionally, the stiles and rails are held together by mortise-and-tenon joints, though some doors of this type have dowelled joints. The spaces between the stiles and rails are filled with panels of solid timber, plywood or glass.

Panel doors come in a wide variety of styles, including traditional and period designs, and in both exterior and interior grades. Most are made of wood, though aluminium doors of this type are available, usually glazed with sealed double-glazing units, and there are fibreglass doors which look like panel doors although they're made by gluing together two moulded skins.

The stiles of moulded doors are usually wide enough, at about 100mm, to accommodate locks and door handles.

Flush doors

These consist of panels of hardboard or plywood, known as facings or skins, applied over a light internal framework. They may be stiffened by a core, typically a honeycomb material made from wood fibres.

Flush doors come in exterior and interior grades, and in a wide range of finishes ranging from unfinished

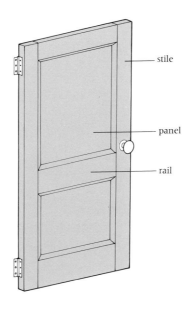

Panel doors

Doors and windows – symptoms, faults and remedies

Symptom	Fault	Remedy	*see page*
Sticking doors and windows	• Build-up of paint	• Strip and re-paint	40
	• Swelling due to changes in humidity	• Plane away excess timber	41
	• Sagging hinges	• Replace	41
	• Rot	• Replace all affected timber	41
	• Loose frame	• Re-fix	41
	• Warps	• Straighten	42
Sash window won't stay up	• Broken sash cords	• Replace	45
Window sill soft or crumbling	• Rot	• Replace sill	44
Broken glazing		• Replace	47

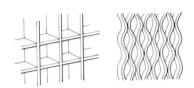

types of internal reinforcement

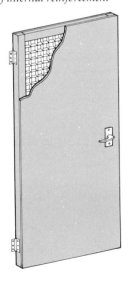

Flush door

edges of flush doors are often fitted with lipping – thin strips of timber held in place by a tongue-and-groove joint or by pinning and gluing. On veneered doors the lippings should match the faces.

Since the internal framework tends to be rather insubstantial, flush doors often have a lock block – extra timber built into the door for fixing locks and door handles. Some doors have lock blocks on both sides, others on only one; new doors with only one lock block should be marked to show where it is. Some flush doors have other blocks to reinforce the door where the hinges are attached. External flush doors may have an internal block or centre rail for fixing a letter box.

Flush doors are available in fire-resistant grades, which are necessary for connecting doors between houses and garages, and with cut-outs for glazing.

Some flush doors have moulded skins to resemble panel doors.

Boarded doors

Boarded doors are more commonly used for sheds, garages and out-houses than for the house itself.

Ledged-and-braced doors consist of a series of vertical boards attached to two or three horizontal ledges and stiffened by diagonal braces. **Framed, ledged-and-braced doors** are similar, but also have frames with mortise-and-tenon joints. They're stronger than the simpled ledged-and-braced type.

or primed for painting to veneered with teak, mahogany or sapele. To neaten and protect the edges of the panels, and to provide some material which can be planed off to fit the door snugly in its frame, the vertical

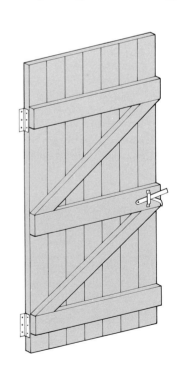

Ledged-and-braced door; the diagonal braces should point upwards from the hinged side

Door sizes

Although all door sizes are now generally quoted in metric measurements, many are still based on feet and inches. The most common sizes are:

	Metric	Imperial
External doors	1981 × 686mm	6ft 6in × 2ft 3in
	1981 × 762mm	6ft 6in × 2ft 6in
	1981 × 838mm	6ft 6in × 2ft 9in
	2032 × 813mm	6ft 8in × 2ft 8in
	1994 × 806mm	no equivalent
Internal doors	1981 × 610mm	6ft 6in × 2ft 0in
	1981 × 686mm	6ft 6in × 2ft 3in
	1981 × 762mm	6ft 6in × 2ft 6in
	1981 × 838mm	6ft 6in × 2ft 9in
	2032 × 813mm	6ft 8in × 2ft 8in
	2040 × 626mm	no equivalent
	2040 × 726mm	no equivalent
	2040 × 826mm	no equivalent

Exterior doors are generally 44mm thick, interior doors 35mm thick.

If your doors don't conform to these standard sizes, the general rule is to buy the next larger size and plane it down. Some doors are specially made so that they can be reduced all round by as much as 50mm.

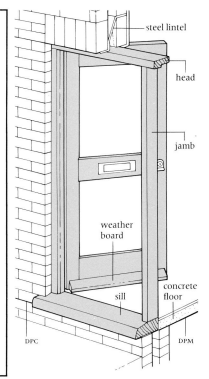

How a door frame fits into the wall

Other types of doors

Sliding doors are usually made by fitting sliding door gear to ordinary flush doors.

Louvred doors allow for ventilation and are commonly used in warmer climates. They have a framework of stiles and rails, filled by a series of horizontal, angled wooden slats.

Stable doors are panel or boarded doors made in two parts, divided roughly in the middle of the door aperture, so that the top can be opened, leaving the bottom closed like a gate. As well as simple versions intended for the use after which they're named, there are smart stable doors suitable for the front or back doors of houses.

Pairs of **garage doors** hung on vertical hinges are usually of the boarded type. They're still available, but have been largely superseded by up-and-over doors. These are made in a wide range of materials and styles. Galvanised steel garage doors are the most common, and the cheapest. They're supplied either in the galvanised finish, pre-treated for painting, or finished. Up-and-over doors are pivotted horizontally, but the pivots are set back so that the door rises as it opens to clear the aperture. The weight of the door is usually counterbalanced by springs rather than weights.

Materials for doors

Exterior doors must be capable of withstanding the rigours of the weather. Timber exterior doors may be softwood, which must be carefully primed and painted, or hardwood, which is more weather-resistant and can be varnished. In either case an initial treatment with a preservative stain suitable for over-painting may be advisable. For more information on paints for exterior woodwork, see Paintwork chapter. Aluminium and fibreglass doors are inherently weather-resistant.

Interior doors are generally softwood, though hardwood interior doors are available, with appearance the main consideration.

Fire doors are constructed to resist the effects of fire for periods of half an hour, one or two hours, depending on where they're used. Although outwardly similar to conventional doors, fire doors have cores of plasterboard, flaxboard or chipboard. Older fire doors may contain asbestos.

Door frames

Doors fit into frames which are fixed to the aperture in the wall. The vertical parts of the frame are known as jambs, the horizontal part at the top is known as the head and the horizontal part at the bottom, if there is one, as the sill.

Door frames may be fixed in place by building the horns – the projecting parts of the head and sill – into the brickwork, or by steel cramps

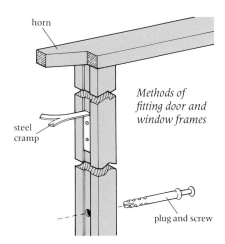

horn

steel
cramp

*Methods of
fitting door and
window frames*

plug and screw

embedded in the mortar, or by plugs
and screws.

Above the door, the weight of the
masonry must be supported by a lintel – a steel, concrete or wooden
beam which spans the opening and
takes the weight off the door frame
itself. Below the sill, the frame of
external doors must be protected
from rising damp by the DPC.

Most door frames are softwood,
often with hardwood sills for exterior use. Some aluminium and fibreglass doors have metal sub-frames
fitted in a hardwood outer frame.

Problems with doors

The most common problem with
doors is sticking, particularly in winter. Doors stick for a variety of reasons:

- the build-up of successive layers of
  paint
- the wood of the door or frame
  expanding and contracting with
  changes in humidity
- wet rot in the timber causing the
  door or frame to swell
- loose or faulty hinges allowing the
  door to droop
- loose joints in the woodwork of
  the door allowing it to sag.

If the hinge side of a door comes
into contact with the frame before
it's fully closed, it's said to be hinge-
bound. Binding may be due to the
build up of paint, swelling due to

increased humidity, or problems
with the hinges themselves.

Door may fit their frames without sticking or binding but still be
difficult to close due to warping or
twisting of the door. This can
happen particularly when there's a
marked difference in temperatures
between the two sides of the door –
when a door is in full sunshine, for
instance.

Curing a sticking door

The first step is to find where the
door is sticking. Watching a sticking
door carefully as you open and close
it usually shows where the problem
lies. With the door open, look for

scuff marks where the door and
frame have been rubbing.

If the door is sticking near the top
on the side opposite the hinges,
check that the gap on the hinge side
is correct. It could be that one or
more of the hinges has worked loose,
allowing the door to droop. You may
need to replace the existing screws
with longer or larger ones – size 10
instead of 8, say – or to plug the holes
with dowels to give the screws a better purchase.

If the door is sticking where it
passes over the floor, this can often
be cured by putting sandpaper –
rough side up – over the high spots
and passing the door across it a few

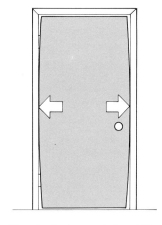

Swelling due to changes in humidity

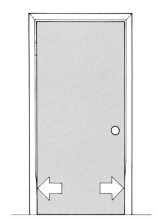

Wet rot in the frame causing it to swell

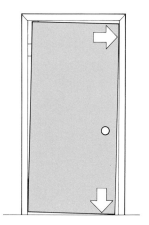

Sagging hinges

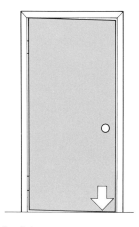

Sagging joints

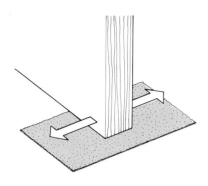

Using sandpaper to cure a door which sticks at the bottom

times. Otherwise, providing that the woodwork is sound, the usual solution is to plane off enough wood from the door to allow it to close freely. You may have to take the door off its hinges to get at the top and bottom, and if the sticking is around the lock or catch you'll have to remove that, too. Aim for a gap between the door and frame of about 2 or 3mm, but don't overdo it if the sticking has been caused by damp – remember that the wood will shrink as it dries out. Treat the planed area with primer or preservative stain right away.

Repairing a rotten door frame

Door frames usually rot near the bottom. Rotten wood will be discoloured (though that may be concealed by paint) and soft. You must remove and replace all the rotten timber. Make a downward-angled cut at least 50mm above the rot and remove the timber below it. Examine carefully the saw-cut in the remaining wood. If there are any signs of rot, cut again 100mm further up, and continue in this way until you're sure that the wood is sound. Treat the cut area with preservative.

Now make a second, upward-sloping cut half-way through the frame at least 50mm above the first, and saw or chisel out the wood between the two saw-cuts. Shape a new piece of timber to fit into the frame, and treat it thoroughly with a

preservative. Aim for an accurate fit between the original frame and the repair piece, both for appearance and weather-resistance. Fix the repair to the original frame with at least two brass woodscrews, and to the masonry using long screws and plugs or special frame fixings. Finally, seal the gap between the repaired frame and the masonry with mastic.

If the door rather than the frame is suffering from rot, it may be possible to replace the rotten timber if only a small area is affected. It's more likely, however, that the rot will have penetrated the joints in the door and the whole door will need to be replaced.

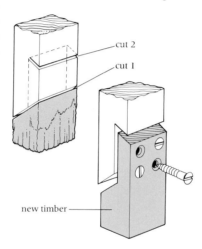

Replacing part of a door frame which has been attacked by wet rot

Curing a hinge-bound door

If a door is hinge-bound, first look at the hinge screws. The problem may be simply that some of the screw heads are protruding and therefore coming into contact with the door before the door is closed. Replace any screws which are damaged or have been put in at an angle and drive them home firmly and straight.

Otherwise, pack out the hinges by inserting pieces of sandpaper, card or hardboard – depending on the thickness you need – in the hinge recesses.

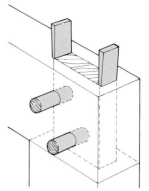

Tightening the joints in a sagging door

Repairing a sagging door

In time, the joints in panel doors can loosen, allowing the door to sag so that it catches on the floor as it is opened. Loose joints can often be repaired by inserting wedges and dowels.

Tap in the wedges first, then bore through and insert the dowels. Both the wedges and dowels should be glued in place.

Boarded doors may sag if the bracing is inadequate, or if the door is hung with the bracing the wrong way round. The bracing should face upwards away from the hinges.

Curing a loose door frame

Door frames are fixed to the surrounding masonry by long screws and plugs or by special frame fixings. To cure a loose frame, first remove any architrave and clear away loose plaster or masonry. Now set the frame in the aperture using wedges or packing to hold it securely. Make sure that the frame is square. You can check this by comparing the measurements across the diagonals and by 'offering up' the door.

Purpose-made frame fixings are much easier to use than conventional wallplugs and screws, since you can drill through the frame and on into the masonry and don't need to remove the frame to insert the plugs. Use a universal drill bit, or drill pilot holes through the frame and follow up with a masonry bit of the

Driving in a special frame fixing

appropriate size. Tap in the frame fixings and hammer or screw them home.

Make good any plaster and replace the architrave, if appropriate. On external doors, seal the gap between the masonry and the door frame with mastic.

Straightening a warped or twisted door

A door which is warped on the hinge side can sometimes be cured by

Straightening a door warped at the top

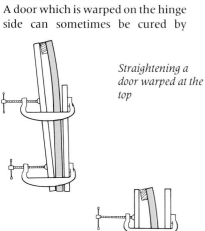

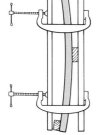

How to spread the load for a more severe warp

adding an extra hinge. Pack the door carefully using wedges between the door and frame when marking out, to make sure that the new hinge pulls the door into shape.

Other methods involve forcing the door into shape using wedges to jam it into the door frame, or stout pieces of timber and G-clamps.

Forcing methods should be used with care, to avoid damaging the door, and aren't suitable for glazed doors. The G-clamp methods have the advantage that the pressure can be stepped up gradually. Leave the wedges or clamps in place for at least two days.

If forcing is impractical or unsuccessful, distortion can sometimes be disguised by moving one or more of the hinges.

Types of windows

Casement windows

Casement windows are the most widely used type in modern homes. The opening parts of the window are hinged to the primary framework,

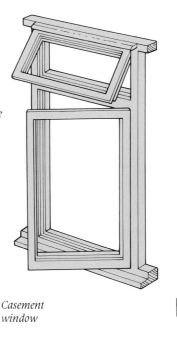

Casement window

usually along their longest edge, which may be either at the side or top. A vast selection of types, styles and sizes is available. Some modern casements have projecting hinges which allow the window to be turned 'inside-out' for cleaning.

Bottom-hung windows are a variation. These generally open into the room, and there are tilt-and-turn types which can also be opened from the side.

Sash windows

In sash windows the secondary frames in which the glazing is mounted slide in vertical channels in the primary frame. In a traditional sash window the secondary frames are counterbalanced by an arrangement of cords, pulleys and weights concealed in pockets in the primary frame. In some modern systems the counterweights have been replaced by spiral sash balances, simplifying the construction of the primary frames. Because the intermediate glazing bars are slim, sash windows have a distinctive appearance which

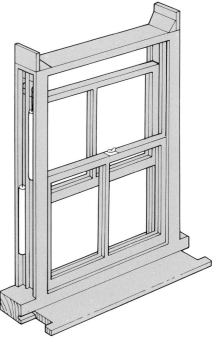

Sash window

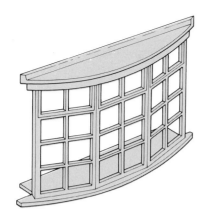

Georgian-style bow window

Bay window

is an essential element in the style of many period homes.

Counterbalancing allows the windows to be opened to any point, giving very good control over ventilation. Properly maintained, sash windows can be a real asset, but they can also suffer from sticking – usually due to the build-up of successive layers of paint – rattling – when the secondary frames are not a good fit in the runners – and problems with the various components of the counterbalancing mechanism.

Pivot-hunt windows

Pivot-hung windows allow both sides of the glass to be cleaned from the inside. The pivot axis is usually horizontal. Pivot-hung windows can be used for odd shapes – circular, for example.

Variations on standard windows

Bow windows curve or bow outwards from the face of the wall. They are essentially Georgian in style, and usually consist of a number of small panes which are flat individually but together give the impression of a curve.

Bay windows are windows set in a projecting part of the wall. The projection may be semi-circular, splayed or square. It may be confined to the ground floor, but often continues up the face of the house to the roof.

Materials for windows

Wood is the most common window frame material. Softwood is used where the frame is to be painted, hardwood where the finish is to be a preservative seal or varnish. Some softwood frames have hardwood sills. Modern wooden frames are suitable for either single or double glazing.

Steel window frames were widely used in the 1930s, but are less popular today. They tend not to be thermally efficient, and so let more heat escape than other types. The steel is galvanised to prevent corrosion, which means that special primers must be used for painting. There are modern versions of the steel window frame designed for double glazing, but these come with a factory-applied paint finish.

Aluminium window frames have been widely used in recent years for double-glazed replacement windows. The aluminium may be anodised (retaining its silvery finish) or painted. Unless the frames incorporate a thermal break – a barrier to insulate the outside of the frame from the inside – double-glazed aluminium windows may waste as much heat as single-glazed wooden windows, and suffer from condensation. Aluminium windows are usually fitted in a hardwood frame, and require little maintenance.

UPVC is an alternative to aluminium for double-glazed windows. UPVC is a type of plastic; the frames look like painted wooden ones but demand much less maintainance.

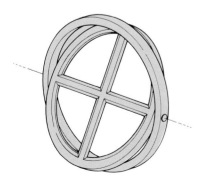

Pivot-hung windows

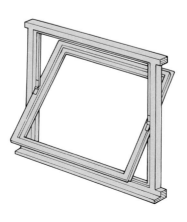

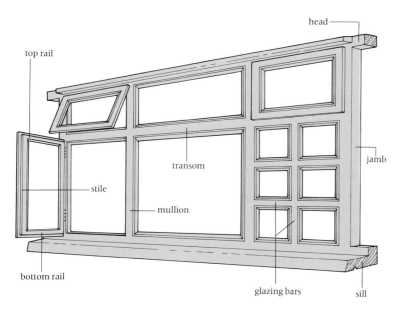

Components of timber window frames; a variety of styles is shown

Window construction

Window frames are fitted into the apertures in walls in much the same way as door frames, either by building the horns – the projecting parts of the head and sill into the brickwork, or by steel cramps embedded in the mortar, or by plugs and screws. The weight of the masonry above the window must be supported by a lintel – a steel, concrete or wooden beam which spans the opening and takes the weight off the window frame itself.

The main frame of the window consists of a horizontal head at the top and a sill at the bottom, with vertical jambs between them at either side. The main frame may then be divided into sections by vertical mullions and horizontal transoms. Fixed lights are glazed direct into the main frame, using putty or glazing beads in combination with putty or mastic. Opening lights – casements or sashes – may be further sub-divided by glazing bars.

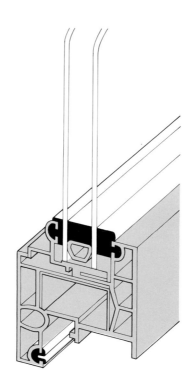

A typical profile of a upvc double-glazed window frame

Double-glazed windows with aluminium, steel or upvc frames generally have a subsidiary hardwood surround, and are usually 'dry-glazed'. The double-glazing units are retained by glazing beads which incorporate inner and outer seals.

Problems with window frames

Some problems with windows – sticking, faulty hinges and loose frames, for example – are similar to those with doors, and similar cures can be applied.

Wooden window sills are prone to rot, and concrete sills can crack or flake. Sash windows need regular (though infrequent) attention to the arrangements of cords, pulleys and counterweights.

Replacing a rotten window sill

If a window sill is rotten, it's quite likely that the rot will also extend into the jambs and mullions – the vertical parts of the frame. If that's the case, the whole frame should be replaced. However, if you're confident that only the sill is affected, it can be replaced leaving the rest of the frame in place. You can buy new window sills in a variety of sizes and shapes. Hardwood sills are more durable than softwood.

Remove all the opening parts of the window and the glazing from fixed lights. Saw through the sill close to the jambs and mullions. Remove the sill and the mortar on which it was bedded.

Saw off the tenons on the bottoms of the jambs and mullions – cut square and as neatly as possible. Treat the cut ends with a wood preservative.

Using the old sill as a pattern, cut the new sill to length and shape it to match the original jambs and mullions. Make sure that the new sill has a drip channel on the underside. Treat the sill with a preservative,

Replacing a rotten window sill

1. Saw through the old sill close to the jambs

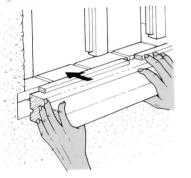

3. Slide in the new sill and wedge it tight to the jambs

2. Cut the jambs flush with the new sill

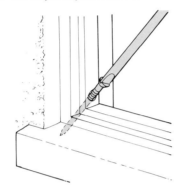

4. Fix with screws driven in at an angle

paying special attention to the ends. Apply water-resistant glue to the ends of the jambs and mullions, and slide the new sill into place, packing it from underneath so it fits as tightly as possible against the old frame. Drill through the jambs and mullions into the sill, and fix it with countersunk screws.

Pack mortar under the sill, pushing it firmly into the recess, and seal the gap between the sill and the masonry with mastic.

This technique for replacing a rotten window sill avoids removing the whole frame. If you're prepared to do that, however, a better repair can be made with the jambs and mullions mortised and tenoned into the new sill. If the old tenons are broken or rotten, they can be replaced by cutting a slot in the old wood and adding a new tongue held in place by glue and dowels.

Repairing concrete window sills

Minor cracks and chips can be repaired using a proprietary cement-based filler. For more substantial repairs, or to resurface a sill which is flaking, remove any loose material and build wooden shuttering around the sill to act as a mould. Dampen the old concrete before applying the new with a trowel. Remove the shuttering when the new concrete has set – about a couple of days.

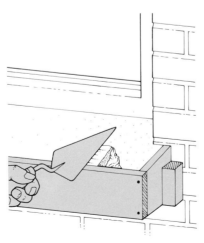

To repair a concrete sill make up wooden shuttering to act as a mould

Replacing the cords in a sash window

If a sash cord breaks, the chances are that other cords are also due for replacement. And replacing all the cords involves not much more work than replacing only one.

The frames of traditional sash windows are quite complicated because they need to provide concealed spaces for the counterweights. Start by lowering both sashes to the bottom of the box frame, then lever out the staff beads which hold the inner sash in place, using a broad chisel. Take care not to damage the beads, so they can be reused.

Swing out the inner sash and cut through the cords. Keep hold of each cord as you cut through and gently lower the counterweight. Remove the cut cords from the sash: they're usually nailed, though some are wedged in place.

To remove the outer sash, lever out the parting beads and cut the cords as before. Remove the pocket cover and take out the weights, taking care not to damage the thin strip of timber, called a wagtail or parting slip, which stops the weights banging into one another. Clean out any debris from the bottoms of the weight compartments.

Check the pulleys at the top of the frame. They may need a little oil at least; at worst they may need to be replaced. If you have to buy new ones, take one of the old pulleys as a guide to size and type.

While you have the window dismantled, check for any loose joints in the sashes and take the opportunity to sand down the paintwork and repaint the frame and sashes.

Replacing the cords in a sash window

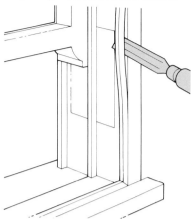

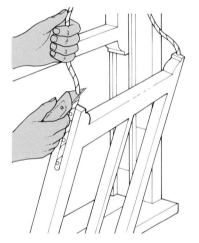

1. *Lever out the beads with a chisel*

2. *Cut through the cords and remove the sashes*

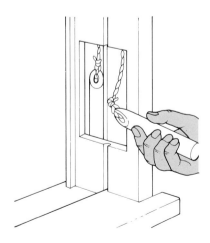

3. *Take out the weights and the old cords*

4. *Mark the upper and lower positions of the bottom of the cord groove on the frame*

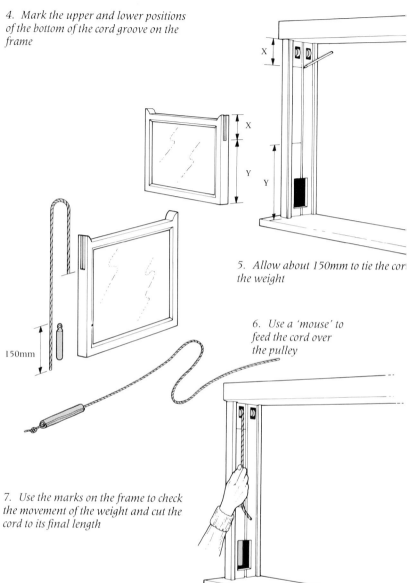

5. *Allow about 150mm to tie the cor[d] the weight*

6. *Use a 'mouse' to feed the cord over the pulley*

7. *Use the marks on the frame to check the movement of the weight and cut the cord to its final length*

To cut the new cords to length, first note the position of the bottom of the cord groove in each sash, and mark the equivalent positions on the frame for the sash fully up and fully down. Taking account of the lengths of the counterweights themselves, and allowing about 150mm for final adjustment and for the knot, cut the cords to length. Measure each cord individually: don't assume that they'll all be the same.

To feed the cords over the pulleys, tie a 'mouse' – a length of string with a weight small enough to pass over the pulleys – to the end of the cord. Put a temporary knot in the other end of the cord to stop it running right through. Then put the mouse over the pulley and retrieve it through the pocket, drawing the new sash cord over the pulley. Tie the cord to the counterweight and feed the weight through the pocket into the weight compartment. Pull on the free end of the cord to raise the weight as far as possible, allow it to drop about 25mm, then hold the cord at a point corresponding to the lower mark on the frame. Now allow the weight to fall, keeping hold of the cord, and check that the holding point moves past the upper mark before the weight 'bottoms' in the frame. Don't let the weight fall too quickly or your fingers may get trapped in the pulley. If all is well, pull the weight up again and put a wedge in the pulley to hold it up. Then trim the cord to its final length by cutting at the holding point. Do the same for the other cords. Replace the pocket covers.

Refit the outer sash in the frame, nailing (rather than wedging) the cords in the grooves with tacks or clout nails. Replace the parting beads using oval brads. Finally, refit the inner sash, attach it to its cords, and replace the staff beads.

Fixing loose joints in sashes and casements

Sashes with loose joints are not only troublesome but can be dangerous. Sash windows share a number of similarities with the guillotine!

Loose joints can be tightened by holding the sash or casement in sash cramps (which can be hired), boring into the joints and inserting dowels using water-resistant glue. The ends of the dowels can be trimmed when the glue has set, and the repair treated with a suitable preservative.

Alternatively, metal plates can be screwed to the surface of the sash or casement. This has the advantage that the window doesn't need to be removed from the frame, but it looks ugly unless the plate is recessed into the wood by chiselling out a suitable space.

Repairing a broken window

Remove the broken glass with great care. Wear stout gloves and use pliers to handle awkward pieces. If the glass is patterned, note which way the pattern runs. In wooden frames where the glass was held in by putty, ease out the putty with a chisel or hacking knife. Pull out the

---

Repairing glazing

Glass
Glass comes in a range of types, thicknesses and finishes.

Float glass	The usual choice for domestic windows. Available in 3, 4, 5, 6 and 10mm thicknesses. 4mm glass is suitable for most windows, 6mm for larger windows.
Toughened glass	For higher-risk applications, such as internal doors, glass panels next to doors, low-level glazing, balustrades, shower screens and tabletops. Usually 6mm thick.
Laminated glass	For the same applications as toughened glass, but offering even greater security – laminated glass is very difficult to penetrate, even when broken. Usually 6mm thick.
Wired glass	Fire-resistant glazing for fire doors, etc. Not a security glazing. Usually 6mm thick.
Patterned or obscure glass	For privacy. Available in 4mm and 6mm thicknesses, and in a wide range of patterns, some tinted.
Solar control glass	Cuts down the heat radiation from the sun while letting most of the light through. Usually 6mm thick. May be tinted grey or bronze.
Mirrors	6mm glass with silvering on the back.
Diffuse reflection glass	Has a finely textured surface to reduce reflections. Used for picture framing. Usually 2mm or 3mm thick.

Alternatives to glass

Polystyrene	Used for secondary double glazing.
Acrylic	Used for secondary double glazing – tougher than polystyrene.
Polycarbonate	Used for security glazing – excellent resistance to impacts.

Fitting a new window

1. Clear out old putty

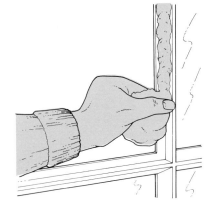

2. Press in fresh putty to bed glass on

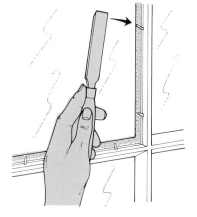

3. Tap in sprigs with the side of a chisel

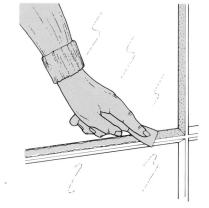

4. Finish with more putty and smooth it with a putty knife

sprigs – the small nails which held the glass in place under the putty – with pliers. In wooden frames with glazing beads, lever them off with a chisel. In metal frames where the glass was held in place by clips, remove these carefully and retain them to use with the new glass.

Clean out all the old putty and brush away debris. Apply a coat of primer (wood or metal as appropriate) to all the newly exposed surfaces. This is most important, as putty will not 'take' on bare wood.

Measure the rebate – the area the glass will fill. Take at least three measurements in each direction, and use the smallest. Check the squareness of the frame by measuring across the diagonals – if they're markedly different, make a sketch to

show the glass merchant.

The new glass should be 3mm smaller in both directions than the rebate. When you buy it, make clear whether the dimensions you give the glass merchant include or exclude this allowance. Take the old glass with you if you can – it will be a guide to the thickness you need for the new glass and to any pattern required, and it's safer than putting fragments of glass in the dustbin. When you get the new glass home, check that it fits the rebate easily.

Linseed oil putty is the traditional material for bedding-in glass in wooden frames. For metal frames, use metal casement putty. Knead a ball of putty until it is soft and pliable, then apply a continuous layer about 3mm thick all round the rebate with

your thumb, pressing it firmly into place. Offer up the new glass, and try to centre it in the rebate to leave an even gap all the way around – use spacers such as matchsticks if necessary. Press around the edge of the pane to bed the glass into the putty, using just enough pressure to squeeze a little of the putty out on the inside. Tap in glazing sprigs using the side of a firmer chisel or, in a metal frame, replace the clips.

Now apply facing putty all around the rebate, squeezing it out of the palm of your hand and pressing it with your thumb. Use a putty knife (a clean filling knife is a good substitute) to smooth it off at an angle of about 45 degrees to the glass and to mitre the corners neatly. Clean up the putty on the inside, leaving a slight angle to encourage condensation to run off. To ensure that the putty is sealed to the glass, run over it with a damp paintbrush or a wetted finger. If the frame has glazing beads, use less facing putty; replace the beads using panel pins and, for extra security, waterproof glue.

Leave the fresh putty for a week or two before painting. Take the paint line on to the glass – inside and out – by about 2mm to form a watertight seal.

Repairs to double glazing

Double glazing in metal and UPVC frames is often dry-glazed – the double-glazing unit is held in place by beads which incorporate weather-resistant seals. In many designs these beads are difficult to remove without special tools – this prevents burglars simply lifting the glazing out – and you will have to contact the manufacturer if a window needs to be replaced.

Double glazing in wooden frames is usually retained by conventional glazing beads pinned to the frames. If you can buy a double-glazed unit of the correct size, replacing these may be a d-i-y job. Most systems use mastic rather than putty to seal the units to the frames.

4 Floors, ceilings and stairs

Problems with floors, ceilings and stairs can range from the simply irritating, such as squeaky or uneven floorboards, to serious structural defects arising from rot or infestation. There is only limited scope for preventive maintenance, but any signs of potential trouble must be dealt with promptly. Replacing a whole floor, ceiling or flight of stairs can be expensive, time-consuming and very disruptive.

Inspecting floors, ceilings and stairs

Once a year, make a methodical inspection of all the floors, ceilings and stairs in your home.

Look for:
- any signs of damp in the floors or around the skirting boards – check for musty smells under floor coverings
- any outward signs of rot – look for threads of fungus, discoloration and cracks
- any outward signs of woodworm – look for holes, typically 1 to 2mm across, and piles of what appears to be fine sawdust
- uneven floorboards and gaps between the boards
- springy or creaking floorboards
- gaps opening up between floors

and skirting boards, especially if cracks have appeared or plaster is flaking away from the ceiling below.
- damp, discoloured or sagging ceilings
- creaky stairs
- cracked or broken stair handrails and balusters

All these problems need immediate attention.

Floors

In older houses both the ground and upper floors are likely to be of 'suspended' construction, with floorboards or sheet flooring supported on a series of wooden joists. In homes built after about 1940 it's more likely that the ground floor will be of solid construction: essentially a concrete slab built up on top of the ground.

Suspended upper floors

The main load-bearing components of any suspended floor are the joists: substantial timbers placed 400 to 600mm apart which span the space between the walls of the house.

On upper floors the joists are supported by the main walls of the house. This is achieved either by building the ends of the joists into the masonry or by using joist hangers, which are built into or fixed to the face of the wall. Where the joists meet the walls, short lengths of joist material, called noggings, are nailed between the joists to support the edges of the flooring.

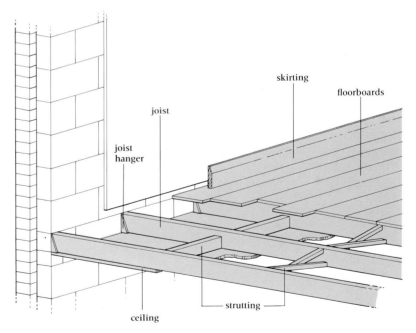

Suspended timber floor – strutting is used to stop long joists twisting

Floors, ceilings and stairs – symptoms, faults and remedies

Symptom	Fault	Remedy	*see page*
Creaking floorboards	• Boards rubbing together	• Lubricate with talcum powder	52
	• Boards not securely attached to joists	• Check joists, re-fix boards with screws or flooring brads	53
Uneven floors	• Wear and tear, or natural shrinkage	• Sand smooth	52
		• Cover with hardboard	52
	• Sagging joists	• Strengthen or replace affected joists	54
Draughty floors	• Gappy floorboard	• Fill gaps with strips of wood	52
Damp	• Inadequate ventilation	• Poke out airbricks	
	• Problems with damp-proof course	• See Walls, p. 20	
Sagging ceilings	• Ceiling separated from joists	• Put in new fixings	56
	• Failed joists	• Strengthen or replace	54
Creaking stairs	• Loose joints	• Reinforce from below with metal brackets	57
		• Tighten joints by inserting screws	57
Broken handrails		• Splice in a new section, or use special handrail bolts	58
Rot or woodworm		• Call in professional help	58

If the joists span more than 3m additional stiffening should be provided to prevent them twisting. This may take the form either of further noggings or angled timbers known as herringbone strutting fixed at mid-span. If the joists span more than 4m, additional timber or steel cross-members known as binders may be required.

The ceilings of rooms on the floor below, whether lath-and-plaster or plasterboard, are generally fixed to the underside of the joists.

Suspended ground floors

The joists of suspended ground floors may be supported by the house walls, either by building the ends of the joists into the masonry or by using joist hangers. More commonly, though, ground-floor joists rely on sleeper walls around the perimeter and at intervals beneath the house. To keep the joists dry, each sleeper wall must have a damp-proof course between the masonry and the wall plate – the piece of timber on which the joists rest.

Damp is the great enemy of suspended ground floors, and the space beneath the floor must be well ventilated. Airbricks in the outer walls allow air to pass beneath the floor, and sleeper walls are often built in honeycomb construction, with spaces between the bricks which allow air to circulate freely.

Flooring for suspended floors

The conventional flooring for suspended floors in tongued-and-grooved timber boarding, about 125 to 150mm wide, laid at right-angles to the joists. Alternatives, particularly in newer houses, are sheets of man-made boards such as plywood or chipboard. These are available in special flooring grades with tongued-and-grooved edges, in sheets which are usually 2.4 by 0.6m. Flooring-grade chipboard for kitchens and bathrooms should be BS5669 type 2/3, sometimes called V313 and tinted green.

Old houses may have butt-jointed floorboards, without tongues and grooves. These are more prone to draughts and tend to be less even, since the boards are supported only by the joists, not by one another. Their only advantage is that they are easier to lift.

Solid floors

Solid floors consist of a series of layers built up from ground level. In modern homes solid floors should always incorporate a damp-proof membrane which is linked to the damp-proof course in the walls. In older homes solid floors may rely on a water-resistant final layer, such as quarry tiles, to keep damp at bay.

Solid floors can be up to 400mm thick. The first layer is hardcore, well graded and firmly compacted, about 150 to 200mm thick. The hardcore is then 'blinded' with sand or a weak mixture of sand and cement, to provide a smooth surface for the damp-proof membrane, usually heavy-gauge polythene. The main load-bearing element – the concrete slab – comes next, between 100 and 150mm thick. Finally, a finishing premature failure, particularly if the loads are applied over small areas.

Damp, caused either by structural faults elsewhere in the fabric of the house, or by leaking water pipes, will certainly reduce the life of a suspended floor, and can quickly ruin coverings on solid floors. On the outside of the house, regularly check airbricks providing ventilation under suspended floors – poke through the holes with a screwdriver to make sure that they're clear. Remove grilles if necessary to clear out debris.

Wooden floors which have been painted or sealed are much less likely to suffer attack by woodworm.

Repairing suspended floors

Uneven floorboards and gaps between the boards are common problems with suspended floors. On their own they're unlikely to suggest more fundamental problems, and are more likely to be caused by everyday wear and tear or by shrinkage, particularly in centrally heated homes.

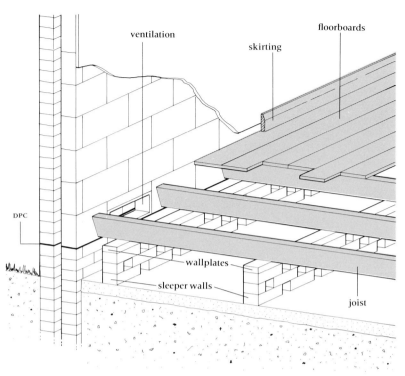

Suspended ground floor resting on honeycomb 'sleeper' walls

screed of sand and cement, about 40mm thick, is applied to produce a smooth surface.

As an alternative to placing the damp-proof membrane under the slab, it can go between the slab and the finishing screed, though this calls for the screed to be about 25mm thicker. In either case the damp-proof membrane must be neatly folded up behind the skirtings and, ideally, tucked into the walls to link up with the damp-proof course.

Looking after floors

Because the principal structural elements of floors are relatively inaccessible, the scope for preventive maintenance is limited. However, it is important to avoid overloading. Heavy items of household equipment or furniture, such as Aga or Rayburn stoves, pianos and waterbeds, can impose stresses on suspended floors which could lead to

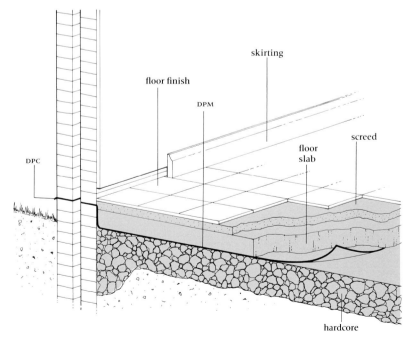

Solid ground floor

Filling gaps between floorboards

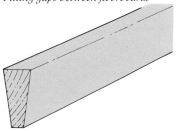

1. *Cut wedge-shaped strips to fit in gaps*

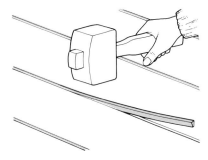

2. *Glue and tap into place*

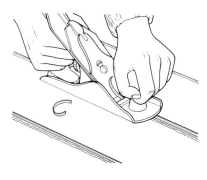

3. *Plane smooth*

To fill gaps, make up softwood strips with a slight wedge shape, apply PVA wood-working glue to the sides and tap them into place. When the glue has set, punch down any nearby nails and plane the strips flush with the boards.

If the unevenness affects a large part of the floor, then sanding it smooth may be the most appropriate treatment. This isn't a job to tackle with a d-i-y electric drill or orbital sander, however, and it's best to hire a professional belt sander.

Before using the machine, fill any gaps between the boards, punch down all the floor nails and remove any tacks or staples left in from floor coverings. Start with a relatively coarse belt and work across the floor at 45 degrees to the boards.

Progress to a less coarse belt, and carry out the second sanding at right-angles to the first. Finally, complete the job with one or two sandings using a fine belt along the grain of the boards. As well as making the floor even, sanding removes ingrained dirt and old paint or varnish, but it's a messy job.

Another way to get a smooth floor is to cover it with sheets of hardboard, fixed with deep-drive panel pins. This is a particularly useful technique in preparation for floor finishes like cork tiles in a bathroom, for example, since it prevents the tile adhesive or subsequent sealer running through gaps between the boards. The hardboard is relatively

cheap, and also means that the tiles can be removed in the future, along with the hardboard, without damaging the floorboards themselves.

Unevenness in just one part of the floor may indicate that one or more floorboards has been removed and replaced carelessly. Plumbers and electricians, who have to remove some floorboards in the course of their work, are not always as conscientious as they might be when they replace them.

Creaking and springy floorboards usually indicate that some of the boards are not securely attached to the joists. Don't simply take up the floor covering and whack in a few extra nails – try to establish the cause of the problem first.

If it's clear that the offending board is one which has been removed at some time, lever it out and make sure that it's properly supported. See Removing and Replacing Floorboards. This will also establish whether there is any plumbing or electrical wiring under the board. Add any additional support required and replace the board using cut floor brads or, better still, countersunk screws.

Slight squeaks may be caused by floorboards rubbing against one another, even though they're securely attached to the joists, especially where the boards are butt-jointed or where the tongue has been removed. Talcum powder, worked into the gap between the

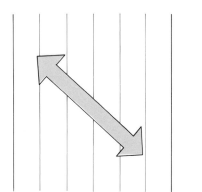
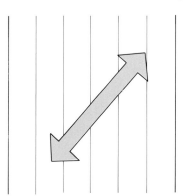
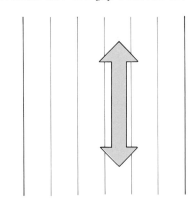

For a smooth floor sand with coarse belts at an angle to the boards, finishing off parallel to the boards with a fine belt

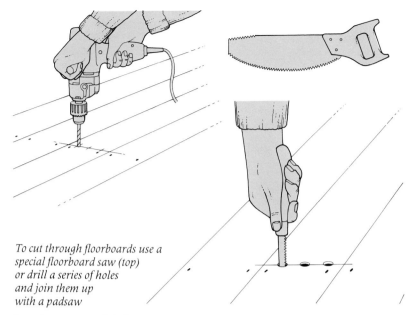

*To cut through floorboards use a
special floorboard saw (top)
or drill a series of holes
and join them up
with a padsaw*

boards to act as a lubricant, can cure the problem.

If several boards are affected, and particularly where the boards show no signs of having been removed before, it may be that one or more joists has sagged or twisted and that more extensive repairs are required. If the corresponding area of ceiling in the room below also shows signs of sagging, then there's little doubt that the joists are in need of attention. See Repairing Floor Joists, p. 54.

Removing and replacing floorboards

If you suspect problems in the structure of the floor beneath the boards, or if the boards themselves have been damaged, you'll have to lift and replace them. Remember that pipes and cables run under floorboards. It's a wise precaution to turn off the

electricity, at least until you can see where the cables run, and to make sure you know how to shut off the water in the event of a mishap. With furniture and floor coverings removed, you will be able to see where the joists run by the lines of nails in the floorboards. Mark out the area you intend to remove.

Unless one of the boards is already loose or has been removed in the past, it will be necessary to cut through one of the boards. If you can, choose a board which already has an end joint in the area you plan to remove. Cut across the board as close as possible to the edge of a joist – about 25mm from the nail heads should just miss the joist itself. Professionals use a special floorboard saw for this – it looks rather like a short panel saw, but the edge with the teeth is curved. If you don't have

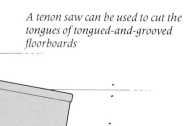

*A tenon saw can be used to cut the
tongues of tongued-and-grooved
floorboards*

one of these, a tenon saw is a possible though a rather inferior substitute. Perhaps the easiest d-i-y method is to drill several holes along the intended saw-cut and use a pad saw to cut through the board.

If your floorboards are tongued and grooved, it will be necessary to cut off the tongue on at least one side of the board. You could do this with a floorboard saw or a tenon saw, or with a circular saw set so that the blade just cuts through the tongue.

Insert a bolster chisel into the original saw-cut and lever up the end of the board. If the boards are not too tight a fit, it should be possible to ease the board up and away from the uncut side. But if this is not possible without damaging the edge of the board or its neighbour, then the tongue on that side will also have to be sawn through.

Gradually work the board out, supporting the raised part with a piece of wood across the adjacent floorboards. When enough of the

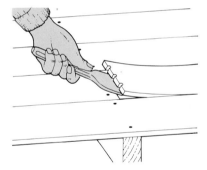

1. Lever out with a bolster chisel

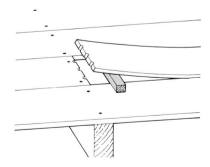

2. Insert a wedge of timber

Lifting a floorboard

board has been raised, make a second cross-cut in line with the centre of a joist.

Once the first board is out, it's relatively easy to lift out as many more as necessary, cutting them across in the same way as the first board but without removing the tongues.

To replace the boards, first screw a batten to the face of the joist where the first cut was made, to support the ends of the floorboards, then replace the boards in reverse order.

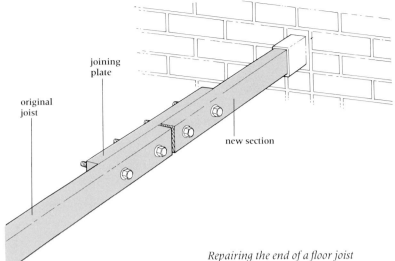

Repairing the end of a floor joist

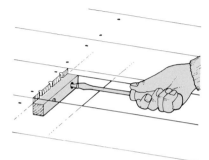

Before replacing the floorboard, screw a piece of wood to the joist to support the end

If you are putting in new boards, cut them longer than the old ones, by half the width of a joist. Then prise out the ends of the remaining boards where the first cut was made, remove the nails, and cut the boards back to the centreline of the joist. A batten will not then be necessary, since the boards will be supported by the joists themselves.

Finally, secure the floorboards to the joists, taking care to avoid any pipes or cables. If the boards will normally be hidden by floor coverings, it may be advisable for future reference to mark the position of pipes and cables on the upper surface of the boards. Coloured self-adhesive tapes are ideal for this.

The traditional fixings for floorboards are cut nails, or brads, hammered well in. But if you think you may need to raise the board again, or are concerned that hammering could damage the ceiling below, use countersunk screws.

Repairing floor joists

If part of the edge of a floor becomes springy, and particularly if a gap opens up between the floor and the skirting board, or if cracks appear or plaster begins to flake away from the corresponding area of ceiling on the floor below, the root of the problem is likely to be where the ends of the joists meet the wall. Joists can need attention for a number of reasons:

● they become dislodged or are inadequately supported where they are attached to the main structure
● the strutting has failed or has become inadequate
● they are too small to carry the load
● they have been weakened by rot or woodworm.

Joists can be repaired or strengthened, and if necessary can be replaced.

Remove the floorboards in the affected area. When joists are installed, whether in recesses in the masonry or using joist hangers, wedges of wood or pieces of slate may be used to bring each joist level with its neighbours. The problem could be that these have shifted, allowing the end of the joist to sag. If there are no signs of damage or decay, the levelling pieces can simply be replaced.

If decay is present, then the cause must be determined and eradicated. If only the end of the joist has been affected, it may be possible to replace just that part of it. Cut away the affected part of the old joist and remove it carefully to minimise damage to the ceiling below. Prepare a new length of joist and a timber 'plate', which will be used to attach it to the remaining part of the existing joist. The plate should be long

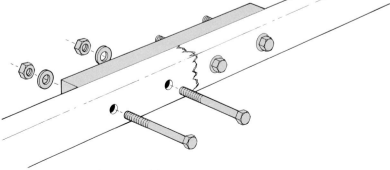

Strengthening a weak-spot in a joist

enough to overlap both the original joist and the new end section by at least twice the depth of the joist. Treat the end of the new section with a timber preservative, and, if it's to be inserted into the masonry, wrap DPC material around it.

Bolt the new section of joist to the plate, then insert the end into the wall or joist hanger and bolt the plate to the existing joist. Make any necessary repairs to the ceiling and replace the floorboards.

For joists which tend to sag in the middle, removing the floorboards may reveal that the cause is failure of some of the struts or noggings rather than of the joists themselves. Replace them, cross-nailing them into the joists. Alternatively, a joist may have a local weak spot, in which case a timber plate can be bolted to the existing joist to strengthen it.

Replacing sections of ground-floor joists

Where a suspended ground floor rests on sleeper walls, it is usually possible to replace sections of joists between two adjacent sleeper walls without having to replace the whole length.

Remove the floorboards to reveal the section of joist to be replaced and the sleeper walls and wallplates on each side of it. Cut out the defective section by sawing through inside the wallplates.

Cut the new section of joist to length so that it will rest on both wallplates and overlap the ends of the remaining parts of the old joist. Use treated timber, and wrap DPC material around the end if it goes into the wall. Nail the new section of joist to the wallplates and to the ends of the old joist, and replace the floorboards.

Replacing whole joists

Replacing the whole length of a joist is a considerable undertaking. Clearly, it will be necessary to remove all the flooring over the joist or joists you intend to renew. If it's an upper floor, it may also be necessary to remove part of the ceiling in the room below. Where a single joist is being replaced, it may be possible to leave the ceiling in place, but you will need to exercise care and some damage is probably inevitable.

Having removed the defective joist, cut the new one to length. If it is supported by joist hangers, this is simply the distance between them, and the new joist can be dropped in and nailed in place through the joist hangers. Where the joist is supported in recesses in the masonry of the inner leaf of cavity walls, the length of the joist should be the distance between the walls plus the amount that the timber can be inserted into one of the recesses. This insertion allowance should be about 165mm –

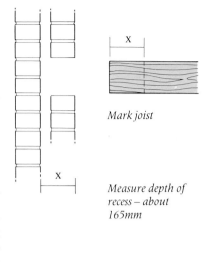

Mark joist

Measure depth of recess – about 165mm

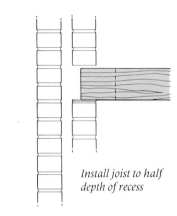

Install joist to half depth of recess

Installing a new joist

115mm of brick or blockwork plus 50mm or so of cavity. Mark this off on one end of the joist.

Treat the cut ends with a timber preservative, and wrap DPC material around them. On the marked end of the joist, use a piece of tape or something similar to indicate the point half-way between the end of the joist and the original mark. Insert the new joist fully into one of the recesses. It should now be possible to manoeuvre the joist into the opposite recess. Centre the joist so that the piece of tape lines up with the inner face of the wall, which will ensure that the joist is equally supported at each end.

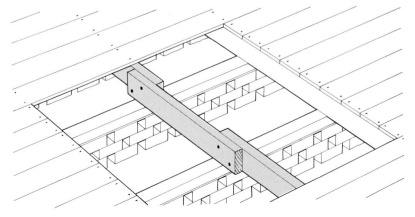

Replacing a section of joist in a suspended ground floor

Solid walls are more difficult, since some of the masonry would need to be removed to put in the new joist. To avoid this, brick up the holes left after removing the old joist and use joist hangers for the new one.

If a suspended ground floor is in very poor condition, it may be possible to replace it with a solid floor. You should get professional advice from a surveyor or your local authority Building Control Officer before embarking on this, however.

Repairing solid floors

A solid floor is very unlikely to suffer any structural failure. When problems arise, they are usually associated with rising damp, either because the damp-proof membrane is inadequate or because the floor does not incorporate one.

It is very unlikely that such problems can be cured by piecemeal repairs to the floor. The only reliable solution is to take up the whole floor and replace it with one which incorporates an efficient damp-proof membrane. This is a very substantial job, and in some cases may involve raising doors and skirting boards.

Insulating floors

All types of floors can be insulated, and any work you have to do on floors – particularly ground floors – may provide an opportunity to add insulation.

Ceilings

In older houses ceilings are generally of lath-and-plaster construction. In newer homes they are usually plasterboard with either a skim of finishing plaster or textured paint.

Laths are thin wooden battens which are nailed to the joists, leaving small gaps between them. Plaster is then pressed on to the laths so that it is squeezed through the gaps, where it spreads out to form a key.

If a lath-and-plaster ceiling gives when pressed, the most likely cause is that some of the laths have parted

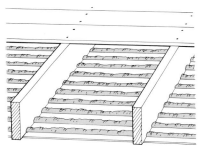

Lath and plaster ceiling

from the joists. If the sag is only slight, it should be possible to reattach the laths to the joists using galvanised screws, covering the heads with proprietary filler.

To repair small areas of ceiling damage, such as a ragged hole where a ceiling rose used to be, a lath-and-plaster ceiling can be repaired with a patch of plasterboard. Strip the damaged area back to the centre of the joists on either side, cutting through the laths. Then cut a piece of plasterboard to fit the hole, and fix it – grey

side down – to the joists with galvanised screws. Finally, bring the patch level with the rest of the ceiling by smoothing on board finish plaster; you'll need more than one coat if the difference in levels is greater than about 3mm.

Plasterboard ceilings can be repaired in much the same way. Slight sags can often be cured by renailing them to the joists. To find the joists, probe with a fine bradawl

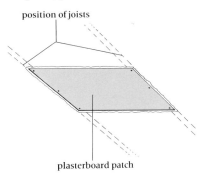

Repairing a ceiling with a patch of plasterboard

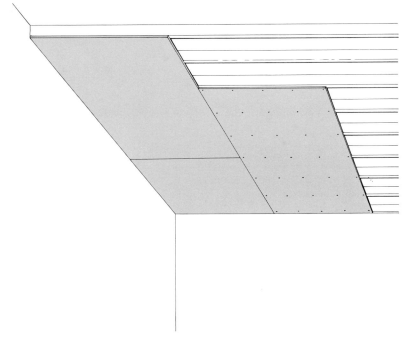

Renewing a whole ceiling with plasterboard – stagger the boards and fit them with the long sides at right angles to the joists

– it will pass through the plasterboard fairly easily and the small holes will be easy to fill. Use galvanised plasterboard nails.

Plasterboard which gets wet will tend to sag and bulge permanently. It must be replaced. If the affected area is small, the patching technique described for lath-and-plaster ceilings may be appropriate.

If a large part of the ceiling – or all of it – has to be replaced, use 9.5mm-thick plasterboard when the joists are not more than 400mm apart, 12.7mm board when the joists are up to 600mm apart. Pull away the old ceiling and remove the old nails. Fix the new boards with galvanised plasterboard nails, driven in just below the surface paper. You'll need someone to help you manoeuvre each board into place: even 9.5mm plasterboard is surprisingly heavy. Arrange the boards with their long sides at right-angles to the joists, and stagger the joints between them. Support the joints with noggings cross-nailed into the joists.

To cut plasterboard, score it deeply with a trimming knife and break it over a straight-edge. The plasterboard should be installed grey side down if you intend to finish it with a skin of plaster, ivory side down if you're going to paint it.

Cracks between ceilings and walls

Cracks at the edge of ceilings, where they meet the walls, are very common. They are caused by tiny movements of the house, such as normal expansion and contraction, and do not indicate any structural shortcomings. They can be a nuisance, nonetheless, particularly as they tend to reappear even if you fill them each time you decorate. The best way to hide them is with coving. This is a curved profile which is glued in place to link the wall and ceiling, concealing the joint between them. Coving is available in expanded polystyrene or, for a more professional result, plasterboard.

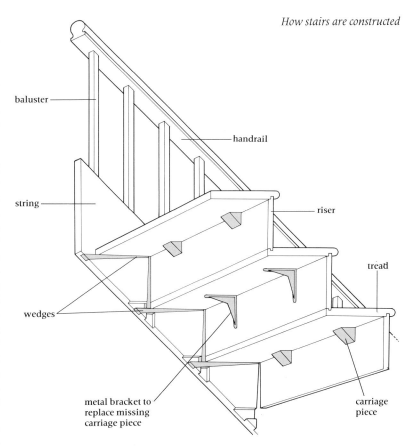

How stairs are constructed

baluster

handrail

string

riser

tread

wedges

metal bracket to replace missing carriage piece

carriage piece

Stairs

Creaking in stairs is caused by some of the pieces of timber rubbing against one another. The construction of stairs is quite complicated, so there's a good deal of scope for this.

If you have ready access to the underside of the staircase, check that all the carriage pieces and wedges are secure. If necessary, metal shelf brackets can be added to stiffen individual treads.

From above, a creaky tread may be cured by screwing through it into the riser below. Use countersunk screws finished flush with the surface of the tread.

Insecure or **broken handrails** can be very dangerous, and should be repaired without delay. A cracked

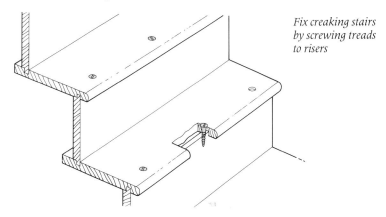

Fix creaking stairs by screwing treads to risers

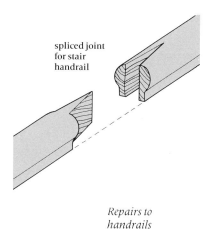

spliced joint
for stair
handrail

*Repairs to
handrails*

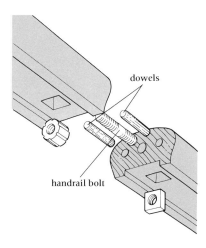

dowels

handrail bolt

handrail can be repaired by squeezing glue into the crack and clamping the handrail firmly until the glue has set.

To deal with more serious problems, new sections of handrail can be spliced into the old, or attached by dowels and handrail bolts. To splice in a new section, cut into the old handrail in a v-shape, and trim the new handrail to fit. Apply the glue to the join, insert the new section and clamp firmly.

Handrail bolts hold sections of rail together. Mark out the ends carefully, and bore into the wood for the bolts and for two dowels to prevent

the handrail rotating. On the undersides, chisel out recesses so that the nuts can be fitted. Apply glue to the dowels and to the ends of the rails, and tighten the nuts securely.

Mending broken balusters

Balusters are the vertical timbers at the side of stairs – together with the handrail they form the balustrade. Cracked balusters can be mended by gluing and clamping, but for the sake of safety badly damaged baluster should be replaced.

Dealing with rot and woodworm

Wet rot

Wet rot thrives in timber which never dries out. It's more common in exterior woodwork which is exposed to the weather, but can arise in floors if a serious degree of damp is present – in bathrooms and lavatories, for example.

Wet rot can be caused by a number of different fungi which thrive in wet conditions. In floors, the most common culprit is the cellar fungus. This causes the wood to darken, swell and soften, and may lead to cracks along the grain. The fungus itself may be visible as a tangle of thin brown threads on the surface of the wood.

Wet rot can be eradicated by removing the cause of the damp. The fungus cannot survive once the wood has dried out. Any affected wood will have been seriously weakened, however, and must be replaced.

Dry rot

Dry rot, in spite of its name, is also caused by a fungus which needs damp conditions in which to start, but can then spread to drier timber and across or even through intervening masonry. An attack of dry rot

is therefore often more extensive than it may appear at first. Inadequately ventilated floor spaces are most susceptible.

Dry rot appears as a covering of white, grey or yellow strands, and wood that has been affected cracks across the grain into cubes which crumble when touched. Prompt action is essential. The first step is to eradicate the cause by seeking out any penetrating or rising damp and by improving ventilation. Then the extent of the attack must be determined and all the affected timber and plasterwork cut away. This is almost always a job for professionals, who can assess the structural implications and apply appropriate spray treatments.

Woodworm

Woodworm is a general name for the larvae of a range of beetles, though the common furniture beetle is the most frequent attacker. The adult beetles lay their eggs on the wood, and the larvae burrow into it and may chomp away for years before emerging as adult beetles. The signs of a woodworm attack are small holes in the timber, sometimes accompanied by tiny piles of what looks like fine sawdust. Favourite targets are cellars and outhouses – woodworm prefer slightly damp conditions – the plywood boards that electricity and gas meters are mounted on, the undersides of staircases and lofts, particularly where these have been used to store old furniture.

A severe attack by woodworm, especially some of the more voracious species such as the house longhorned beetle, can seriously weaken timber. Although d-i-y woodworm treatments are available, if you suspect an attack you should call in professional woodworm treatment specialists.

5 Fences, outside walls and gates

Fences, walls and gates come in a variety of types and materials, and most need regular maintenance to keep them in good condition. The great enemy is damp, which penetrates wooden fences and fence posts and promotes rot, causes brickwork to crumble when frost strikes and gives rise to rust in nails, fencing wires and hinges.

Maintenance can be complicated by disputes between neighbours over the ownership of fences. Traditionally, the structural components of a fence are on the inside of the property to which it belongs, with the fence boards or panels applied to the outside. As a rule of thumb, if you can see the framework of the fence from your side, the fence probably belongs to you – although this is certainly not a hard and fast rule. If you need to determine whether a fence or wall lies on your land or on the adjacent plot, ask to see the plans held by your local authority Department of Planning and Building Control. Where doubt still remains, try to come to an agreement with your neighbour over the maintenance of the fence – it's in nobody's interest to simply ignore it.

Inspecting your fences, walls and gates

Problems with fences, walls and gates often make themselves apparent without anyone specifically looking for them. Regular inspections are worthwhile, nonetheless – twice a year, say, in spring and autumn – since minor repairs carried out promptly can often prevent major remedial work later on. Wooden fences treated with creosote or other preservatives need re-treatment every two or three years to keep rot at bay.

Fences:
- examine fence posts carefully for signs of rot, particularly at ground level: rotten posts must be replaced
- in fences which have horizontal rails jointed into the fence posts, check for rot caused by water penetrating the joints
- check fence boards or panels for damage or decay
- check that the bottom of the fence is not in direct contact with the ground; fencing should be fitted clear of ground level, with gravel boards to span the gap
- check gravel boards for rot
- wooden fences are often held together by nails – these inevitably rust in time and need to be replaced
- in chain link fences, check throughout for rust and for slackness in the tensioning wires.

Walls:
- check for frost damage on the tops of brick walls, causing the bricks to crumble
- check that walls are upright and straight, particularly where the wall marks a change in level and is supporting higher ground on one side.

Gates:
- make sure gates swing freely on their hinges and don't 'bind' on the gateposts
- check that catches and locks work efficiently
- check for signs of rot or damage.

Fences

Wooden fences
There are three main types of wooden fence:
Panel fences consist of pre-fabricated panels attached with nails or clips between wooden fence posts, or slotted into moulded channels in concrete fence posts.

Boarded fences are built up on site. Horizontal rails are attached between the fence posts, and the fence boards are then attached to the rails, usually on the outside. The fence boarding may be in a 'stockade' style, with gaps between the boards, or 'feather edge', with tapered, overlapping boards.

Ranch-style fences have no vertical fence boards, but consist only of a series of horizontal rails spanning the fence posts.

Fence posts
Fence posts for timber fencing come in wood or concrete. They're usually supported by concrete

Fences, walls and gates – symptoms, faults and remedies

Symptom	Fault	Remedy	*see page*
Loose fence post	• Rot caused by water getting into post at ground level	• Replace post – either:	
		• dig out base of post, replace with new post set in rubble or concrete,	62
		• install concrete spur and bolt post to it, or	62
		• fit new post set in steel fence post socket	63
Decayed gravel boards	• Rot caused by water seeping up from the ground	• Replace the gravel boards	64
Loose joints in boarded fencing	• Rot caused by water getting into joints	• Fit arris rail brackets • Replace affected timber	63
Loose fence boards or panels	• Nails have rusted away	• Re-nail or fit fencing clips	63
Holes in chain link fencing	• Rust	• Replace	64
Slack chain link fencing	• Loose or broken tensioning wires	• Tighten or replace tensioning wires	64
Crumbling bricks on top of wall	• Frost damage	• Replace any badly affected bricks – add water-resistant capping	64
Sagging or bulging walls	• Inadequate foundations • Foundations undermined by tree roots	• Rebuild the wall • You must sacrifice either the tree or the wall – you'll have to decide which	64
Gate won't close (or won't open)	• Gateposts rotten • Loose hinges • Sagging joints in gate	• Treat as for fence posts • Re-fix or replace • Secure joints with dowels or wedges	62 41 65

around the base below ground level. A hole is dug, the fence post is put in and held upright by a temporary support, and wet concrete is poured around it. When the concrete sets the post should be secure.

The best timber posts are hardwood – usually oak – but these are expensive, so softwood is often used for economy. Whatever the wood, it must be thoroughly treated with preservative, especially at the base.

Concrete fence posts come in a variety of forms and sizes. For panel fencing, concrete posts are available which have channels moulded in either side, so that the panels can be slotted into place between pairs of posts.

Provided that they don't get damaged, concrete posts can be expected to last many years. But wooden posts tend to have a much more limited life. The problems arise where the posts meet the ground. The conditions here are ideal for rot, and posts often fail at this point even though they're in good condition elsewhere. There's not a great deal that can be done to prevent this for existing posts, but for new ones it's worthwhile taking trouble to protect the post before it is installed.

Gravel boards

Whatever its type, wooden fencing should be installed so that it is clear of the ground, to prevent rot. Preser-

vative-treated gravel boards should be fitted at ground level between the fence posts to fill the gaps. The gravel boards are bound to rot, but are simple and relatively inexpensive to replace.

Chain link fencing

Chain link fencing is made of steel wire. It may be plastic-coated (usually green), or galvanised, and is available in a range of widths and wire sizes, expressed as the 'gauge' of the wire – the smaller the gauge number, the thicker the wire.

Chain link fencing is supported by tensioning wires strung between the fence posts. Fence posts for chain link fencing up to about 1.8m high are usually concrete. The posts have holes for attaching the tensioning wires at the corners, or to allow them to pass through intermediate posts. Corner posts usually have extra diagonal supports to prevent them sagging under the tension of the wires.

For taller chain link fencing – around a tennis court, for example –

the fence posts are often 'angle iron'. This is actually steel which has been painted or galvanised. They're usually set in concrete like other types of post.

Just as the conditions at ground level tend to promote rot in wooden posts, steel posts tend to rust at this point.

Repairing fences

Fences usually fail as a result of high winds. The most common problem is that a fence post which has been weakened by rot gives way at the base. If you're unlucky, there can then be a domino effect with other posts failing along the run.

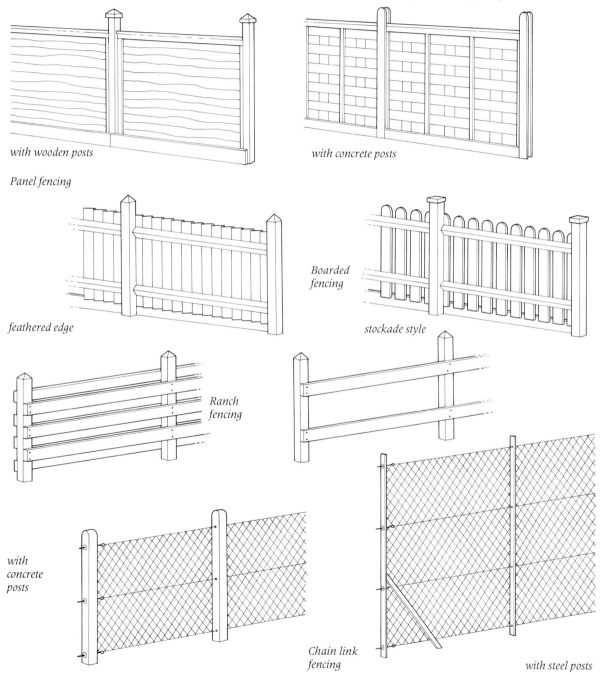

with wooden posts

with concrete posts

Panel fencing

Boarded fencing

feathered edge

stockade style

Ranch fencing

with concrete posts

Chain link fencing

with steel posts

61

If you spot the initial failure early enough, it's worthwhile rigging up some temporary support – a couple of diagonal braces, for example – to minimise the damage. Once fence panels come adrift they're likely both to get damaged themselves and cause further damage elsewhere. If they look as though they're likely to break free it may be worth removing them, but take care and don't attempt this on your own – a fencing panel freed from its mountings is very hard to handle in a wind.

Don't attempt permanent repairs until the wind has died down, and don't skimp the repair – it's never worthwhile.

Replacing a fence post

There are at least three ways to replace a fence post. If the part of the post which was above ground level is in good condition, you could cut off the decayed stump and bolt the remaining post to a concrete spur. If you need a new post, it can be installed in concrete or – if you soil is strong – in rubble surrounded by compacted earth. If you'd rather avoid the hard work of digging out the old stump, you can install the new post in a steel fence post socket driven into the old stump.

Whether you're using a new post or the remains of an existing one, stand the base in a container of wood preservative for at least 24 hours.

Installing a fence post spur

Spurs are concrete bases to which fence posts are bolted. Because the post is held clear of the ground it's much less likely to rot, and the concrete spur itself should last for many years.

Dig out the old stump, line the bottom of the hole with rubble, bolt the post to the spur and set it in the hole. Make sure that the base of the post will be above ground level. If necessary, add more rubble to bring it up to the right level. Make sure that the post is upright and support it with a couple of temporary struts.

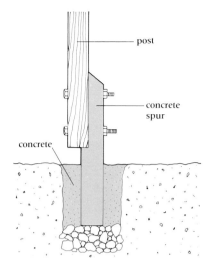

Repairing a wooden post using a concrete spur

Using a mix of about 1:2:4 of cement, sand and coarse aggregate, surround the spur with concrete. Allow the concrete two or three days to cure before removing the struts.

Installing a new post in concrete

Buy the new post, allowing for about 0.5m below ground. Install the post as described for a post spur (above), but bring the concrete above ground level and smooth it off away from the post. This will encourage water to

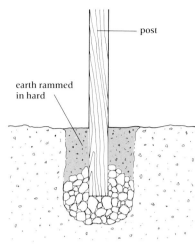

In firm ground you may not need to use concrete

run off and reduce the risk of rot in the future.

If you have at least fairly heavy soil, you may prefer to surround the base of the post with rubble – broken bricks, for example – and then fill the hole with soil, ramming it down hard. This technique has the advantage that water tends to drain away from the base of the post, but will only be successful where the soil is strong enough to give the necessary support.

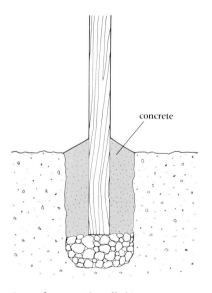

A new fence post installed in concrete

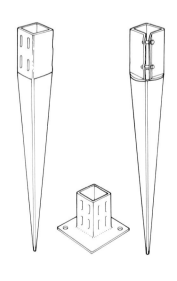

Steel fence post sockets

Using a steel fence post socket

Steel sockets for fence posts are intended primarily to be driven into virgin soil, for new fences. They're available in various sizes, to suit fences of different heights. But they can also be used to rejuvenate old fence post stumps, by driving the socket into the soft stump of the old post without the need to dig out the concrete.

Most types have a tapered x-shaped spike. If you're driving a socket into the stump of an old post, choose a socket with a relatively short spike, or one with an l-shaped spike which is specifically designed for this purpose. Drive the socket in with a sledgehammer, using a 'dolly' (available from the supplier of the socket) to prevent damage to the socket.

You must make sure that the socket is driven in accurately, so that the new post will be upright. Since the post should be a very tight fit in the socket, it's not possible to insert and remove it at stages to check that

the socket is aligned correctly. Having someone to watch while you drive in the spike can be very helpful, or you can use a smaller piece of wood to check the alignment at intervals. Alternatively, you can buy sockets which can be tightened after being driven in.

Repairing fencing panels

Fencing panels rely for much of their strength on a secure attachment to the fence posts. Once they start to come adrift – because the fixing nails have rusted away, for example – they tend to come apart.

Prevent this by promptly replacing fixings which have given way or show signs of weakness. The panels are often nailed direct to the fence posts, but putting new nails into old panels can itself cause damage. To avoid this, use fencing panel clips which can be screwed to the panels

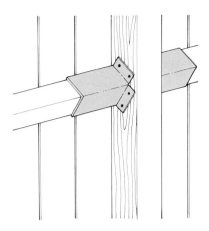

Arris rail repair bracket

holes will have to be drilled and plugged. You'll need a powerful drill, preferably with hammer action, and a masonry drill bit.

Individual fencing boards are fairly easy to replace. Take care not to damage sound boards when levering out the old nails, and always use galvanised nails when replacing them. Put the nails through the thick part of feather-edged boards taking

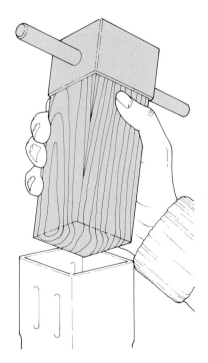

Dolly for driving in steel fence post sockets

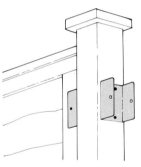

Fencing panel clips

and to the posts. Use zinc-plated screws – or better still brass – to prevent rusting in the future.

Repairs to boarded fencing

Boarded fencing is attached to horizontal rails strung between the fence posts. The rails are generally triangular – known as arris rails. They're susceptible to rot at the joints between the rails and the fence posts. If the damage isn't too great, arris rails can be repaired using a special metal bracket which fits over the rail and is nailed or screwed to the fence post.

With concrete posts, the screw

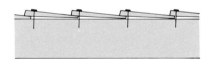

Nailing pattern for feather-edge fencing

care to miss the thin part of the board beneath.

In time, feather-edged boards tend to curl, so that gaps open up in the fence. If the problem is not too severe, soak the fence with enough water to make the boards pliable, and nail them flat. Take care not to split them, especially when working near the edges. If you think that there's a danger of splitting, drill holes through the boards first. When you've sorted out the boards, the whole fence will need a fresh coat of preservative, but wait until the water has dried out.

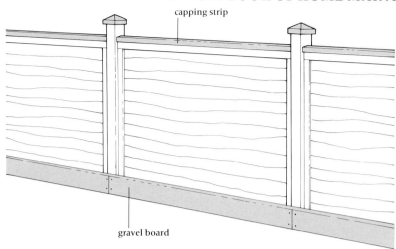

capping strip

gravel board

Capping and gravel boards protect fence panels from the worst of the weather and can easily be replaced

Replacing gravel boards

Gravel boards take the worst of the weather, and if they need to be renewed it's worthwhile using timber which has been pressure-treated with preservative. They're generally nailed to the faces of the fence posts.

Preserving your fences

Fence posts will last longer if they have caps of timber or rust-proof metal – lead, copper, zinc or aluminium. Fence panels and feather-edged boarded fences will also benefit from a saddleback capping strip.

Wooden fences need to be regularly treated with a suitable preservative. Choose dry weather if possible, to encourage the wood to soak up the preservative. Tie back plants to give you free access to the fence, and apply at least two generous coats.

If your fences are close to garden plants, choose a grade of preservative which won't damage them. Creosote will shrivel up almost any plant it touches before it's dry.

Repairs to chain link fencing

Rust is the principal enemy of chain link fencing, though with plastic-coated types it may not be immediately apparent. The rust eats away the steel wire inside the plastic coating, so that the fence can be very weak although it still appears to be in reasonable condition.

The only permanent repair to chain link fencing is to replace it. Holes can be patched, but the chances are that once the effects of rust have appeared, the whole fence has reached the end of its useful life.

If chain link fencing has simply sagged, however, the problem is more likely to be the tensioning wires than the fencing itself. For replacements, use only galvanised wire. Don't overtighten the tensioning devices at the ends of the wire – they need only be tight enough to prevent the fence sagging. Excessive tension puts undue strain on the wires themselves and on the supporting posts.

Walls

Garden walls tend to be the poor relation of the walls which form part of the house. They often have only modest foundations, can be dis-turbed by the roots of trees, and are completely exposed to the weather. Fortunately, the consequences of this are often not too severe. However, where walls mark a change in level, so that they are supporting higher ground on one side, it is especially important to keep them in good condition.

Sags and bulges

A wall which sags or bulges may have inadequate foundations, or simply be too weak to carry the load it has to bear. Or it may be that the pointing has failed, allowing water to penetrate. Whatever the cause, it's too late to put the wall back to the way it once was. It may be possible to give it extra support in the form of piers or struts, and so prevent the problem getting worse, but the only permanent solution is to rebuild it.

Garden walls can sometimes be affected by the growth of tree roots. This almost always means that either the tree or the wall will have to be sacrificed if the other is to be saved.

Preventive maintenance of walls

Pointing The mortar pointing between the bricks or stones of a wall helps to keep damp out, and to maintain the structural integrity of the wall. For details of repointing brickwork see Walls, p. 22.

Capping Because the tops of garden walls are exposed, the brickwork can be damaged by frost, causing it to flake and crumble. This can be avoided by capping the wall with waterproof masonry such as engineering bricks or moulded concrete cap-stones or copings.

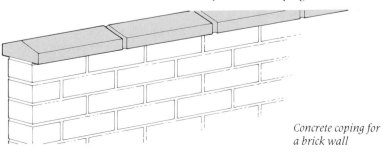

Concrete coping for a brick wall

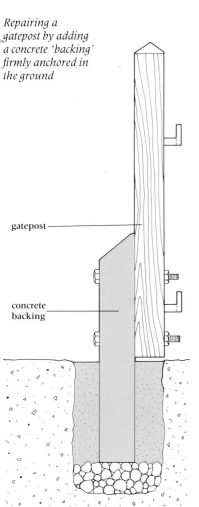

Repairing a gatepost by adding a concrete 'backing' firmly anchored in the ground

gatepost

concrete backing

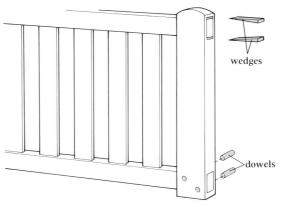

Add wedges and dowels to cure slack joints in a wooden gate; be sure to use a waterproof glue

wedges

dowels

Gates

Gateposts

Gateposts suffer the same ills as fence posts and respond to the same treatments. Gateposts must always be well-anchored. Loose gateposts which are otherwise sound can be backed with a concrete post.

Wooden gates

Wooden gates usually have mortise and tenon joints. In time, successive wet and dry cycles can cause the joints to become slack, so the gate sags. They can generally be rejuvenated by boring through the joints and inserting dowels, using a waterproof adhesive. If the outer ends of the tenons are visible, they can be tightened by driving in thin wedges.

Metal gates

Metal gates should need no more than a regular coat of paint every two years or so. Don't paint over rust – clean it back to the metal with a wire brush and apply a metal primer, or use one of the special one-coat paints designed for outdoor metal.

Hinges, locks and catches

The 'furniture' on external gates will benefit from an occasional drop of oil. As well as helping hinges and locks to work smoothly, the oil will tend to keep the water out, so helping them to resist corrosion.

6 Paintwork

Paint is more than a decorative finish: it is essential for preserving and prolonging the life of many parts of the house. The term paint covers a wide variety of coatings which are applied as liquids and dry to form a protective film over a surface.

All paints deteriorate with time, depending on the severity of the con- ditions to which they are exposed and on how well they are applied to start with. Paints used outdoors generally need to be renewed more frequently than paints for interior use. There's no hard-and-fast rule about how long any coat of paint is likely to last, but we give a guide in the Tables on the next few pages.

Types of paint

Primers and sealers

Alkali-resisting primer	• For cement, concrete, render, plaster and brickwork
Stabilising primer	• For loose and flaking surfaces on cement, concrete, plaster, etc. • Alkali-resisting
Knotting	• Used to seal knots and other resinous areas in softwood
Pink primer	• Traditional primer for wood • *May contain lead* – check label
Aluminium wood primer	• Alternative to pink primer • Contains particles of aluminium, but no lead
Quick-drying primer and primer/undercoat	• For wood – dries in an hour or so to allow the undercoat or topcoat to be applied the same day
Red lead	• Traditional primer for iron and steel – *contains lead*
Zinc phosphate primer	• General-purpose primer for metals • Alternative to red lead for iron and steel
Zinc chromate primer	• For aluminium and other non-ferrous metals • Rust-inhibiting primer for iron and steel
Calcium plumbate primer	• For galvanised metal such as garage doors and some window frames • *Contains lead* • Galvanised surface should be weathered before being painted

Never use primers or other paints which contain lead indoors, or for items such as children's play equipment outdoors

Paints for outside walls

Water-repellent solutions are used to fill the pores in brickwork. They can be useful in some cases of penetrating damp as an alternative to rendering or cladding. They're applied direct to the masonry by brush and dry clear, so there's virtually no change to the outward appearance of the wall. The surface of the masonry must be in good condition – a water-repellent solution won't make up for crumbling pointing.

Exterior emulsion paint adheres readily to masonry, and can be a cheap alternative to masonry paint for walls which are in good condition and not subject to very severe weather. Emulsion paints will not fill cracks, however.

Masonry paints contain fillers which help to fill and seal small cracks in the surface. They're available in a range of textures. Properly applied, masonry paints will protect a wall against even severe weather.

For paints for exterior timber claddings, see Paints for Exterior Woodwork.

Paints for exterior woodwork

Varnish doesn't provide adequate protection for exterior woodwork. If you want to retain a natural appearance for wood, use a preservative woodstain.

Preservative woodstains contain chemicals toxic to fungi and

Paints for outside walls

		Approx. life
Brush-on water-repellent treatments	• Do not change the outward appearance	10 years
Exterior emulsion paints	• Wide range of colours • Relatively cheap and readily available	5 years
Masonry paints	• More weather-resistant than exterior emulsion paints • Available in a range of textures • Best choice for filling hairline cracks	5 years

Paints for exterior woodwork

		Approx. life
Varnish	• Not recommended	
Preservative woodstains	• Limited choice of shades • Very good resistance to fungal attack • Most types suitable for over-painting	5 years
Conventional oil-based primer/undercoat/gloss	• Wide choice of colours and very readily available • Durable if applied conscientiously • Time-consuming to apply	3 years
Microporous paints	• Need no primer or undercoat • Limited choice of colours • Not as glossy as conventional oil-based paint, but equally durable • Effective only if applied to bare wood	3 years

insects, to keep rot and woodworm at bay. They penetrate dry wood well, and once dry (allow at least two days) can be painted over.

Conventional oil-based paints are applied in three stages: primer, undercoat and one or two topcoats. An almost infinite range of colours is available. The surface must be prepared thoroughly and the paint applied carefully to achieve satisfactory performance; the whole process can be time-consuming. For repainting, however, fresh topcoats can be applied over old paint which is still sound.

Microporous paints are a relatively recent innovation. They allow the wood to 'breathe', so that water vapour can escape without blistering the paint, and offer durability equivalent to conventional oil-based paints. They need neither primer nor undercoat, but should be applied direct to the bare wood – there's no advantage in using microporous paint on top of conventional paints.

Outdoor paints for metal

Conventional oil-based paints must have an appropriate primer when used on outdoor metal. Any corrosion must be scrupulously removed before painting.

Bitumen paint is a thick, tar-like paint for waterproofing. Not to be confused with bitumen based emulsions which are used on concrete or roofs.

Enamels have an attractive, high gloss finish. All corrosion must be removed, and the surface treated with an appropriate primer. Enamels do not usually need an undercoat. They're available for brushing and also in aerosols, for painting small areas to a high standard, in a fair range of colours.

Rust-killing paints do not require a primer, and need only loose rust to be removed before they're applied – they neutralise the remaining corrosion.

Paints for interior use

Most paints suitable for exterior use can also be used inside the house. Primers which contain lead must not be used indoors, though.

However, whereas the primary function of exterior paints is to protect materials from the weather, inside the house their main purpose is decorative. This opens up the field to allow a wider choice of paints and finishes.

Outdoor paints for metal

		Approx. life
Conventional oil-based primer/undercoat/gloss	• Wide choice of colours and very readily available • Durable if applied conscientiously • Time-consuming to apply	3 years
Bitumen paint	• Black or brown only • For the inside surfaces of guttering	5 years
Enamels	• Fair range of colours • High gloss finish • Need an appropriate primer	3 years
Rust-killing paints	• Need no primer • Smooth or hammered finish • Limited choice of colours • Relatively expensive	5 years

Paints for interior walls and ceilings

		Approx. life
Distemper	• Water-based finish now superseded by emulsion paints	
Emulsion paints	• Prodigious choice of colours • Matt or satin finish • Easy to apply	5 years
Textured finishes	• Available ready-mixed or in dry powder form • Wide range of textures possible • Useful for sealing cracks and blemishes • Usually need a decorative topcoat of emulsion	25 years

Paints for interior walls and ceilings

Emulsion paints are water-based and relatively fast drying. Two coats – applied by brush, roller or paint pad – are usually needed to give adequate coverage. 'One-coat' emulsions contain a high density of pigment to cover in a single coat.

Textured finishes in dry powder form are considerably cheaper than ready-mixed. They're applied very generously with a brush, and then combed or stippled to achieve the required texture.

Paints for interior woodwork

Varnishes based on polyurethane are particularly tough, to withstand everyday knocks and scrapes. Varnishes with staining pigments built in can be used to change the colour of the wood, as an alternative to staining before varnishing, though they lack the clarity of separate stain and varnish treatments.

Satin finish paints for interior woodwork are an alternative to gloss paints; they're applied in the same way and offer similar durability.

Repainting

Regular repainting will ensure that you preserve and maintain exterior wood and ironwork. Ideally, you should always repaint before the old paintwork has deteriorated to the point where the surface underneath has been damaged by the elements. Even so, you're likely to find a few spots which have been affected by rot or rust, and you must put these right before painting afresh. Painting over potential problems simply means a bigger repair job in the future.

Preparing the surface

Success in painting depends on thorough preparation. To get the best out of any paint it's essential to remove all dirt, grease and corrosion, and any old paint which is unsound.

Wash down with a solution of sugar soap, a proprietary paint cleaner, washing soda or simply household detergent. Pay particular attention to areas which tend to accumulate grime, such as the parts of window frames which are normally hidden or areas around and above open fires and warm air outlets.

If old paintwork is sound, there's little point in removing it. But areas of old paint which show signs of flaking or blistering should be stripped

Paints for interior woodwork

		Approx. life
Varnish	• Durable indoors • Available clear or with 'staining' pigments	10 years
Conventional oil-based primer/undercoat/gloss	• Wide choice of colours and very readily available • Durable • Time-consuming to apply	10 years
Satin finish	• Oil based • Semi-matt finish • More limited choice of colours than gloss paint	10 years

Because interior paints aren't exposed to the elements, the chances are that you'll want to redecorate simply to spruce up the paintwork or to change your colour scheme rather than because the protection offered by the paint is in danger of breaking down.

off. Use a wire or stiff nylon brush to test how well the old paint is adhering to the surface – if it flakes away: strip it. Pay special attention to windowsills which receive the full force of both sun and rain, and the bottom corners of door and window frames where deterioration of the old paint may have allowed water to penetrate.

It's rarely necessary to remove all the old paint, unless:

• most of it is flaking or blistering
• the old paint finish is very poor
• successive layers of old paint have built up making doors or windows difficult to open
• you want to change to a different type of finish – a preservative stain rather than gloss paint, for example.

Carry out any repairs which are necessary, and rub down the surface with a fine grade of abrasive paper to provide a 'key' for the new paint to hold on to. Smooth off sharp external corners – sharp edges result in thinning of the paint film.

Removing old paint

There are three techniques for removing paint: **heat**, applied with a traditional blowlamp or a hot air gun; **chemical strippers**, which soften the paint and allow it to be scraped away; **rubbing down** with sandpaper or a similar abrasive.

Using a blowlamp or hot air gun

Blowlamps and hot air guns use heat to soften the paint, causing it to bubble up and separate from the surface underneath so it can be scraped away. If you're right handed, hold the blowlamp or hot air gun in your left hand, so you can hold the scraper or shavehook in your right (vice versa for left handers). Wear heat resistant gloves and keep the heat just ahead of the scraper. You're likely to need a little practice to develop an effective technique.

Take care not to scorch woodwork and, if possible, catch the hot scrapings in a metal bucket. On windows, keep direct heat away from the glass or you may crack it.

Chemical paint strippers

Chemical strippers are particularly useful on intricate surfaces. Always wear rubber gloves and goggles; if you do get splashed wash the paint stripper off straight away. Protect adjacent surfaces and floors with polythene sheets and have something like an old baking tin standing by to put the scrapings in.

Solvent strippers are usually thick liquids. Using an old brush, apply a fairly generous coating of stripper. After a few minutes the paint should blister and can be scraped away. Stubborn or thick

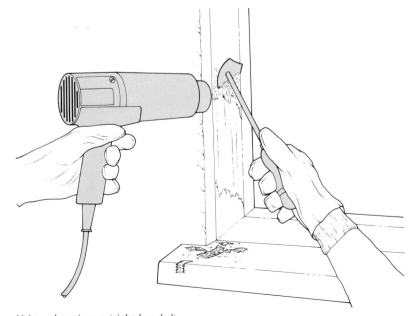

Using a hot air gun (right-handed)

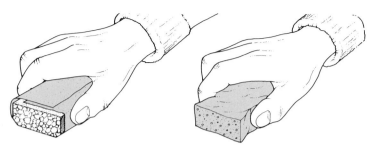

Sanding blocks: cork (left) and plastic foam (right)

paints may need two or more applications of stripper. Always wash down thoroughly with white spirit before repainting.

Caustic strippers are usually pastes which are supplied either as a powder to be mixed with water, or ready mixed. They're applied as a thick layer, and in some cases should be covered by a blanket (supplied with the paste). After a few hours the paste can be removed, bringing the old paint off with it. Wash down with plenty of water containing a little vinegar. Caustic strippers may darken the wood considerably.

Using abrasives

Removing large areas of paint by rubbing down is likely to involve a good deal of time and hard work. Aluminium oxide and silicon carbide 'wet or dry' papers are more durable and less prone to clogging than traditional glasspaper.

Sanding by hand is usually much easier if the abrasive paper is wrapped around a sanding block. This can be any suitably sized piece of timber or a purpose-made block of cork. Sanding blocks are also available made from resilient plastic foam with the abrasive material glued to the surface. They can be washed out under the tap to remove dust.

Removing corrosion

Metals containing iron are prone to rust. Unless you use a rust-killing paint, all rust must be removed before repainting or it will continue to spread under the new paint.

Start with a wire brush, either a hand brush or one fitted to an electric drill, and remove as much rust as you can. Finish off with wire wool and abrasive papers, and then apply primer as soon as possible.

How much paint do you need?

This depends on the type of paint, the difference in colour between the new paint and the surface to which it's being applied, the porosity of the surface and its texture. The Table below gives a rough guide to the coverage per litre (for a single coat) of various types of paint:

paint	coverage per litre
primer	6 to 12sq m
smooth masonry paint	12sq m
textured masonry paint	6sq m
undercoat	16sq m
gloss paint	16sq m
non-drip gloss paint	12sq m
matt emulsion paint	14sq m
silk emulsion paint	13sq m

Paint brushes

Buy the best brushes you can afford. If you clean them thoroughly and store them properly they'll last many years and repay the initial investment. Just two sizes will be sufficient for painting woodwork around the house:

- a 25mm-wide brush for narrow sections like window frames
- a 50mm-wide brush for larger areas like fascia boards, doors and skirtings.

The 50mm brush will also be useful for painting around the edges of walls with emulsion, and around light fittings, power-points and ceiling roses when the main means of painting is to be a roller. If you want to paint entire walls and ceilings by brush, you need one 100mm wide.

A couple of special brushes may also be useful:

- a cutting-in brush – a narrow brush with angled bristles for getting into the corners of window frames
- a radiator brush, with the bristles set at right angles and a long handle to get behind radiators.

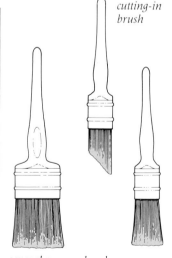

cutting-in brush

general purpose brushes

radiator brush

Paint brushes

Brushing technique

Transfer some paint from the can into a paint kettle or any suitable container with a handle. Put the lid back on the can.

Dip the brush in the paint to about one third to one half of the depth of the bristles – no more or paint will work its way up to the top of the bristles and from there to the handle. Estimate the area you'll cover with one brushful and apply the paint in dabs about 60mm apart. Brush the paint out to produce an even coating, using both vertical and horizontal strokes. Finally, 'lay off' the paint with light, vertical, upward strokes. Repeat the process, laying off the second area so that it merges into the wet edge of the first, and so on.

If the coating is uneven, you're applying the paint too thin or not brushing it out enough. If the brush drags, you're probably trying to spread the paint too thin. If the paint sags or runs, you're applying it too thickly. Don't try to correct mistakes which appear as the paint dries by brushing over them with fresh paint; the brush will drag off the surface film and just make matters worse. Wait until the paint has dried, rub down and repaint.

Before you use a new brush, stroke it vigorously back and forth across the palm of your hand, to remove as many loose bristles as possible. Even so, a few bristles are sure to appear in the paint when using a new brush. If you spot them right away, you can flick them off the paint with the tip of the brush. Otherwise, wait until the paint has dried, remove the bristles, rub down and repaint.

For windows, start by painting around the concealed edges of opening casements or sashes. Next, paint around the glass – use a cutting-in brush or, if you have difficulty getting a clean edge with a conventional brush, apply masking tape around the sides of the pane. Paint the horizontal edges first, then the verticals. Next, paint the outer faces of the

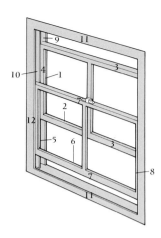

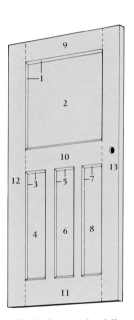

Painting doors and windows in the right order will give best results: follow the numbers above (left-handers should work from right to left)

opening parts of the window. Move on to the fixed parts of the frame – start with the normally-concealed edges and finish with the outer faces and the sill. As a rule, work on horizontal areas first and finish on verticals.

For doors, paint edges and small details such as the beading around panels or glazing first, and finish on the main parts of the frame. As with windows, the general rule is horizontal surfaces first and vertical surfaces to finish.

Cleaning brushes

Brushes used with oil-based paint must be cleaned promptly with white spirit or a proprietary paint brush cleaner. First, squeeze out as much paint as possible. Then work the white spirit or cleaner thoroughly into the bristles – you can't be too conscientious about this – and squeeze again. Wash out all the cleaner with soap or detergent and water, repeatedly squeezing the brush to try to remove all traces of the paint colour. Finally, wrap the

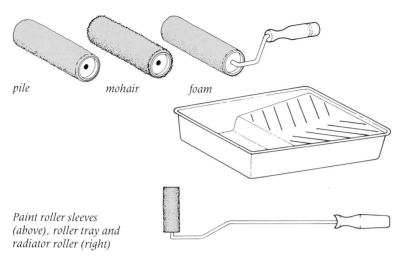

pile   mohair   foam

Paint roller sleeves (above), roller tray and radiator roller (right)

brush in absorbent paper to maintain the shape of the bristles and leave to dry. Looked after like this, you brushes will last for years and will get better with age.

Brushes used with emulsion need only be thoroughly washed out in water, and then wrapped in absorbent paper to maintain their shape.

Paint rollers

Rollers are very useful for painting large areas, particularly those with a textured surface. They're especially suitable for emulsion paints because they enable you to work quickly, so each new area of paint can be merged into a wet edge on the previous area – this can be difficult with a brush because emulsions dry relatively quickly.

Rollers consist of a frame with a handle, and a sleeve which applies the paint to the surface. A number of types of sleeve are available:

- foam sleeves are cheap and suitable for both emulsion and gloss paints, but don't give a very good finish
- pile sleeves, with natural (sheepskin) or synthetic fibres, are very good for emulsion paints but not suitable for gloss
- mohair sleeves are for gloss paints
- special sleeves are available for creating patterns with textured paints.

Special small rollers with long handles are available for reaching behind radiators, and spring-loaded rollers for painting around pipes.

Roller frames with a hole in the end of the handle can be used with a broomstick to help reach high walls and ceilings.

Paint roller technique

Before starting with the roller, paint edges and around switches, sockets and ceiling roses with a brush.

A paint roller must be used with a tray. Special trays are available with a shallow well to hold the paint at one end and a sloping area like a draining board at the other, to help you load the roller evenly. Fill the well with paint, dip the roller in it and then run it up and down the sloping part until it's evenly coated.

Estimate the area to be covered with the first load of paint, and apply

it in a series of zig-zag strokes. Spread the paint evenly with strokes in all directions and finish with parallel strokes and a light pressure on the roller. You should be able to work quickly, but don't move the roller too fast or paint will tend to flick off the ends of the sleeve. Apply the second load so that it slightly overlaps the wet edge of the first, and so on until the job is complete.

If you're using gloss paint, it may have a stippled look at first, but don't worry: if you have spread the paint correctly it should dry to a smooth finish.

Cleaning rollers

Remove as much paint as possible by rolling it out on newspaper. For emulsion clean out the roller in plenty of water – use the sloping part of the tray to squeeze the water through the pile. Keep going as long as your patience allows – it's unlikely that you'll be able to remove every trace of the paint from the roller, though. Squeeze out the excess water and leave the roller standing on end to dry.

Cleaning mohair rollers used with gloss paint can be messy. Start by squeezing out as much paint as possible, clean out the tray and put some white spirit or a proprietary paint brush cleaner in the well. Now use the tray to work the cleaner thoroughly into the roller. Finally, use soap or detergent and water to wash the cleaner from both the roller and the tray.

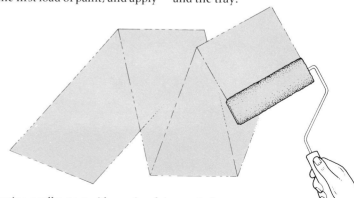

When using a roller start with a series of zig-zag strokes

Part Two
HOUSEHOLD SERVICES

7   **Electricity**

It takes only the briefest power cut to make us realise how much we depend on electricity. It's not just the lights and the TV which go out, but most central heating systems – though they may use other fuels as the source of heat – as they also rely on electricity to control them.

Like other household services, home electrics need regular maintenance to keep them working safely and efficiently.

But don't contemplate maintenance or repairs to your household electrics unless you're completely confident that you understand what you are doing. You should *always* disconnect the supply before doing any work on the electrical system. Electricity is potentially dangerous – it can, and does, kill. Professional advice is readily available, and in some cases may be free.

Inspecting the electrical system

It's not always easy to tell when a house needs to be rewired.

Things to look for are:
- old round-pin power points and round light switches
- rubber insulated cables
- fuses which blow repeatedly
- power points and other outlets which don't work
- power points wired in flex rather than cable, or in cable which is too small for the power passing through it.

If your home still has round-pin power points or round light switches, then it's quite likely the house needs to be rewired. But even new fittings don't guarantee that all is well: old power points and switches may have been replaced without changing the original wiring, or by renewing only part of it.

If your house still has old rubber-insulated wiring, then it's almost certainly time it was rewired. Rubber insulation has a dull appearance, in contrast to the shiny plastic of modern cables, and tends to crumble where it gets hot – in ceiling roses, for example. It may also have a lead sheath. If you find old wiring with crumbling insulation, don't interfere with it – take out the appropriate fuses (to make it safe) and get it replaced without delay.

If fuses blow repeatedly, first check that it's not a particular appliance that is causing the trouble by trying other appliances in the same outlet. If the fuse still blows, the problem is likely to be rooted in the wiring.

If power points or other outlets don't work, then there's clearly something wrong with the wiring.

Many problems with household electrics are caused by unsatisfactory d-i-y work. A common error is wiring an extension power point in flex rather than cable or in cable which is too small for the power. All fixed wiring to sockets should be in 2.5mm² two-core and earth cable (see Household Wiring, p. 77).

Getting your wiring inspected professionally

A full test and inspection of household wiring requires specialist equipment and calls for a professional approach. To ensure that your wiring is in good condition, you should have it inspected every ten years or so. Suitably qualified electrical contractors will be members of the National Inspection Council for Electrical Installation Contracting (NICEIC) or the Electrical Contractors Association (ECA) (see Useful Addresses, p. 136). These bodies guarantee their members' work and ensure that it conforms to the Wiring Regulations. Electricity companies are all members of NICEIC.

Contractors will charge a modest fee for a written report for an average house, though some contractors occasionally offer free inspections.

Spotting danger signs

You don't need a professional to spot other danger signs:

- broken fittings – power points, ceiling roses and so on
- fittings that show signs of overheating – discoloration, distortion, charring or suspicious smells
- power points which are overloaded – a double or triple socket in place of a single is much safer than an adaptor
- long, trailing flexes from power points to appliances.

Understanding electricity

To do its work, electricity has to flow in a circuit. In household terms, it

Electricity – symptoms, faults and remedies

Symptom	Fault	Remedy	*see page*

Fuse blown or miniature circuit breaker tripped	• Circuit overloaded
	• Appliance faulty
	• Wiring faulty
		• Replace fuse, but first:
		  • Disconnect suspect appliances
		  • Reduce load or share between several circuits
			80

Broken, hot or discoloured fittings	• Old age • Internal faults	• Replace	80
Sockets overloaded or long, trailing flexes to appliances	• Not enough sockets	• Have single sockets converted to doubles or triples • Have extra sockets installed, or house re-wired	81 81
Wiring not tested for 10 years or more	• Wiring may be out of date or deteriorating	• Arrange for professional inspection • Have house re-wired if necessary	75 81

flows up the wire from the sub-station to the meter in the house, from the meter to the consumer unit (the up-to-date term for the fuse box), from the consumer unit to the various power points and light fittings, through the appliances and back by a parallel route to the source.

This circuit involves two wires. The incoming flow is carried in the live wire – red in fixed wiring, brown in electrical flex – and the return flow in the neutral wire – black in fixed wiring, blue in flex. Household wiring also has a third wire: the earth connection, which is coloured either green or green and yellow. The earth connection protects us, the consumers, by providing a safe pathway for electricity to 'escape' if something goes wrong.

The earth has an almost infinite capacity to absorb electricity. Without an earth connection, it would be possible for a fault to occur so that the body of, say, an electric kettle was connected to the live supply. A person touching the kettle would receive an electric shock – perhaps a fatal one. By connecting the body of the kettle to earth, the dangerous live connection is short-circuited. In practice, the fuse in the plug would blow almost at the instant the fault occurred, cutting off the live feed.

The Wiring Regulations

Electrical wiring in all buildings is governed by *Regulations for Electrical Installations* – usually called the IEE Wiring Regulations – published and updated regularly by the Institution of Electrical Engineers. They're not legally binding in England and Wales, though in Scotland they're incorporated in the Building Regulations.

The Wiring Regulations are a guide to good wiring practice, to ensure that it can safely meet the demands placed on it. They cover all aspects of wiring. Anyone can buy a copy, and most public libraries will have them, though you may find them difficult to understand unless you already have a good deal of relevant expertise.

Some electrical wholesalers offer guides to the Regulations – though these are aimed at electrical contractors rather than d-i-yers – and may summarise relevant parts of the Regulations in their catalogues.

Working safely with electricity

It cannot be said too often that electricity is dangerous. Before you start work on any part of your wiring, SWITCH OFF AT THE MAINS. Switching off at a wall switch is not enough. If it's *essential* to keep some circuits working while you work on others – to use an electric drill, for example – it is possible to remove the fuses or switch off the circuit breakers for just some of the circuits. But you must be quite certain which fuses or circuit breakers are involved. In older homes particularly, this may not be obvious. Extra power points may have been fitted, for example, and you should not assume that all the power points in one room are necessarily connected to the same ring main. At all times, err on the side of safety: IF IN DOUBT, STOP. Get advice from a qualified electrician or from your local electricity showroom. NEVER TAKE CHANCES.

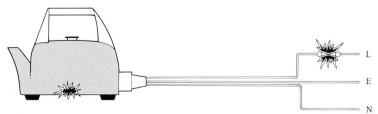

Earthing prevents faulty appliances becoming 'live'

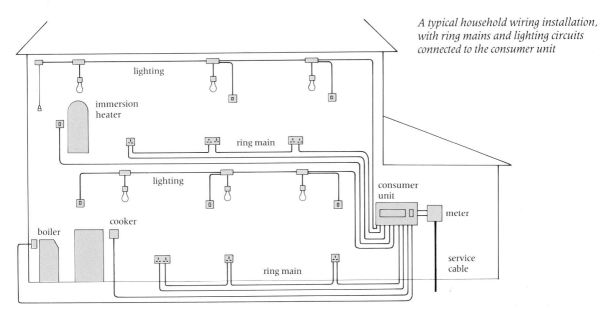

A typical household wiring installation, with ring mains and lighting circuits connected to the consumer unit

Household wiring

The electricity supply to a house comes through an underground service cable or, in some rural areas, through overhead wires. It goes into the electricity meter via a service fuse, and then on to the consumer unit. The incoming cable, the service fuse and the meter, all of which should have tamper-proof seals, belong to the supplier, and should be maintained by them.

The meter measures the amount of electricity drawn from the supply. If you use off-peak electricity, for storage radiators for example, you may have an Economy 7 meter which records separately the electricity used during the day and for a seven-hour period at night. Older installations may have two meters, or a white meter.

The householder's responsibility begins at the consumer unit. This is the up-to-date term for the fuse box, and is the point from which electricity is distributed to the various wiring circuits in the home. Each circuit will be protected by a fuse or miniature circuit breaker (MCB), and some of or all the circuits may also be connected to a residual current device (RCD) which provides additional pro-

tection against the worst effects of an electric shock. The consumer unit has a master switch which disconnects all the circuits in the house.

Fuses and circuit breakers

Electrical cables and fittings can cope with only a certain amount of electrical power. If the current becomes too great, they may overheat and catch fire. A **fuse** is a short length of wire which is designed to melt – breaking the electrical connection – when the flow through it exceeds the fuse rating. Fuses are rated in *amps* – from 5 amps to 45 amps for most domestic wiring.

A **miniature circuit breaker** (MCB) does the same job as a fuse, but mechanically switches off the current when the rating is exceeded. MCBS have the advantage that they can be reset when the fault has been put right, whereas a broken fuse must be replaced.

Fuses and MCBS protect whatever lies 'downstream' of them in the electrical circuit. The fuses and MCBS in a domestic consumer unit therefore protect the fixed wiring in the house. Flexes to appliances – and the appliances themselves – should be protected by further fuses in the plugs.

Residual current devices (RCDS) protect you rather than the wiring or the appliances. In an electrical circuit which is working correctly, the

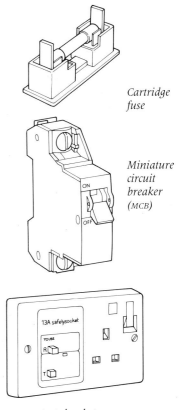

Cartridge fuse

Miniature circuit breaker (MCB)

RCD-protected socket

returning current in the neutral wire will be exactly equal to the incoming current in the live wire. But if something's amiss – some of the current leaking away to earth, for example – the currents won't balance. RCDS sense this difference and shut off the supply if it becomes too great. The importance of this is that it can protect you against electrocution. If you touch a live wire or terminal, you get a shock – some of the electricity 'leaks' out of the circuit and through you to earth. An RCD won't stop you getting a shock, but it will 'trip' and shut off the supply before you receive enough electricity to kill you. A fuse or MCB won't act anything like fast enough to give you any protection in these circumstances.

RCDS can be incorporated in consumer units, where they protect some of or all the circuits in the house, and are also available built into plugs, sockets and adaptors, to protect individual appliances. RCDS are essential when working with electrical appliances outdoors.

Circuits

The wiring **circuits** to power points, lights, immersion heaters and so on radiate out from the consumer unit. Thirteen-amp outlet power points are generally supplied by **ring mains**, where the cable containing the live, neutral and earth wires is connected as a loop starting and finishing at the consumer unit and connected to each of the power points in turn on the way. This means that the current to any outlet can be shared between the two arms of the loop.

Individual outlets, in a garage for example, and supplies to high-power appliances like immersion heaters and cookers, will be wired in **radial circuits**, where a single cable containing live, neutral and earth wires connects the consumer unit to the outlet. Old installations, with round-pin sockets, may have all the sockets wired as individual radial circuits.

Lights may be wired in **loop-in**

Electrical cables: different sizes of cable are used according to the current they have to carry (see below)

size	typical application
1.0mm^2	lighting circuit
2.5mm^2	ring main for 13-A power points
2.5mm^2	radial circuit to 13-A outlet or 3kW immersion heater
4.0mm^2	radial circuit to 6kW electric shower
6.0mm^2	radial circuit to cooker or 7kW electric shower
10mm^2	radial circuit to large cooker

circuits, where the supply cable runs from the consumer unit to each ceiling rose in turn, with a cable running out to the corresponding switch, and finishing at the furthest rose. Alternatively, they may be wired in a **junction box** circuit, where the supply goes to a series of junction boxes, which are in turn connected to the lights and their switches.

Fixed wiring

Most fixed wiring in the home – the wiring in the circuits described above – consists of three solid copper conductors, one each for live, neutral and earth. In high-power cables the live and neutral conductors consist of several copper strands. The live conductor has red insulation, the neutral black, and there's an overall grey or white insulating sheath. In modern wiring the insulation and sheathing is PVC plastic.

Ceiling roses and light switches

The most common form of outlet for lighting circuits is the ceiling rose. The wiring in ceiling roses can be rather complicated: in a typical loop-in lighting system, three cables and the flex to the light fitting may all come together within the rose.

Four terminals are needed:

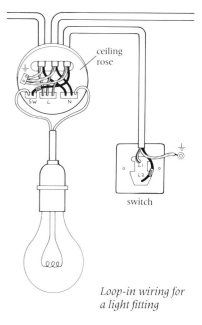

Loop-in wiring for a light fitting

- terminal 1 connects the neutral wires for the incoming and outgoing supply cables (black) and the neutral wire in the flex (blue)
- terminal 2 connects the live wires for the two supply cables and the live feed to the switch (all red)
- terminal 3 connects the returning live feed from the switch (black with a red sleeve) to the live wire in the flex (brown)

- terminal 4 connects all the earth wires.

Confusion arises because the returning live feed from the switch is a black wire, whereas all other live wires in the fixed wiring are red. This wire should have a short length of red sleeving on it to distinguish it from the neutral wires, but electricians are not always as conscientious as they might be in doing this. The exposed earth wires should have green/yellow sleeving, both in the ceiling rose and behind the switch.

In a **junction box** lighting system, or to accommodate a ceiling fitting which doesn't have enough terminals, the necessary connections are made in a separate four-way junction box rather than in the ceiling rose, but otherwise the same principles apply.

Some lights may be controlled by **two-way switching** – a landing

light with switches at the top and bottom of the stairs, for example. This doesn't affect the wiring in the ceiling rose, but calls for special wiring between the switches. The two switches are connected by a three-core and earth cable, with two red wires, one black and one earth.

Lighting circuits in older homes may not have an earth conductor.

Thirteen-amp power points

Power points are usually supplied by ring mains. The cables representing two arms of the ring are simply connected together in the appropriate terminals of the socket: red to live or L, black to neutral or N and the earth wires to the terminal marked earth, E or ⏚.

The exposed earth wires should be covered by green/yellow sleeving. If the socket is on a radial circuit, it will have only one earth cable.

Razor socket

Switch with indicator light

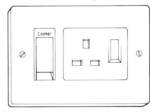

Cooker outlet with socket

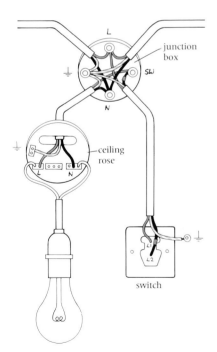

Junction box wiring for a light fitting

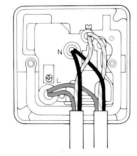

Wiring a 13-A power point

You may find sockets where three cables are connected, with the third cable – known as a spur – leading to an additional socket or other outlet.

Other electrical outlets

Although 13-A power points are the most common form of outlet, there are a number of others:

Razor sockets are special outlets which are safe for use in bathrooms, where the Wiring Regulations outlaw ordinary 13-A sockets. They should conform to BS3052.

Switched outlets are commonly used for immersion heaters, central heating boilers and electric storage

radiators. They have a switch, often with a neon light to show when they're on, and an outlet for the flex.

Cooker controls have a large switch to isolate electric cookers, and may also include a 13-A socket.

Switches, sockets and other outlets are either **flush-** or **surface-mounted**. Flush-mounted fittings

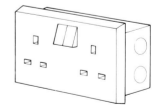

Flush-mounted socket

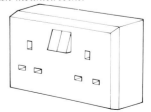

Surface-mounted socket

have metal boxes recessed into the wall. Surface-mounted fittings use a plastic **pattress** which is fixed to the surface of the wall.

Earth bonding

All the metal pipework in a house needs to be earthed to prevent it from becoming live if a fault develops. This is called **bonding**, and increasingly strict standards for bonding have been a feature of recent editions of the Wiring Regulations. Additional (supplementary) bonding is now required for metal surfaces in kitchens and bathrooms, for example. Unless your home has been rewired in the last ten years or so, it's quite likely that it doesn't meet current standards for earth bonding. This doesn't necessarily mean that it's unsafe, though.

Making your electrics safer and more up-to-date

Most of the ideas in this section involve work on the fixed wiring of the house. Don't contemplate this unless the earlier parts of this chapter make sense to you.

Label your consumer unit

This is a simple task which is often neglected, but which can be very important if problems develop or you suffer some catastrophe like a fire or flood. Make sure all the fuses or MCBS in your consumer unit are clearly marked to show which circuit they apply to: upstairs lights, downstairs ring main, cooker, etc.

If you don't know which is which, test them by removing each fuse in turn or switch off each MCB, and simply go around the house finding out what doesn't work. For safety, turn off the mains before you pull out the fuse, then on again once it's out. Do the same when replacing it.

Replacing a blown fuse

Fuses may be rewirable or of the cartridge type (similar to but generally larger than those in 13-A plugs). Either way, when fuses blow they must be replaced, and *always* with fuse wire of the appropriate rating or the correct cartridge fuse. 'Repairing' fuses in any other way – with other wire or by wrapping silver paper around blown cartridge fuses, for example – is very dangerous. Turn off the master switch, pull out the fuse and replace it.

Before you turn the mains back on, try to find out why the old fuse blew. Fuses deteriorate with time, and may blow even though there's no fault in the system. More likely, however, is that an appliance or one of the outlets has developed a fault. Disconnect any suspect appliances, and look for scorch marks or other signs of overheating in outlets or ceiling roses.

If in spite of that the replacement fuse blows when the supply is restored, unplug all appliances on that circuit, or remove the appropriate lightbulbs, and try again. If the fuse blows a third time, there must be a fault in the wiring.

MCBS are easier than fuses, because they don't need to be replaced, simply reset. Try to find the fault which caused the MCB to 'trip' in the first place, and switch off at the master switch before resetting the MCB.

Replacing a power point

There are a number of reasons why you might want to replace a power point. It may be a single power point where you need at least a double or an unswitched power point where a switched one would be more convenient, or it may be an old 15-A round-pin type. Don't replace an old 5-A power point with a 13-A type because the wiring may not be suitable.

Whatever the reasons, it's hard to make a case for installing a single power point. It costs little more in time or trouble to install a double, and extra power points are always useful.

First, decide whether the new power point is to be flush- or surface-mounted. For a flush-mounted power point, you'll need a metal box of the appropriate size, which will be recessed in the wall. For surface-mounting, you'll need an appropriate pattress. Surface-mounting has the advantage that no masonry work is involved, but flush-mounted power points are neater.

To install a flush-mounted box, switch off at the mains, remove the old power point and chisel out a recess a little larger and deeper than the box. If you have a cordless drill, you can 'honeycomb' the area with holes to make the job easier, and to help get the bottom of the recess even. When the recess is right, mark, drill and plug two holes in the wall, fit a grommet to the box for the cable, and fix the box to the wall.

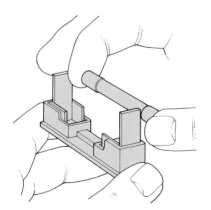

Replacing a cartridge fuse

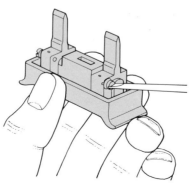

A rewirable fuse is more fiddly

Make good the plasterwork, attach the wires to the appropriate terminals, and fit the power point to the box. Suitable screws should be provided with the power point. Take care not to crush the cables as the power point goes into the box, and make sure that the exposed earth is covered by green/yellow sleeving.

The procedure is much the same for a surface-mounted socket, except that the wall does not need to be cut away. Drill and plug the wall for the pattress, then attach the socket to the pattress.

You can also buy double and triple 'conversion' power points which fit existing boxes for single, flush-mounted power points. These stick out further from the wall, but are a quick and easy way of adding extra power points. The triple power points usually have a built-in fuse to make sure that they don't overload the fixed wiring.

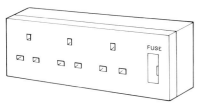

Triple 'conversion' socket with fuse

Moving or replacing a ceiling rose

Ceiling roses need to be attached to something substantial. The ceiling – particularly if it's of the lath-and-plaster type – isn't strong enough to support them. They must therefore either be attached through the ceiling to a joist, or to a noggin – a piece of timber spanning two joists.

To replace an old ceiling rose, switch off at the mains and remove it. Don't separate any wires which are twisted together, particularly if you find a plain black wire connected to the live feed on the lighting flex. This will be the live return from the switch (see Ceiling Roses, p. 78).

It should have a short piece of red sleeving on it to distinguish it from the neutral wires – if it hasn't, add one or wrap around a piece of red insulating tape. Fix the new ceiling rose with screws long enough to penetrate through the ceiling and into the joist.

To move a ceiling rose, you'll need access from above. Remove the old ceiling rose and replace it with a junction box attached to the side of the joist, with a spur of cable leading

Moving a ceiling rose

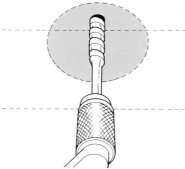

Mark out and drill through the ceiling

Add extra support if necessary

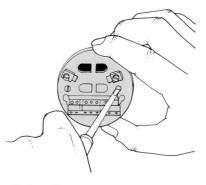

Fix the ceiling rose

to where the new rose is to be sited. For details of the wiring, see Ceiling Roses, p. 78.

Pick a spot for the new rose under a joist, or fix a noggin in place between the joists. Make a hole in the ceiling for the cable, fix the new rose in place and connect up the wires. Make good the hole where you removed the old rose (see Ceilings, p. 56).

Getting your house rewired

If you home needs to be rewired, use an electrical contractor approved by NICEIC or ECA (see Getting Your Wiring Inspected Professionally, p. 75). Get more than one quote, as prices can vary considerably.

Having a house rewired provides an opportunity to have not just the wiring but the whole installation brought up to date. So give careful thought to the number of power points you need, where they will be most conveniently sited, and whether there are new appliances – such as an electric shower – which you'd like to have installed at the same time. All this adds to the bill, of course, but it will work out cheaper than having a basic rewiring job and then having extra work done at a later date.

Make a room-by-room assessment of your needs, listing all the appliances you already have and taking account of those you might be adding in future. Think about where they'll be used, and whether they need a full-time power point or can 'borrow' one when they need one. Remember that cookers, showers and immersion heaters need their own circuits.

The Wiring Regulations impose no limit on the number of sockets you can have, but instead say that each ring main should cover no more than 100sq m of floor space. The logic behind this is that however many appliances you have you won't want to use them all at once.

8 Plumbing

Hot and cold running water is the definition of domestic comfort and convenience. But, like all aspects of the home, plumbing needs a degree of routine preventive maintenance to keep it in good condition, and problems that arise need to be dealt with promptly. With plumbing, a minor problem can easily develop into a messy and expensive catastrophe.

Water supply plumbing is largely regulated by water by-laws. These are increasingly being harmonised around the country, but some differences remain between regions. If you're in doubt about the regulations in your area, consult your water company – it is listed under Water in the telephone directory.

Waste water plumbing is covered by the Building Regulations, which are administered by the Department of Building Control, which will be listed under your local authority.

Inspecting plumbing

As long as your plumbing is working effectively, there's nothing to be gained by disturbing it. There's plenty of scope for preventive maintenance, however, particularly to guard against pipes freezing in cold weather, and to identify the early symptoms of possible problems. You should check your plumbing system at least once a year, as follows:

Outside the house:
- clear any debris from around the water company's stopcock
- check that none of the overflows is dripping

- if you have cast-iron waste pipes, check for corrosion and cracks. Cast iron is very heavy, so check the brackets holding the pipes to the wall, too.

In the loft:
- check the lagging around water pipes and cisterns
- check inside the cold water cistern for accumulated silt and to make sure that nothing has fallen in
- if you have a metal cistern, check for corrosion.

Inside the house:
- 'exercise' the stopcock on the rising main – simply turn it off and on a few times. Do the same with other valves, such as those on the outlets from the cold water cistern. If the main stopcock or other valves are stiff, try lubricating them with penetrating oil
- check all taps to make sure that they're not dripping
- check sinks, basins and baths to make sure that they drain efficiently
- check supply and waste pipe connections for leaks
- track down the source of any smells.

Household plumbing

Water supply

For practical purposes the water supply to a house starts at the water company's **stopcock**. You'll generally find this just outside the boundary of the property, under a small metal cover in the footpath. It will pay you to know where to find the stopcock for your home, and to have a means of turning it off in an emergency. If you can't find it, ask your water company where it is. Check it occasionally, and remove any debris which has fallen in.

You may already have a steel key for operating the stopcock – it's likely to be over 750mm below ground-level. You can buy keys from builders' merchants or make your own from wood.

Water from the water company's stopcock is carried to the house in the underground **service pipe**. Once under the house, the service pipe turns upwards to become the **rising main**. As it enters the house, it passes through the **main stopcock**. This controls the flow of all the water coming into the house, so it's important that you know where to

steel   *wood*

Stopcock keys

Plumbing – symptoms, faults and remedies

Symptom	Fault	Remedy	*see page*
Dripping tap	• Worn tap washer	• Replace washer	91
Dripping overflow pipe	• Punctured float • Faulty ballvalve	• Replace float • Repair or replace valve	91 92
Basin or sink not clearing	• Blocked waste pipe	• Remove blockage by: (a) plunging (b) clearing trap	92
wc not clearing	• Blocked waste pipe	• Remove blockage by: (a) flushing with hot water (b) plunging (c) using a drain rod	93
Tap doesn't work	• Frozen pipes • Airlock	• Defrost with care • Flush out air	91 93
Spluttering taps	• Air in pipes	• Flush out air	93
Stiff taps	• Packing too tight	• Ease off gland nut	91
Leaking pipes	• Frost damage • Leaky joints	• Replace affected pipe • Tighten or replace joints	89 89
Water dirty or discoloured	• Water company working on mains • Dirt or debris in cistern	• Contact water company • Drain and clean out cistern	93 93
Noisy pipes	• Air in pipes • Worn tap washers • Wrong type of ballvalve	• Flush out air • Replace washers • Fit equilibrium ballvalve	93 91 92
Hot water too hot or too cool	• Thermostat faulty or wrongly adjusted	• Adjust thermostat; replace if defective	93

find it and that you can rely on it to work in an emergency. Main stopcocks often become stiff simply because they don't get used. It pays to turn the stopcock on and off a few times every six months or so, just to keep it in good working order.

If you have a **water meter**, it will usually be fitted just above the main stopcock, or it may be combined with the water company's stopcock under a larger inspection cover.

From the stopcock on the rising main, there are two basic systems for piping the water to where it's needed: indirect and direct plumbing.

Indirect plumbing

In an indirect plumbing system water at mains pressure is piped direct to only one tap – almost invariably the cold tap on the kitchen sink. This is to ensure a clean source of water for drinking. All the other taps and fittings are supplied from a cold water **cistern**, usually in the loft. The level in the tank is controlled by a ballvalve, and there's an overflow pipe – usually emerging from the eaves – to prevent a flood if the ballvalve develops a fault. The cistern will have at least two outlet pipes, one feeding the hot water system, the other wcs and cold taps in the bathroom. There may be other outlets for some kinds of showers and bidets, too.

Each outlet should have a **valve** to isolate that part of the system for repairs or maintenance. The valves may be close to the cistern – as in the drawing – or where the pipes emerge inside the house – in the airing cupboard, for example.

Cold water enters the hot water cylinder near the bottom, and hot water is drawn off from the top. To allow air and steam to escape, there is also an expansion pipe leading from the top of the hot water cylinder and over the rim of the cold water cistern.

Direct plumbing

In direct plumbing systems, the rising main is connected direct to all the cold taps, wcs and other fittings needing a cold feed. The cistern in the loft feeds only the hot water cylinder, so there will usually be only one outlet fitted with a control valve.

House with indirect plumbing and single-stack waste system

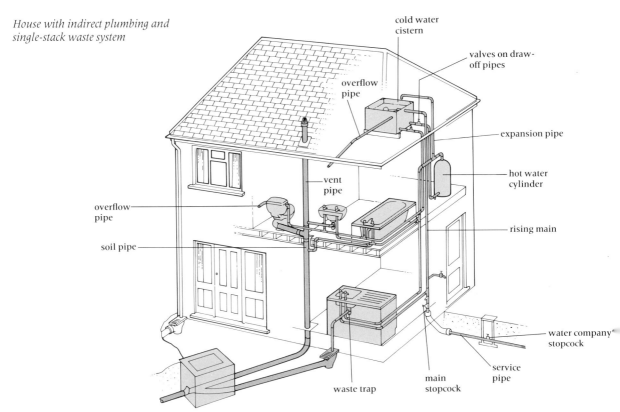

- cold water cistern
- valves on draw-off pipes
- overflow pipe
- expansion pipe
- hot water cylinder
- vent pipe
- rising main
- overflow pipe
- soil pipe
- water company stopcock
- service pipe
- waste trap
- main stopcock

House with direct plumbing and two-pipe waste system

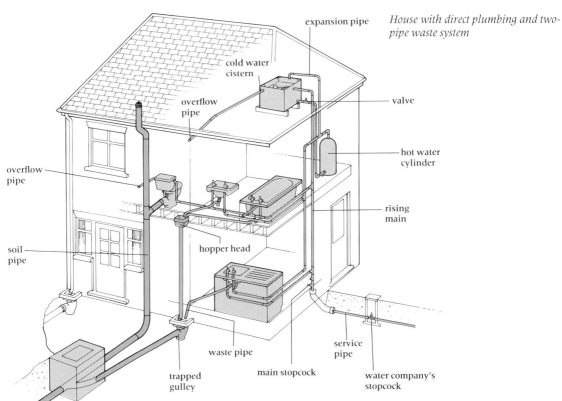

- expansion pipe
- cold water cistern
- valve
- overflow pipe
- hot water cylinder
- overflow pipe
- rising main
- soil pipe
- hopper head
- waste pipe
- main stopcock
- service pipe
- trapped gulley
- water company's stopcock

Why the difference?

Direct plumbing systems tend to be simpler and cheaper to install, but **indirect** plumbing reduces the danger of back-siphonage: water being drawn back into the mains, with a consequent risk of contamination of the water supply. Indirect systems also have the advantage that the pressures to both the hot and cold taps in the bathroom are roughly equal and aren't affected by variations in the mains pressure. The cistern also provides a store of water if the mains supply should be interrupted for any reason, which was its original purpose. By and large, direct plumbing is more common in older houses, indirect plumbing in newer homes.

In practice, individual homes may have plumbing which combines elements of both direct and indirect systems. To find out more about the plumbing in your home, turn off the water supply at the main stopcock. Any cold taps and WCs connected direct to the mains should be shut off almost immediately: you may get a little water, but the flow should stop within a few seconds. Taps and WCs which draw their supply from the cistern will not be affected until all the water has drained from the cistern, though.

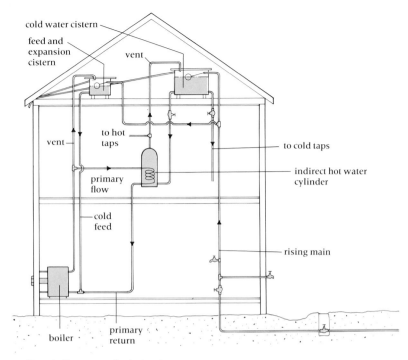

Indirect boiler system for hot water

Hot water systems

Hot water for sinks, baths and showers is stored in the copper hot water cylinder, which in most homes is in the airing cupboard. The cylinder is supplied by the cold water cistern, which is usually in the loft. Note that some kinds of showers require a minimum pressure – usually expressed as a 'head' measured in feet or metres – to work satisfactorily. The head is determined by the height of the cistern, not the hot water cylinder.

In older homes the water in the cylinder may be heated directly by a boiler. Usually, **direct boiler systems** rely on thermocycling – the natural tendency of hot water to rise and cold water to fall – to circulate water between the boiler and the cylinder. This means that the cylinder must be installed above the boiler, otherwise a circulating pump must be fitted.

More modern homes generally have **indirect boiler systems**, often combined with the central heating (see Chapter 9). In these, the hot water cylinder contains a coil in

Direct boiler system for hot water

which water circulates to and from the boiler without coming in direct contact with the water in the cylinder. The boiler has its own cold water cistern and vent pipe.

Immersion heaters

Most houses with boilers also have an electric immersion heater. This is a large heating element, similar to that in an electric kettle, which heats the water in the hot water cylinder.

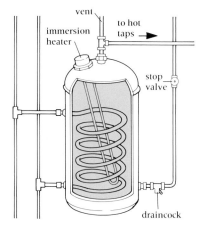

Indirect hot water cylinder with immersion heater

Instantaneous water heaters

These may be powered by gas or electricity, and include electric showers. They're generally used for supplying hot water to a single point, though **gas multi-point heaters** work on the same principles but can be used to supply hot water all around the house. Instantaneous water heaters have the advantage that no heat is wasted in keeping water hot, but the disadvantage of a relatively modest flow rate.

Unvented hot water systems

Unvented hot water systems are common in the USA and other countries – they've been mandatory in West Germany for over 30 years. But they've only recently become available in Britain. In an unvented system, both the hot and cold supplies are connected direct to the mains – there is no storage cistern. A special

hot water cylinder is required, and other fittings may also have to be specially designed to eliminate the risk of back-siphonage.

The advantage is that both the hot and cold water is at mains pressure. This is particularly useful for showers, and means that you get a strong flow of water which isn't affected as other taps are turned on and off. The only potential disadvantage is that there's no stored water to draw on if the mains supply should be cut off. Even this can be avoided by fitting a high-pressure water storage tank, however.

Waste systems

Water carried into the house by the supply system has to be carried away by the waste system to the drains. To make sure that foul air and smells can't get into the house, each fitting – sink, bath, shower, bidet or wc – must have a trap. Traps are u-shaped pipes which allow water to pass through to the drains, but retain a relatively small volume of water to seal the waste pipe when the flow stops. In wcs, the trap is an integral part of the pan; in other fittings it forms part of the outlet pipework.

Single-stack waste systems

Houses built in the last 30 years or so have single-stack waste systems. In these, the waste from sinks, baths and wcs is connected to a single **soil pipe** or **soil stack** (as in the drawing of an indirect plumbing system on p. 84). The stack is a relatively large pipe, usually 110mm in diameter, which runs vertically either inside or down the outside wall of the house. The stack will be vented above the roof, or it will be fitted with a one-way valve to let air in while preventing smells escaping.

Single-stack systems have to be designed carefully to ensure that the water flowing down from the stack won't suck the water out of the traps on individual fittings. The Building Regulations include detailed specifications for the slope, length and

size of branch pipes, and where they can be connected to the stack.

Two-pipe waste systems

Older houses generally have waste systems where wcs discharge into a **soil pipe**, which is connected direct to the sewer or septic tank, but waste from sinks, baths, showers and bidets is carried by a separate waste pipe to a **trapped gulley**. This arrangement is shown in the drawing of a direct plumbing system on p. 84.

The soil pipe is vented above the eaves, as in a single-stack system. The waste pipe, on the other hand, has an open **hopper head** at the top, where the outlet pipes from the bath, basin and so on come together. The waste pipe and kitchen sink discharge into the gulley: a water trap at ground level which leads off to the drains.

This arrangement prevents any chance of sink or bath traps being sucked dry by water draining out of other fittings, so two-pipe systems do not require the same stringent design standards as single-stack systems.

For more details of drains, see Chapter 12.

Pipes and fittings

In old installations, pipes for both supply and waste may be lead or iron. In modern homes, the supply piping is most likely to be copper, with soldered or compression joints, and the waste plumbing plastic, with push-fit or solvent-cemented joints.

Copper piping

Copper pipe for domestic plumbing comes in two main sizes: 15mm and 22mm. These sizes are measured over the *outside* diameter of the pipe, and replace pipes of $^1/_2$ and $^3/_4$in, which were measured over the *inside* diameter. The size used depends on the rate of flow through the pipe and the amount of pressure loss which can be accepted. 15mm pipe is used for individual connections to sink and basin taps, 22mm pipe for the outlets from the cold water cistern and hot water cylinder and for connections to bath taps. 28mm pipe (which replaces 1in) may also be used where high rates of flow are required: for central heating boilers, for example.

Fittings for copper pipe come in both compression and solder types. A wide variety is available, including tees (for connecting three pipes together), bends, tank and tap connectors, valves and adaptors for connecting pipe of different sizes (including adaptors to connect new metric pipe with old Imperial-size pipes).

Plastic supply piping

Plastic piping is available in the same sizes as copper pipe, and for both hot and cold water supplies. Plastic piping is much less susceptible to frost than copper.

CPVC plastic piping is relatively rigid, and is usually joined using solvent-welded fittings – the plastic equivalent of a soldered joint on copper pipe.

Polybutylene pipe is more flexible, and is usually joined using 'Acorn' push-fit connectors which include a

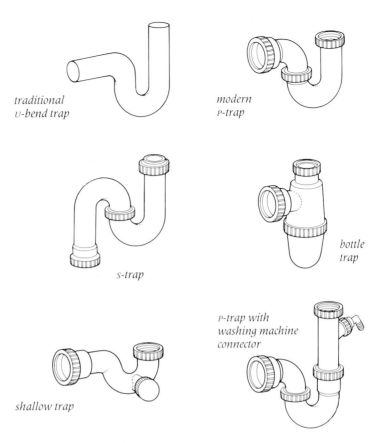

traditional u-bend trap

modern p-trap

s-trap

bottle trap

shallow trap

p-trap with washing machine connector

Types of trap for sink, basin and bath wastes

rubber o-ring seal and a grab ring to hold the joint in place. These fittings can also be used with copper pipe.

Waste piping

The traditional materials for waste pipes were lead for the branch pipes leading from each sink, basin or bath, and cast iron for the hopper head and vertical waste pipe on the exterior wall.

Modern waste piping for sinks, basins and baths is ABS or UPVC plastic, and comes in three sizes: 32mm (1¼in), 40mm (1½in) and 50mm (2in). It is usually white.

Connections may be solvent-cemented, push-fit or compression types, and a wide range of fittings is available including traps of various types, elbows and tees. The compresson joints have rubber sealing rings and should be tightened by hand –

not with a spanner or wrench. Larger pipes – for the waste from WCs and for the soil stack – should be UPVC, with push-fit or solvent-cemented joints.

Traps

All sinks, basins, baths and showers – and appliances like washing machines and dishwashers which have been plumbed in – must be fitted with a trap to seal off the waste pipe (WC pans already incorporate one).

The traditional sink or basin trap is a simple **u-bend** formed from lead pipe, with an access plug at the bottom. The modern equivalent is the plastic **p-trap**, but this is only one of many types now available. Note that the outlet points slightly downwards to prevent water running back into the trap.

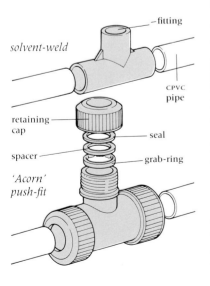

solvent-weld

fitting

CPVC pipe

retaining cap

seal

spacer

grab-ring

'Acorn' push-fit

Fittings for plastic pipes

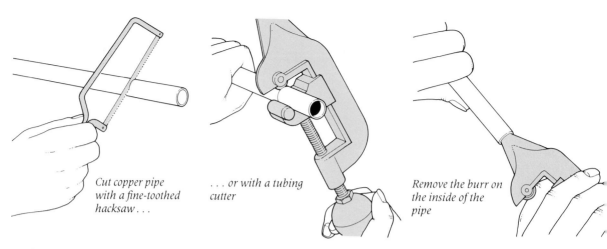

Cut copper pipe
with a fine-toothed
hacksaw . . .

. . . or with a tubing
cutter

Remove the burr on
the inside of the
pipe

Cutting copper pipe

s-traps are similar to p-traps, but have the outlet pointing vertically downwards. **Bottle traps** are compact, but get blocked more easily than p- and s-traps. **Shallow traps** may be used where space is limited – under baths, for example – but should be used only with a two-pipe waste system. With single-stack systems, only deep traps should be used.

Traps with connectors are available for plumbing in washing machines and similar appliances.

Overflows

An overflow must be provided wherever there is a ballvalve – in cold water cisterns and wcs. In older homes, overflows may be copper or lead. Modern overflows are usually 22mm pvc with push-fit connections.

Maintaining your plumbing

As long as the plumbing in your home has been properly installed, routine repairs should amount to little more than curing dripping taps, clearing blocked sinks and keeping ballvalves working efficiently. However, there may also be times when more substantial repairs are required, as a result of frost damage, for example.

Working with copper pipes

Replacing or repairing sections of copper piping is well within the scope of the d-i-yer, although work

Push on the nut
and then the olive

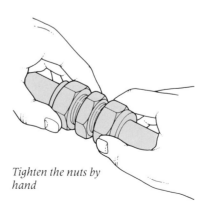

Tighten the nuts by
hand

Making a compression joint

on lead or iron pipes is best left to a skilled professional.

Copper pipe may be cut with a saw or a special pipe cutter. For sawing, use a fine-toothed hacksaw (24 teeth

Push the pipe into
the fitting until it
meets the internal
stop

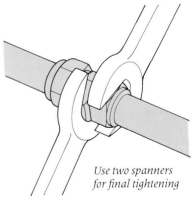

Use two spanners
for final tightening

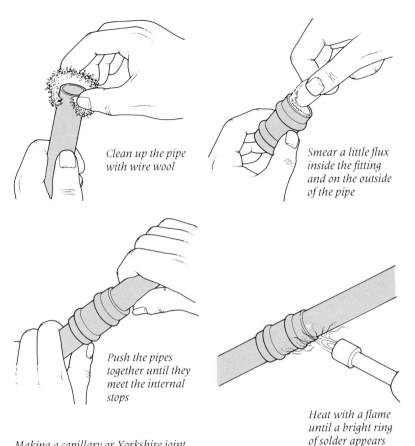

Clean up the pipe with wire wool

Smear a little flux inside the fitting and on the outside of the pipe

Push the pipes together until they meet the internal stops

Heat with a flame until a bright ring of solder appears

Making a capillary or Yorkshire joint

per inch) and gentle pressure. Take care to cut squarely across the pipe, and clean up the edges – inside and out – with a file. Pipe cutting tools leave a rounded edge on the outside of the pipe, and usually incorporate a deburring tool to smooth off the inside.

Copper pipe is quite easy to bend, but will kink if it's not supported. Professionals use tools which draw the pipe around a former – these can be hired. For d-i-y plumbing, however, a pipe bending spring is a good investment. You tie a string to one end, push the spring into the pipe, make the bend around your knee and withdraw the spring.

Copper pipes can be joined using either **compression** or **soldered** fittings. Compression fittings work by squeezing a compression ring or 'olive' on to the outside of the pipe, holding it firmly in place and sealing

it. No heat is involved. Solder joints are simply copper sleeves which fit closely over the pipe. Some – known as Yorkshire fittings – have a ring of solder built in which melts when the fitting is heated. With others – known as end feed fittings – the solder has to be applied externally. All solder fittings need the pipe and the inside of the fitting to be thoroughly cleaned with wire wool, and a smear of flux applied, before they're heated. After making the joint, any flux residue should be removed, otherwise it will go green and 'bleed' through paint.

When making soldered joints, use a heat-resistant mat behind the joint to protect the wall and woodwork.

Emergency repairs
Emergency plumbing problems usually arise either when frozen pipes thaw out or the plumbing is

damaged during other work – putting a nail through a pipe when replacing floorboards, for example. Whatever the cause, the first priority is to shut off the supply.

Close the main stopcock to cut off the mains pressure. If this doesn't staunch the flow, turn off boilers and water heaters, close the valves on the outlets from the cold water cistern and open all the taps to drain water out of the pipes as quickly as possible. Attach hoses to any draincocks and open them, too.

If this doesn't work, the leak must be coming from the cistern itself, or from the pipes upstream of the outlet valves. Open the outlet valves again and drain all the water out of the cistern through the taps.

Frost causes damage because water expands slightly as it freezes. This expansion can force a pipe out of a compression joint, or may split the pipe. The problem isn't apparent immediately because there's not indication of a leak until the ice melts.

A 'blown' compression joint can usually be reassembled, though you should renew the sealing ring or 'olive' – they're readily available separately. Burst or damaged pipes can be temporarily mended using special clamps or tapes, but for a permanent solution you must replace the affected section of pipe, using

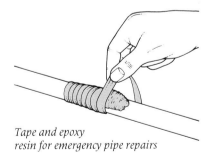

Tape and epoxy resin for emergency pipe repairs

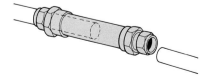

Slip fitting for a permanent replacement

either a slip fitting or a short length of new pipe with straight connectors at each end.

A leaking galvanised cistern probably means that it has rusted beyond repair – replace it with a plastic one.

If you have to replace the hot water cylinder, buy one with factory-applied foam insulation – it's a good investment.

Guarding against frost

Water pipes in lofts – particularly lofts which are well insulated – are prone to freezing. Outside wcs are also vulnerable. All exposed pipework must be lagged to insulate it from the cold. For the pipes themselves, the easiest material to use is pre-formed foam pipe lagging. It comes either as a strip which you wind around the pipes, or moulded into a tube which is split down one side so you can put it around the pipes. The edges of the split are either coated with an adhesive or fitted with a sort of zip connector. For extra security, it's worth adding a few turns of insulation tape at intervals, especially near bends and fittings. Wrap-around foam insulation can also be used for compression fittings, valves and other more bulky items, though traditional felt is easier to work around awkward shapes. Secure it with insulation tape. Cold

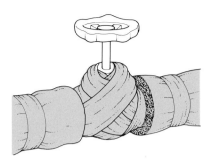

Felt lagging for a valve

water cisterns in the loft should be well lagged, but leave a gap in the loft insulation immediately below the cistern, so that a little warmth from the house can come through.

For very exposed pipes, you may have to provide some form of heating to keep frost at bay. Outside wcs can be a particular problem, so make sure that their doors and windows are adequately draught-proofed, and leave the light on in very cold weather.

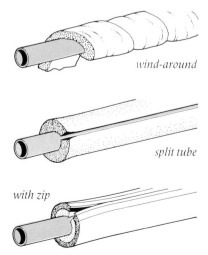

wind-around

split tube

with zip

Foam pipe lagging

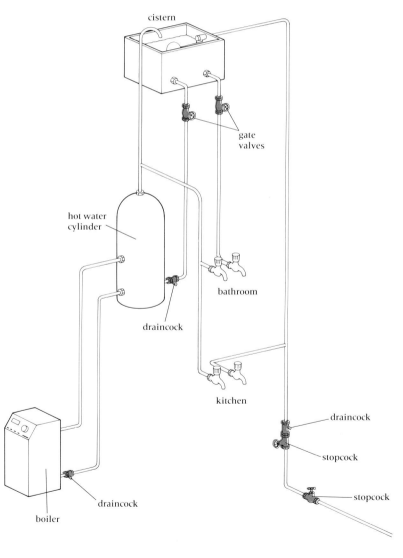

Control valves and draincocks in a typical plumbing system

Defrosting frozen pipes

If a tap or wc fails to work in very cold weather, it may indicate a frozen pipe. Use a hairdrier or towels soaked in hot water to thaw out the pipe, working back from the affected tap or valve. Lag the pipe thoroughly to prevent it freezing again.

Frozen traps on sinks and basins can generally be cured by filling the bowl with hot water.

Draining the plumbing system

If you have time to plan what you're doing, rather than having to respond to an emergency, drain only that part of the system you want to work on.

Start by finding all the control valves and draincocks in the system, and make a note of them for future reference. Isolate the part of the system you want to work on by shutting off the relevant control valves and opening taps and draincocks. Note that opening the hot water taps will not drain the hot water cylinder because the outlet is at the top; you will need to drain it from the appropriate draincock.

If you have to drain the boiler, let it cool down first.

If you find that the main stopcock won't turn, you can still cut off the supply to the cold water cistern by tying up the ballvalve.

When refilling part of the system, open all the taps a little to prevent air being trapped in the pipes.

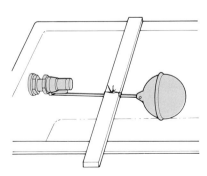

Shutting off the supply to the cistern by tying up the ballvalve

Curing a dripping tap

If a tap drips when it's turned off, the most likely cause is a worn sealing washer. 'Supataps' are designed to allow the washer to be replaced without turning off the water, but with all other types this is the first step in making a repair. Isolate the appropriate part of the system and open the tap to drain the water away.

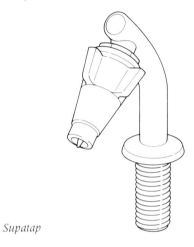

Supatap

Remove the top of the tap. On cross-head taps, the top is usually secured by a grub screw. On shrouded taps, the shroud may simply push on the spindle or be retained by a screw concealed under a plastic disc.

Crosshead tap

Shrouded tap

Unscrew the cover – use a cloth to protect the finish if you have to use a spanner – to reveal the small nut holding the packing and the larger nut which holds the valve mechanism into the body of the tap. Unscrew the large nut and take out the valve mechanism. The washer is a small disc of rubber at the bottom of the valve mechanism. It seals against a seating in the body of the tap.

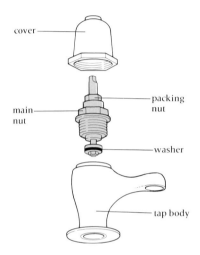

Replacing a tap washer

Replace the washer: you may have to remove a small retaining nut to do this. Replace the mechanism, cover and top, and turn the water back on.

If a tap leaks out of the top when it's turned on, the packing isn't sealing properly. Tightening the small nut on the top of the valve mechanism a little may do the trick. Otherwise you'll have to replace the packing: either impregnated wool or a rubber o-ring, depending on the type of tap. A stiff tap probably indicates that the packing has been squeezed too tightly.

Curing a dripping overflow

A dripping overflow means that a ballvalve isn't shutting off properly. This can be caused by a leak in the ball, making it lose some of its buoyancy, or by a problem in the valve itself.

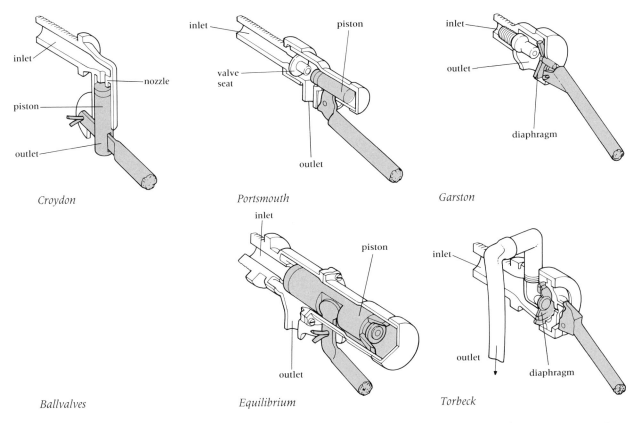

Croydon

Portsmouth

Garston

Ballvalves

Equilibrium

Torbeck

A leaking ball will have to be replaced, but you may be able to make a temporary repair by tying a plastic bag around the ball or – if the ball isn't completely waterlogged – by adjusting the float arm to compensate for the ball's reduced buoyancy.

Leaks in the valve itself can arise from wear in the seals or because grit has got in. In either case, the water supply will have to be turned off and the valve dismantled and repaired.

There are five distinct types of ballvalve. The Croydon (now obsolete) and Portsmouth are simple piston valves. The Garston or BRS ballvalve has a diaphragm rather than a piston. Equilibrium ballvalves allow the inlet water pressure to act on both sides of the piston: this helps to overcome problems of water 'hammer' caused by ballvalves shutting off too quickly. The Torbeck is a brand of equilibrium valve which uses a diaphragm, and has a very small float and a short float arm.

Ballvalves can be noisy, though this rarely indicates that they're not working properly. With piston valves, a good deal of the noise arises because the flow is reduced progressively as the float rises. When the cistern is nearly full, the water is squeezing into it through a small hole. Diaphragm valves are better in this respect, since the flow remains constant up to the very last movement of the float arm.

Ballvalve noise can be much reduced if a silencer tube is fitted to extend the outlet below the water-level in the cistern. Because of the risk of back-siphonage, however, rigid silencer tubes are no longer permitted, although the Torbeck has a collapsible silencer tube which is still allowed.

Curing a blocked sink

A blocked sink almost invariably means that debris has accumulated in the trap. Kitchen sinks are especially vulnerable, because grease combines with solids to form a clogging mass.

Before you resort to removing the trap, though, it's worth trying to clear the blockage with a sink plunger. You'll need at least a few inches of water in the sink or basin for the plunger to work. Place the plunger directly over the plug hole, and squelch it up and down vigorously. You may have to put your hand or a cloth over the overflow to get sufficient suction.

If the plunger doesn't work, you'll have to clean out the trap. Remember that the water will gush out as soon as you release the trap, so have a bucket or large bowl strategically placed to catch it. Clean the trap thoroughly before replacing it. Look for sharp edges and projections where hairs or fibres might catch.

If cleaning out the trap doesn't solve the problem, then the blockage must be further down in the system. If the waste pipe is straight, you may be able to push the blockage through with a stick. Otherwise, try shifting it using some form of plumber's snake. These can be hired, or you can make your own from net curtain wire with a hook in the end.

To avoid repeated blockages, flush waste pipes occasionally with hot water and a washing soda, and try not to put grease, vegetable waste, tea leaves or rice down the sink.

Curing a blocked wc

This can be a very unpleasant job. Try to flush the blockage through with hot water to which you've added some washing soda and disinfectant. If that fails, a large sink plunger may do the trick – types without a rigid backing disc are the best for this, since they can be turned inside out to make them fit the base of the pan. Wear rubber gloves and be sure to clean and disinfect them and the plunger afterwards.

For stubborn blockages, you may have to resort to a drain rod fitted with a rubber disc.

Dealing with noisy plumbing

Plumbing can generate noise for a number of reasons.

Creaks and **groans** frequently occur as pipes expand and contract, rubbing against joists or other parts of the house structure. If you can pin down the source of the noise, it can usually be cured by slipping a piece of wadding under the pipe.

Water hammer is a loud knocking which occurs when taps or ballvalves shut off. It's caused by the pipework 'tensing' and relaxing as the pressure in the pipes changes. You may be able to cure water hammer by fixing pipes more securely – adding extra pipe clips, for example.

If it's being caused by a ballvalve shutting off, replace it with an equilibrium ballvalve (see p. 92). Any air trapped in the pipes will tend to encourage water hammer (see below).

Gurgles and **irregular flow** from taps indicates that air has been trapped in the pipes. To remove it, connect one end of a length of hose to the affected tap and the other to another tap – if possible one connected direct to the mains. Turn on

Using a hose to clear air from pipes

both taps to drive out the air. If that fails, drain the affected part of the system, open all the taps a little, and refill slowly. Persistent problems with air locks usually indicate a design fault in the system, such as pipes which slope in the wrong direction or pipes which are too small.

Dirty, discoloured or cloudy water

If the water emerging from the taps is dirty or discoloured, the cause should be investigated immediately.

If the affected taps are supplied from the cold water cistern (this includes all the hot taps, of course), check the cistern for silt or contamination. The outlets on cisterns are placed 50mm or so above the bottom

of the tank, to prevent silt being drawn in. But if the water gets stirred up – because you've been working on it or because the level has dropped lower than usual as a result of a heavy demand, or because the ballvalve is faulty – some of the accumulated debris will find its way out.

If the discoloured water is emerging from taps connected direct to the mains, then the most likely cause is that the water company has been working on the supply pipes. This inevitably stirs up silt which has accumulated in the pipes, but which is very unlikely to be harmful. If the water doesn't clear after running the tap for a few minutes, contact the water company for advice.

Getting the right temperature

The temperature of domestic hot water is controlled by thermostats on boilers, on electric immersion heaters and, in some cases, on the outside of the hot water cylinder itself. There's no point in heating water excessively – it's simply a waste of money – so thermostats should be adjusted to provide an adequate hot water temperature for the minimum energy consumption.

Thermostats are often marked with numbers rather than temperatures, or may just have a 'high' and 'low' scale. In such cases, finding the ideal setting is a matter of trial and error: start at the bottom and work up. If there is a temperature scale, 55°C (130°F) is a good starting-point. If you have to remove cover plates to get at the adjusting knob or screw – with an electric immersion heater, for example – *always* turn off the electrical supply first.

9 Central heating

Central heating has brought us a degree of flexibility and control over the interior temperature of our homes which could never be achieved with traditional fires and stoves. It's also eliminated the dirt and draughts which were associated with coal or wood fires. Central heating means that heat is generated at a central point and then distributed around the house. Systems differ in the fuels they use – gas, electricity, oil or solid fuel – and in the method by which the heat is distributed – hot water piped through radiators or warm air carried in ducts. Most central heating systems also provide hot water for baths and sinks.

Fuels differ in cost, and systems vary in efficiency, but all central heating systems consume a substantial amount of energy and are therefore relatively costly to run. Regular maintenance is essential to ensure that the systems are running efficiently and therefore providing the maximum comfort at the minimum cost.

Inspecting the central heating system

The best time to look at the central heating system is the spring, so that any work which is necessary can be carried out over the summer.

Inside the house:
- check radiators, valves and pipe fittings for leaks
- listen for gurgles and knocks and try to track them down to their source
- check for cold spots near the tops of radiators which indicate trapped air, and cold spots near the bottom which suggest accumulated sludge
- check that the thermostats in the system are working
- check the relative room temperatures throughout the house
- for warm air systems, clean out the filters.

In the loft:
- check the water-level in the feed and expansion cistern and make sure that the ballcock is working
- check that the pump isn't pushing hot water out of the vent pipe.

How central heating systems work

Systems using hot water and radiators

'Wet' systems using boilers and radiators are the most popular choice for domestic central heating.

Water heated by the boiler is pumped through the radiators in one or more circuits, and indirectly heats the hot water in the hot water cylinder. The flow is maintained by a pump and controlled by valves.

Most systems are of the open vented type, with a feed and expansion cistern, usually in the loft. This keeps the system topped up with water, allows room for expansion and provides an escape route for steam and air bubbles. In the USA and the colder parts of continental Europe, sealed or closed systems are more common. These have specially designed closed expansion vessels, and need no cistern in the loft.

Warm-air systems

In 'dry' or warm-air systems the air is directly heated and blown by a fan through a series of ducts, emerging through grilles in the floors or skirting boards. The outlets have shutters to control the air flow. Many gas warm-air systems include a water heater. Electric warm-air heating systems generally rely on an immersion heater for hot water.

Other heating systems

Electric storage radiators are sometimes referred to as a form of central heating, but this is not strictly accurate since each radiator is self-contained – there is no central source of heat. And by and large electric storage radiators cannot offer the same degree of control over room temperature that can be achieved with true central heating systems.

Electric underfloor heating is similar in operation to storage radiators, except that the heat is stored in the floor itself rather than in a stack of special bricks inside the radiator. Like storage radiators, electric underfloor heating isn't as flexible or responsive as central heating based on radiators or ducted warm air.

Boilers

The term 'boiler' is something of a misnomer, since the water should never be heated to boiling point. Boilers incorporate thermostats which are usually set to provide

Central heating – symptoms, faults and remedies

Symptom	Fault	Remedy	see page
Leaking radiator valve	• Weepy joint between valve and radiator	• Tighten valve and seal threads with PTFE tape if necessary	102
	• Weepy gland	• Tighten gland nut	102
Leaking radiator	• Corrosion pin-hole	• Replace radiator	102
Knocks and gurgles	• Air in system	• Bleed system to remove air	102
	• Pipes inadequately supported	• Put in extra support	103
Cold spot near top of radiator	• Air trapped in radiator	• Bleed radiator to remove air	102
Thermostat not working	• Faulty wiring	• Turn off electricity and check wiring	104
	• Faulty thermostat	• Replace	104
System cycles on and off too rapidly	• Boiler or cylinder thermostats set too low	• Increase thermostat settings	103
	• No cylinder thermostat	• Fit cylinder thermostat and three-port valve	98
Low water-level in feed and expansion cistern	• Ballcock set incorrectly	• Reset by bending float arm	103
	• Ballcock jammed	• Dismantle, clean and refit	92
Hot water being pumped through vent pipe	• Excessive flow through circulating pump	• Reduce pump setting	104
Some rooms too cool	• Radiators too small	• Check radiator against room size; replace if necessary	104
	• Insufficient flow through radiators	• Check inlet/outlet temperatures and adjust flow rates	104
Some rooms too hot		• Reduce flow rates	104
		• Fit thermostatic radiator valves	105

water at a temperature between 80 and 85°C (176 and 185°F).

Older gas boilers and almost all boilers using oil or solid fuel are floor-standing, and need a flue to carry the exhaust gases to the outside. With boilers like these, you must also ensure an adequate supply of fresh air, so there will probably be a ventilator fitted in a nearby window. On no account should ventilators like these be blocked off.

A more modern development is the wall-mounted gas boiler with a balanced flue – known as 'balanced' because a special vent both draws in air to burn with the gas and gets rid of the exhaust. The boiler doesn't need a chimney, and can be fitted to virtually any outside wall.

The latest development in gas boilers is the condensing boiler. This is very compact and efficient – converting about 90 per cent of the energy in the gas to heat, compared with roughly 75 per cent for a conventional gas boiler.

Pipework

Radiators in houses are usually connected in a **two-pipe system**. The feed pipe brings hot water from the boiler to the radiator and the return pipe carries it back. To keep the water flowing there's a pump.

With systems using 15mm, 25mm or 28mm pipes, each pair of feed and return pipes can serve several radiators. With 8mm or 10mm microbore systems, each radiator has its own

feed and return pipes connected back to a central fitting known as a **manifold**. The manifold will be connected to the boiler with larger pipes – 25mm, say.

Pipes from 15mm upwards are rigid, and use the same fittings as conventional hot and cold water plumbing. Microbore pipes are much more flexible, and the piping is supplied in rolls. This makes it easy to install – more like installing electrical cable than conventional plumbing – and neater where the pipes are on show.

Single-pipe systems

It is possible to pipe radiators on a single-pipe system, with one pipe leading from each radiator to the next in turn. The circulation within

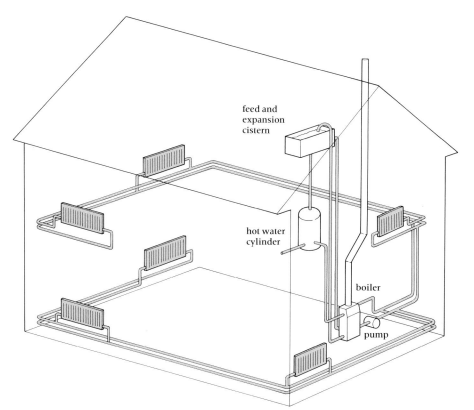

Central heating system with boiler and radiators

each radiator is by gravity, with the inlet at the top on one end and the outlet at the bottom on the other. A variation is the loop-in system, where the supply pipe loops in and out of a special valve which incorporates a by-pass.

Hot water

Central heating boilers usually also provide domestic hot water, but indirectly. Feed and return pipes from the boiler are connected to a coil inside the hot water cylinder, so that heat is transferred to the cylinder's contents, but there is no direct contact between the boiler water and the water which comes out of the hot taps.

In many systems this hot water circuit relies only on 'gravity-fed' circulation, sometimes called 'thermo-siphoning', rather than a pump. Since hot water is less dense than cool water, there is a tendency for hot water from the boiler to rise up

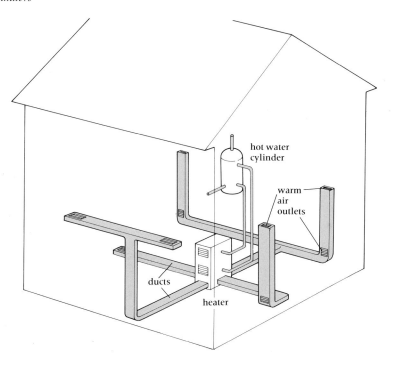

Warm air central heating system

the feed pipe to the heating coil in the hot water cylinder. Conversely, having transferred its heat, the cooler water tends to return to the boiler down the return pipe, and a continuous flow cycle is established. More sophisticated systems use the pump for both the radiators and the hot water circuit – seen Controlling the System, below.

The feed and expansion cistern

The boiler, the radiators and the heating coil in the hot water cylinder form an essentially closed circuit, with the same water circulating all the time. This helps to minimise corrosion in the system. But there must still be room for the water to expand as it heats up, and a means of replenishing the system when necessary. These are the functions of the feed and expansion cistern, which is normally located in the loft.

The feed and expansion cistern is very similar to the main cold water storage tank, but usually a good deal smaller. It has a cold water feed from the mains, via a ballcock, and a vent pipe leading from the top of the heating coil in the hot water cyclinder.

Controlling the system

One of the great advantages of central heating is the ability to control the temperature inside the home, and to respond rapidly to changing conditions without wasting costly energy. The system controls make this possible.

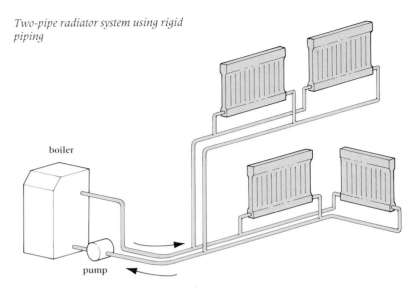

Two-pipe radiator system using rigid piping

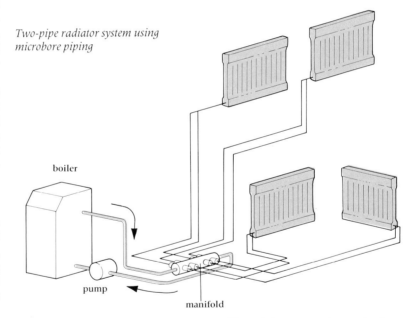

Two-pipe radiator system using microbore piping

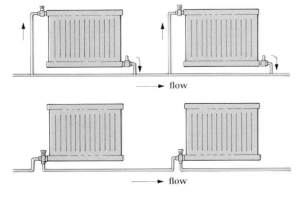

Single-pipe system

Single-pipe loop-in system

The minimum requirement – for a system with a gravity-fed hot water circuit – is a programmer, a boiler thermostat and a room thermostat. More sophisticated systems – with pumped hot water circuits – may also have motorised valves to direct the flow of hot water where it's needed, a cylinder thermostat, radiator thermostats and an external thermostat to guard against frost.

The **programmer** is the central control, and determines which parts of the system are in operation and at

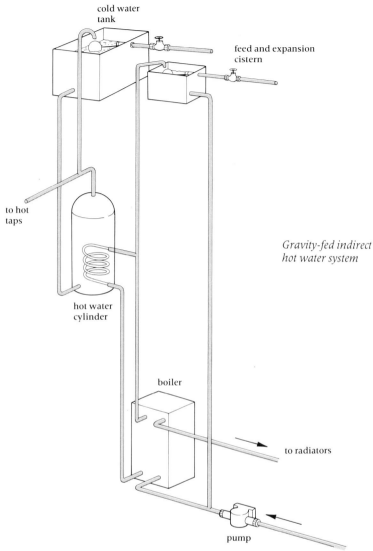

cold water tank

feed and expansion cistern

to hot taps

Gravity-fed indirect hot water system

hot water cylinder

boiler

to radiators

pump

located in the main living-room.

A cylinder thermostat is used in conjunction with a motorised valve, where the hot water system is pumped rather than relying on gravity flow. It works in the same way as the room thermostat, turning on the pump when the temperature of the water in the cylinder drops below the pre-set value. The motorised valve responds to inputs from both the cylinder thermostat and the room thermostat, directing the outflow of the pump accordingly.

An external thermostat is used to override the other controls when the outside temperature drops to a level where frost damage might occur.

Thermostatic radiator valves (TRVs) control the flow through individual radiators. They're very useful in rooms which might otherwise get too warm before the temperature in the living-room has reached the level set on the room thermostat. Most TRVs incorporate the thermostat within the valve itself, but there are types with remote thermostats which can be placed on the wall some distance from the radiator.

Radiators and their valves

In spite of their name, radiators give up most of their heat by convection of the air flowing over them. But 'radiators', as a name for devices where the heated surface is in direct view, distinguishes them from 'convectors', where the heating element is contained within an outer casing.

Although radiators are available in a variety of materials, including cast iron, aluminium and plastic, steel panel radiators are by far the most common in current use. At their simplest they consist of two steel panels welded together with a watertight seal all around the edge. Single- and double-panel types are available, and either may have banks of fins or flutes behind the panels, which increase their output by about 30 per cent. Most radiators have four threaded connection points, one in each corner.

which times. Simple programmers offer a choice between hot water only or hot water plus central heating, for one or two periods in each 24-hour cycle. Simple programmers are not very flexible; for example, it is not generally possible to programme them to provide hot water only for one on-period and hot water plus heating for the other in the same day. More sophisticated digital programmers are available which work on a 7-day cycle, with more on-periods in each 24 hours and a more flexible choice of hot water only or hot water plus central heating.

Thermostats are simply temperature-controlled switches. The boiler thermostat controls the temperature of the water flowing out of the boiler. If the temperature is below the setting of the thermostat, and the programmer says that the system is on, then the boiler comes on. The room thermostat senses the temperature inside the room and switches the heating on if it has the 'permission' of the programmer to do so. In practice, in a simple system this means starting up the pump to circulate water around the radiators. The room thermostat is usually

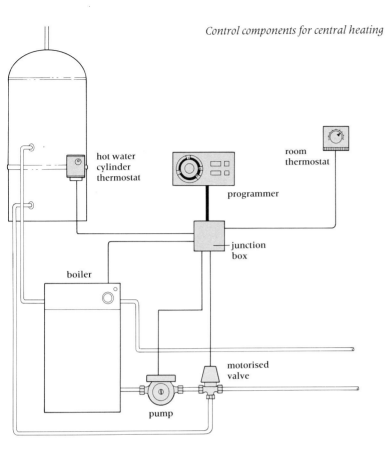

Control components for central heating

In systems using supply pipes of 15mm or more, each radiator is usually fitted with two valves: a **wheelhead** valve on the inlet which can be used to turn the radiator on and off and a **lockshield** valve on the outlet which is used to control the rate of flow, and should be used only when the system is being set up.

In microbore and some single-pipe systems, twin-entry radiator valves are used. These are actually two valves in one. A tube attached to the valve inside the radiator carries the supply water to the far end of the radiator.

Convectors

Skirting convectors (sometimes perversely referred to as skirting radiators) fit along the bottom of walls in place of skirting boards. They're unobtrusive, and give an even distribution of heat in the room. Matching empty casings are available so that the skirting all around the room can have the same appearance.

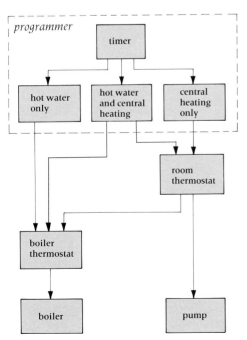

Simple control diagram

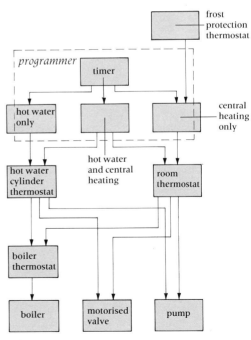

Sophisticated control diagram

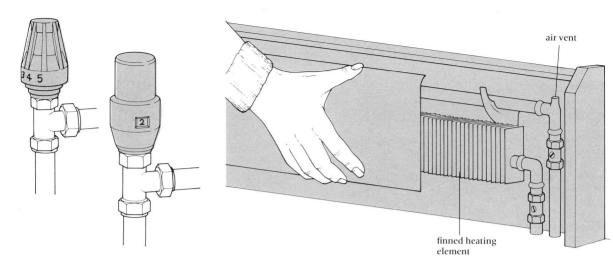

Thermostatic radiator valves (TRVS)   *Skirting convector*

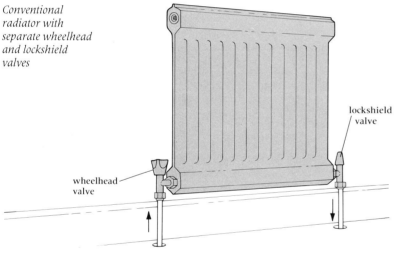

Conventional radiator with separate wheelhead and lockshield valves

Kick-space convector

Kick-space fan convectors fit under kitchen units, into the bottom of a flight of stairs to heat a hallway, or wherever a wall-mounted heater would be impractical.

Underfloor convectors, which may be natural-draught or fan-assisted, fit in the space under suspended floors.

Other components of the system

Draincocks must be provided at the low points in the system to enable it to be drained when necessary.

Isolating valves should be fitted on either side of the circulating pump so that it can be removed for service or repair without draining the system. Other parts of the system may also have isolating valves, for the same reason. A similar type of

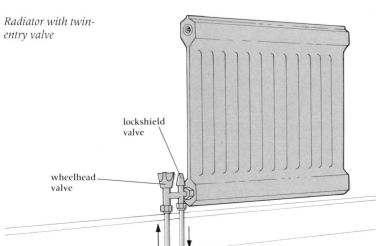

Radiator with twin-entry valve

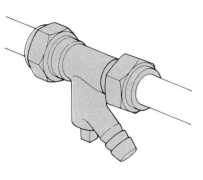

Draincock

valve is sometimes used to restrict the flow to the heating coil in the hot water cylinder, to prevent it taking more than its fair share of the flow from the boiler.

Air vents are required to 'bleed' the air out of the system. Most radiators have manual air vents either as an integral part of the radiator or with a threaded body which fits in one of the upper connections on the radiator. There are also automatic air vents which can be placed at strategic points in the pipework to prevent air accumulating. These are generally of the hydroscopic type, containing a number of fibre discs which hold the valve closed as long as they're moist. If air under the valve allows the discs to dry out, they shrink and open the valve. Once the air has been expelled the valve closes automatically.

Safety valves are essential in sealed systems, and are sometimes fitted to open-vented systems. They're designed to open when a pre-set pressure is exceeded, but should never do so unless there is a major fault in the system.

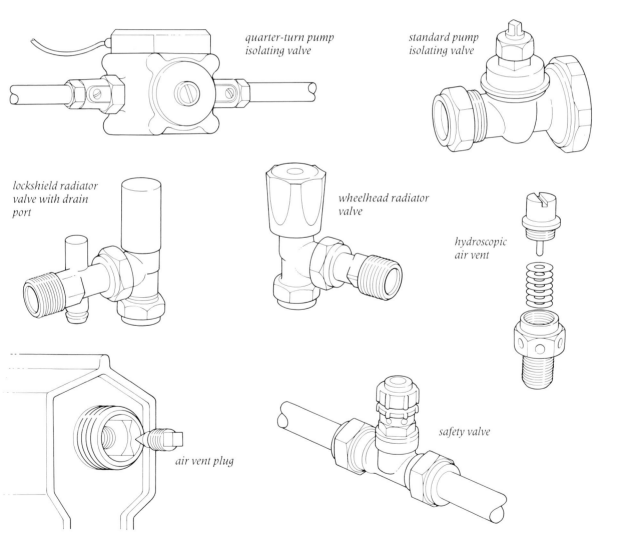

quarter-turn pump isolating valve

standard pump isolating valve

lockshield radiator valve with drain port

wheelhead radiator valve

hydroscopic air vent

air vent plug

safety valve

Central heating valves and air vents

Maintaining your central heating

Dealing with leaks

The most frequent sources of leaks in central heating systems are:

- weepy compression fittings
- leaky threaded couplings on radiator valves, bleed valves, boiler connections, etc.
- leaky glands on radiator valves
- corrosion pin-holes in radiators.

'Weepy' compression fittings (see Plumbing chapter, p. 82) can often be cured by tightening up the fitting slightly. If this doesn't work, the compression ring or olive inside the fitting has been distorted and must be replaced. This usually means draining down at least part of the system so that the fitting can be dismantled.

If you have to replace an olive, try to slide the old one off the end of the pipe, but don't damage or distort the pipe or you'll make matters worse. If you have to, cut off the old olive, but cut through only the olive, not the pipe. If the pipe does get damaged, cut off the affected section and replace it with a length of new pipe attached with a solder ring coupling.

Leaky threads on radiator valves can be sealed with PTFE tape. Shut off

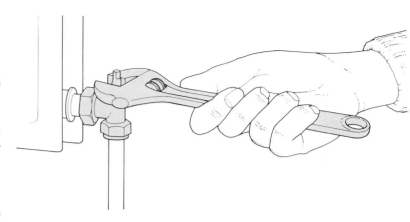

Gently tighten the gland nut to cure a weeping gland on a radiator valve

the wheelhead valve, remove the cover from the lockshield valve and shut that, too. Use pliers on the top of the lockshield valve and note the number of turns so you can open it the correct amount when you have finished the job.

Have something like a washing-up bowl standing by to catch the water from the radiator. Remove the leaking valve gently to prevent water gushing out. Wrap three or four turns of PTFE tape around the threads, stretching it gently as you wind it on. PTFE tape has no adhesive, but tends to stick to itself when stretched. Replace the valve and make sure all the threads are tight. Open the lockshield valve to the original setting and then the wheelhead valve. Check for leaks. Finally, remove air from the radiator by opening the bleed valve at the top with an air vent key.

Leaking threads elsewhere in the system should respond to the same treatment, but you'll have to drain the system down unless the part you need to work on can be isolated or you hire a pipe freezing kit.

Leaky glands in radiator valves result in water weeping out around the central spindle. They can often be cured by removing the cover and gently tightening the gland. If this fails, the gland will have to be repacked, which means draining down at least part of the system.

Corrosion can lead to pin-holes in steel panel radiators. As a temporary measure, an affected radiator can be isolated by shutting off both the wheelhead and lockshield valves, but the only real cure is for the radiator to be replaced. If you buy a new radiator of the same size and type as the old one, this should involve no alterations to the plumbing and therefore no need to drain down the system. However, if corrosion has taken place this suggests that either there is no corrosion inhibitor in the water or it has become ineffective. In these circumstances the system should be drained, flushed through and filled afresh with water containing a suitable corrosion inhibitor.

The colour of the water in the system is a good guide to the extent of corrosion. Black water is caused by a chemical reaction between different metals in the system. It can be cured by adding corrosion inhibitor. Red water indicates that there is air in the system: see Bleeding the System.

Bleeding the system

Air in the central heating system can cause knocks and gurgles, cold spots in the tops of radiators and accelerated corrosion. All radiators should have bleed valves, and there may be others at 'high points' in the system such as the upper connection to the heating coil in the hot water cylinder.

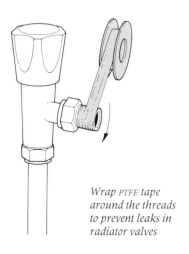

Wrap PTFE tape around the threads to prevent leaks in radiator valves

Before bleeding the system, make sure that the pump is off, otherwise it's possible for air to be drawn in instead of being pushed out. Have a cloth ready to put over the bleed valve to stop water spurting out when all the air has been removed. Start at the lowest point in the system. Using a radiator air vent key, open each bleed valve a little, let out any air and close the valve when water rather than air is produced. Start the pump, run the system for a while, and check the air vents again.

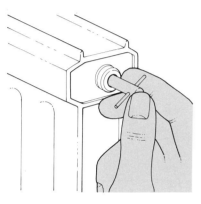

Bleeding a radiator using an air vent key

Making sure that pipes are secure

Noises in central heating pipes can also arise if the pipes aren't properly supported. Track down the source of the noise and add extra support as required: extra pipe clips or noggings under pipes between joists, for example. Noises caused by pipes rubbing on walls and timbers can be cured by gently squeezing pieces of foam pipe insulation into the gaps.

Draining down the system

There's no point in draining the central heating system unless you have to. But there are times when draining the system is necessary to enable maintenance and repairs to be carried out.

The water in central heating systems must contain a corrosion inhibitor. If you're working on a system which has been filled only recently,

you may want to retain and reuse the water. Bear in mind that the amount of water in the system might be as much as 200 litres, though, so you'll need large containers to store it in. In general, if you have to drain the system it's worth taking the opportunity to flush it through and refill with fresh water and a fresh supply of inhibitor.

Switch the system off, locate the draincock and attach a length of hose to carry away the water. Make sure all the radiator handwheel valves are open. In the loft, turn off the water supply to the feed and expansion cistern or tie up the ballvalve. Open the draincock. As the system empties, open the air vents on the radiators – starting from the top – to make sure all the water drains away.

When the water has drained away, close all the vents and the draincock, and turn the water supply to the feed and expansion cistern back on. As the system fills, bleed the radiators to get rid of all the trapped air. When the pipes and radiators are full, open the draincock again and let the water flow through. When you're satisfied that the system is clean, drain it once again as before.

If the old water is very murky, there are chemical descalents and flushing additives which you can use to help clean the system out. All chemicals should be added through the feed and expansion cistern. Individual radiators can be cleared of sludge by removing them while the system is empty and flushing them through with a hosepipe.

To refill the system, close the draincock, turn the water supply back on, add a corrosion inhibitor to the feed and expansion cistern and refill, bleeding the radiators as the system fills up. Finally, run the pump for a while and bleed again.

Using a pipe freezing kit

If you need to work on just one part of the system, and you really don't want to drain the whole system, an alternative is to use a pipe freezing

kit. These use carbon dioxide gas to freeze the water in the pipes at either side of the area you want to work on, forming plugs of ice. They can be hired from d-i-y hire stores.

The feed and expansion cistern

When the system is cold, there need only be 100 to 150mm of water in the feed and expansion cistern. As the water expands, the level rises and the float is submerged. The only water loss is by evaporation and any leaks in the system.

This can mean that ballcocks on feed and expansion cisterns are called upon to open very infrequently, and they tend to jam as a result. If yours jams, don't simply release it by 'exercising' the float arm. This may seem to cure the problem, but there's a chance that the valve will then jam open and you'll get an overflow. Dismantle the valve and clean it thoroughly; for more details, see Plumbing, p. 92. Diaphragm and Torbeck-type valves tend to be more reliable than conventional ballvalves for feed and expansion cisterns.

Getting the water temperatures right

There can be a conflict between the ideal temperatures for the domestic hot water, maximum boiler efficiency and optimum radiator performance. By and large, boilers work best with their thermostats set towards the top of their range – that is, the hotter the better. If the boiler thermostat is set too low, the boiler will tend to turn itself on and off frequently, which can be both irritating and wasteful. The exception to this general rule is the gas condensing boiler, which should be set to the minimum temperature which provides satisfactory operation of the system.

A high water temperature also suits the radiators, which can then respond more quickly when they get the signal for action from the room thermostat. But in a system without a thermostat on the hot water cylinder, this also tends to mean that the domestic hot water is heated far more than is necessary.

The solution to this conflict is to fit a cylinder thermostat and a three-way motorised valve. Cylinder thermostats usually strap on to the outside of the hot water cylinder and are wired back to the system's electrical junction box. If you have a cylinder with factory-applied foam insulation, the insulation will have to be cut away so that the thermostat makes contact with the metal of the cylinder. The motorised valve controls the flow from the boiler, directing it to the radiators, the hot water cylinder or both, as appropriate.

The details of the wiring vary from system to system – if you don't have a thorough understanding of electrical matters, it's a job best left to a professional. If you do decide to d-i-y, *turn off the electricity at the mains*. Remember that all the control wiring for central heating systems is at mains voltage.

Now the boiler will start up only when its own thermostat *and* either the cylinder thermostat *or* the room thermostat call for heat, and the three-way valve will direct the water where it's needed.

The dials of thermostats are not generally marked in degree scales – a simple scale from 1 to 5 or even just 'cold' at one end and 'hot' at the other are more usual. For boilers and radiators the conventional 'design temperature' is 82°C (180°F). For domestic hot water 60°C (140°F) is usually ample.

Checking that thermostats are working

The **room thermostat** usually controls the circulating pump. Turn the programmer to central heating only, and switch on. Changing the room thermostat setting should turn the pump on and off. Room thermostats are generally marked in actual temperature scales. These may not be very accurate, but that's not too important as long as they're consistent.

If the thermostat is not working, the fault may lie in the wiring or in the thermostat itself. Either way, *turn off the electricity at the mains* before you attempt any investigation or repair. Room thermostats are usually quite easy to replace.

The **boiler thermostat** is the last element in the chain of command to the boiler. To check it turn the programmer to central heating and the room thermostat to maximum. If the boiler is cold, it should come on immediately; otherwise, you should be able to turn it on and off by varying the position of the thermostat control. If the thermostat appears to be faulty, *turn off the electricity at the mains* before attempting any further investigation. Boiler thermostats are usually built into the boiler, and are likely to be quite difficult to obtain through normal retail outlets.

Adjusting the flow through the pump

Most central heating pumps are adjustable. They should be set to the minimum flow which keeps all the radiators supplied. Start from the minimum flow and work up. If you find that hot water is being pumped out of the vent pipe into the feed and expansion cistern, then the flow rate is too great. The position of the control for maximum and minimum flow rates should be clearly marked on the pump.

Pumps can sometimes jam, particularly on systems with gravity-fed hot water, when the pump may not be used for several months in the summer. If you suspect that a pump has jammed, shut down the system at the programmer, and look for a means of turning the pump by hand. Most pumps have this, usually a disc with a slot, which can be turned with a screwdriver. Turn the pump in the normal direction of flow to free it. If this fails, you'll have to shut off the isolating valves, remove the pump and dismantle it, or call in a professional heating engineer.

To prevent pumps jamming on systems with gravity-fed hot water, set the programmer to central heating, turn up the room thermostat and run the pump for just a minute or so every couple of weeks throughout the summer.

Getting the room temperatures right

For a central heating system to work properly, the sizes of radiators should be chosen to suit the room they're in. As a rough guide, the recommended temperatures for various types of room are:

- Living- and dining-rooms   21°C (70°F)
- Bedrooms   18°C (65°F)
- Kitchens   20°C (68°F)
- Bathrooms   21°C (70°F)
- Hallways   18°C (65°F)

Working out how much heat you need in a particular room can be quite complex, involving the size, type of structure, how many outside walls there are, the size and type of windows and a number of other factors, and is beyond the scope of this book. But the simple fact is that you may find that some of your rooms are too hot or too cold.

Before you decide to buy new radiators, though, it's worth checking that the system has been properly 'balanced'. Balancing means setting the flow rates so that all the elements of the system are getting their fair share of the water.

For radiators, this is achieved by adjusting the lockshield valves. Radiators are designed to work with a temperature difference between the inlet and outlet of 11°C (20°F) for a nominal input temperature of 82°C (180°F). In other words, water entering a radiator at 82°C (180°F) should be leaving it at 71°C (160°F). To measure the temperature difference, you may be able to devise a consistent technique using a conventional thermometer, but the

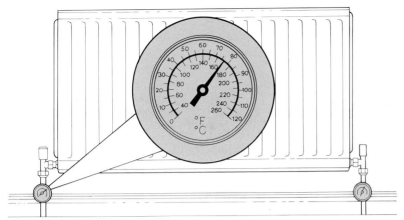

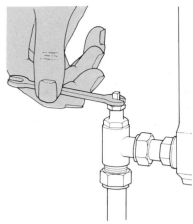

Use a pair of clip-on pipe thermometers to show the difference in temperature between inlet and outlet: it should be 11°C

Adjust the flow rate through the lockshield valve; replace the cover afterwards

easiest way is with a pair of clip-on pipe thermometers attached to each side of the radiator. These cost a few pounds each, from plumbers' merchants – they're not widely available for hire.

Start with the radiator closest to the boiler and work away from it. Adjust the valves until the temperature difference is 11°C (20°F) for each of the radiators. You may have to work around the circuit several times, since each adjustment to one radiator tends to affect at least some of the others.

If a room is still too cold, the options are:

- replace the radiator with a larger or more efficient one (a two-panel in place of a one-panel, or a finned in place of a plain)
- improve the insulation in the room to make better use of the available heat
- add a second source of heat

If a room is too hot, a very effective answer is to fit thermostatic radiator valves. These simply replace the existing handwheel valves and shut off the flow when the set temperature is reached. Some thermostatic valves tend to seize closed during the summer, however. Leave them on their highest setting when the central heating is not in use for a prolonged period, to ensure that they are at least opening and closing slightly.

10   Gas

For roughly 160 years, the gas used for domestic lighting and heating was 'town gas' extracted from coal. Today, however, town gas has been replaced by natural gas from the North Sea. Natural gas has roughly twice the energy content of town gas, which meant that existing gas appliances had to be converted to natural gas in the 1960s and 1970s. What natural gas lacks is town gas's characteristic smell, so a smell is added to ensure that potentially dangerous gas leaks don't go unnoticed.

The Gas Regulations

Gas is dangerous, and should be treated with great respect: gas explosions can be devastating. There are strict rules for the supply of gas to homes, known as the Gas Safety Regulations, which are designed to ensure that people using gas present no danger to themselves or to the public at large. The Regulations cover not only the installation of pipes, meters and appliances, but also their use. Under the Regulations:

- only competent persons are permitted to install or service gas systems or appliances
- you must not use, nor permit anyone else to use, any gas appliance which you know or suspect to be dangerous
- if you suspect a gas leak, you should turn off your gas supply immediately at the isolating valve next to the meter
- if you can still smell gas after turning off the isolating valve, you must inform your local gas service centre immediately. If turning off the supply does stop the smell, you've eliminated the immediate danger, but you will still need to locate the fault and put it right.

For the majority of gas users, the Regulations mean that the installation and maintenance of gas pipes and appliances should be entrusted to a qualified professional. British Gas have their own engineering staff who can be contacted through gas showrooms, but you'll also find independent gas engineers and gas installers in Yellow Pages. Qualified contractors have to be members of CORGI – the Council of Registered Gas Installers – as of 31 March 1991.

Routine maintenance

Regular maintenance of gas appliances is essential, both for safety and to ensure that they are working efficiently and therefore at minimum cost. British Gas advise that gas appliances, and particularly gas central heating boilers, should be serviced annually. The best time is probably the spring, just after the system has been working at its hardest over winter. British Gas, and most independent contractors, offer annual maintenance contracts varying from a simple boiler service to an annual check on the whole gas installation.

You shouldn't even contemplate undertaking this maintenance work yourself unless you have read the Gas Regulations and can honestly say that you have understood them. The onus is on you to establish your own competence. The Regulations are published by HMSO, and copies are generally available in the reference section of larger public libraries.

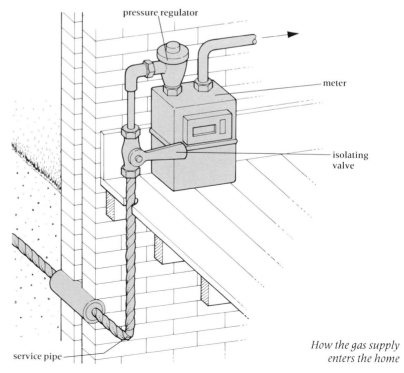

How the gas supply enters the home

service pipe

pressure regulator

meter

isolating valve

Emergency precautions

If you suspect a gas leak, the first thing to do is to turn off the supply at the isolating valve next to the meter. Then open windows all round the house to let the gas escape.

- *don't* switch any lights on or off – the spark generated inside the switch could set off an explosion
- *never* under any circumstances search for a gas leak with a lighted match.

If in doubt, and especially if you can still smell gas after turning off the isolating valve, contact British Gas immediately: they're listed under Gas in the telephone directory.

Gas in the home

The service pipe and meter

The **service pipe** brings gas into the house from the gas main. In older homes the service pipe usually passes through the walls of the house below ground-level and then emerges through the floor. In newer installations the gas meter may be accessible from the outside, so that the gas supply passes through the isolating valve and meter before it enters the house.

The service pipe is connected to the **isolating valve**. This controls the flow of gas into the house. The valve is on when the handle is in line with the pipe, and off when the handle is at 90 degrees to the pipe – this is the general rule for all gas valves and taps.

From the isolating valve, the pipe leads to a **pressure regulator**. The regulator reduces the pressure of the gas from the mains, and keeps it constant despite fluctuations in the mains pressure. The gas now passes through the meter and from there to the gas plumbing and appliances in the house.

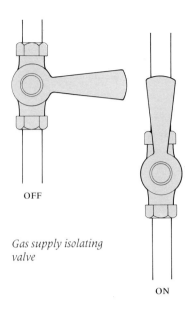

Gas supply isolating valve

OFF

ON

All the components up to and including the meter are the property of British Gas, and any work on this part of the installation may be carried out only by British Gas or a contractor nominated by them.

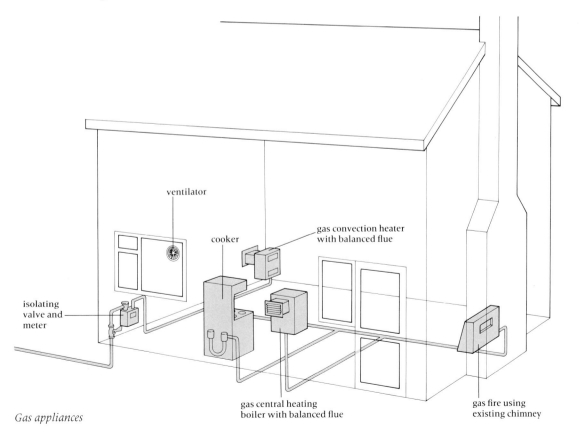

ventilator

cooker

gas convection heater with balanced flue

isolating valve and meter

gas central heating boiler with balanced flue

gas fire using existing chimney

Gas appliances

Gas plumbing

Copper pipe is used almost universally for gas plumbing, and installations must conform to a British Standard Code of Practice and to the Gas Safety Regulations.

The size of the pipes depends on the amount of gas demanded by the appliances being served. However, it's normal for all the concealed gas pipework to be in 15mm pipe, with reduced couplings fitted where the pipes emerge through walls or floors for appliances which have 10mm or 8mm inlets.

Pipe joints must be of the capillary soldered type – compression fittings like those used for water plumbing are not permitted. PTFE tape should not be used to seal threaded gas fittings – a special gas jointing compound must be used.

Pipes must be protected where they pass through walls and all pipework must be adequately supported.

All gas pipework must be tested to ensure that it has been correctly installed. The tests are designed to ensure both that the pipework is gastight and that there is sufficient gas pressure at the appliance for it to work properly. Most gas appliances incorporate a pressure test point where this can be measured.

The Wiring Regulations for electrical installations require gas (and water) pipework to be electrically earthed, to prevent it becoming live if a fault were to develop in the electrical system. This is called 'bonding', and involves fitting a special earthing clip to the gas plumbing close to the meter, with a cable connecting it to the electrical earth at the electricity meter. Connecting it to a household earth wire will not provide sufficient protection.

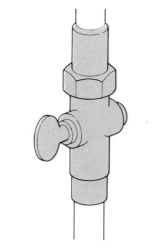

Service cock for a gas appliance (shown ON)

Connections to appliances

Most appliances are connected to the supply by rigid pipes. A service cock should be fitted in each case, so that the appliance can be isolated, and some appliances also require a restrictor to help regulate the flow of gas.

Free-standing cookers are generally connected by a flexible pipe, so that the cooker can be trundled for-

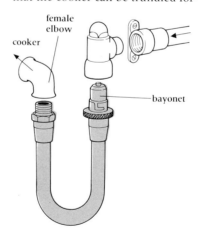

Gas cooker connection

ward to clean behind it. This pipe should be of the self-sealing plug-in type, with a bayonet connector. To prevent the cooker toppling forward and pulling on the flexible connection, a stability bracket may be fixed to the wall behind the cooker, or a length of chain fixed between the cooker and the wall to limit the cooker's movement.

Flues and air supplies

All gas appliances need an adequate supply of air. Without it, the gas may not burn properly and carbon monoxide could build up inside the house. With the exception of cookers, most gas appliances also need flues to carry away the exhaust gases.

In some gas boilers and heaters, these needs are satisfied simultaneously by using a **balanced flue** (see p. 95). Ventilators are often incorporated in the windows of kitchens where gas cookers and gas boilers have been installed. On no account should these ventilators be blocked off.

Getting an old gas system replaced

Like everything in the home, the gas installation won't last forever. If you have old pipes which need to be replaced, or you want to extend the system to add more gas appliances, call in a professional. Get a number of quotes, and make sure that they specify in detail the work which is being proposed, so that you can compare them accurately.

Is there any scope for d-i-y?

The short answer is: very little, and it's not worth taking chances.

11 Rainwater removal

Chapter 12 deals with 'foul water' drainage – how the waste from sinks, baths, basins and WCs is carried from the house to the sewer or to a cesspool or septic tank. This chapter is concerned with 'storm water' drainage – coping with the water which falls on the roof of the house as rain – which is the job of the gutters and downpipes. These are usually connected to soakaways – porous pits beneath the ground some distance from the house – rather than to the sewers. In some older homes, and in cases where the lie of the land, the type of soil or the position of the house in relation to others – in cities, for example – means that soakaways would not be practical, rainwater may be drained into the sewer. This usually entails an extra payment on your water charges, which should be shown as a separate item on your bills.

In heavy rain the gutters and downpipes of a typical house may have to cope with up to 100 litres of water per minute. To make sure they're up to the job, inspect your gutters and downpipes at least once a year (twice is better), keep them clear of debris and repair them promptly when necessary. Iron gutters and pipes must also be painted regularly to stop them rusting.

Inspecting the gutters and downpipes

The most important time at which to look at your gutters and downpipes is the onset of winter. Autumn leaves tend to settle in gutters, where they mix with silt from the tiles or slates to form a clogging mass. If left, this will reduce the efficiency of the gutters substantially and may block the downpipes.

Each year:
- scrape out the gutters and wash them down. Look for leaks and confirm that the water drains away efficiently through the downpipes
- if the downpipes discharge into gulleys at ground-level, clear out any debris there too
- check that the gutters are firmly supported by their brackets, and that each run of guttering is at least level or has a steady fall towards its downpipe. Sagging gutters will allow water to spill out on to the walls when it rains
- check for cracks, breaks and leaky joints. If major repairs and renovations are needed, you may prefer to postpone these until the following spring or summer, but you shouldn't delay making emergency repairs to prevent water falling on the brickwork which can give rise to penetrating damp.

Inspect the gutters again in spring to see how well they've survived the winter:

- once again, check for cracks, breaks and leaky joints
- with iron gutters, assess whether they will need to be painted before the following winter.

Rainwater systems

Modern gutters are made of plastic, which won't rust, needs no painting and is very much lighter than the cast iron which was used until about 20 years ago. Before cast iron became available, the traditional material was lead.

Gutters can be laid level, but they work more efficiently and are less prone to silting up if each length of guttering slopes down evenly towards the downpipe. The slope, or 'fall', needs to be only slight: 1 in 250 is typical, equivalent to 25mm over a length of 5m.

Plastic gutters

Lengths of plastic guttering are joined by couplings which incorporate rubber seals and plastic clips which hold the guttering in place while allowing room for expansion in warm weather. These joints also

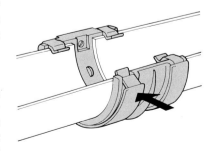

Clip-on joint for plastic guttering

Gutters and downpipes – symptoms, faults and remedies

Symptom	Fault	Remedy	*see page*
Gutter leaks	• Damaged joint seal	• Replace seal	111
	• Cracked, broken or rusty guttering	• Replace affected length	109
Gutter overflowing	• Gutter blocked	• Rake out	111
	• Broken, damaged or rusty bracket(s)	• Replace faulty bracket(s)	112
	• Blocked downpipe	• Clear blockage in downpipe	112
Downpipe leaks	• Damaged joint seal	• Replace seal	112
	• Cracked, broken or rusty downpipe	• Replace affected length	112
Water spills out of gulley at bottom of downpipe	• Blocked gulley	• Clear blockage	
	• Soakaway silted up	• Dig out soakaway	112

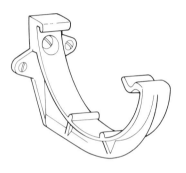

Plastic gutter bracket

avoid the need for adjoining lengths of gutter to overlap, so plastic guttering can be cut and joined at any point. The gutters clip into plastic brackets fixed to the fascia boards or to the rafters. The brackets should be spaced at intervals of one metre or less.

Plastic gutters and downpipes can be obtained in up to 4m lengths, and in a range of sizes and profiles. The usual choice for domestic use is 112mm half-round guttering used with 68mm downpipes. A wide range of brackets, connectors and fittings is available for both the guttering and the pipes, including adaptors to connect new plastic guttering to old cast-iron gutters.

Plastic gutters cannot rot, but do tend to become more brittle with age due to the effects of ultra-violet radiation from the sun.

Cast-iron gutters

Cast-iron gutters are usually supported on metal brackets attached to the sides or tops of the rafters. The guttering is not attached to the brackets – it relies on its considerable weight to stay in place. Each length

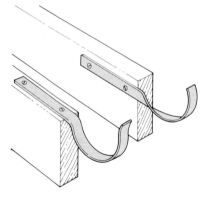

Brackets for cast-iron gutters

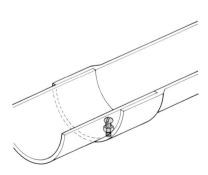

Joint in cast-iron gutter

of cast-iron gutter has a short enlarged section at one end, so that it will overlap the adjoining length. The joint is sealed with putty or mastic and secured by a small nut and bolt.

Cast-iron gutters and downpipes are heavy, prone to rusting and need to be handled carefully as they tend to be rather brittle. Cast-iron downpipes will almost certainly crack if they freeze up with water inside them.

Other gutter materials

Lead gutters and downpipes are rare, but may be a very important feature of an old house. Lead doesn't rust but can become brittle with age, and lead pipes may crack if they freeze up with water inside. Permanent repairs to lead guttering should be entrusted to a specialist plumber.

Aluminium guttering is available from specialist firms; it combines corrosion-resistance and light weight. It's usually tailor-made on-site to suit the house, however, and for anything but minor repairs you will probably have to contact the original installers.

Some houses built in the late 1940s and early 1950s may have asbestos cement gutters. These need no painting but tend to be very brittle. If major repairs are necessary you would be well advised to replace them with modern plastic guttering.

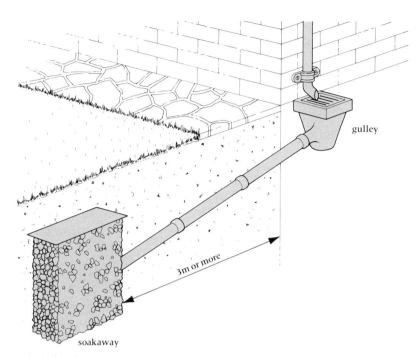

A typical soakaway

get rid of the remaining sediments and to check that the water flows away efficiently.

If you don't have them already, invest in balloon gratings which fit in the mouth of the gutter outlet. If your gutters seem to collect a lot of rubbish – because there's a large tree nearby, for example – it may be worthwhile fitting covers over the whole gutter. These are available readymade, but it's easy (and a good deal cheaper) to make your own from plastic or galvanised steel mesh.

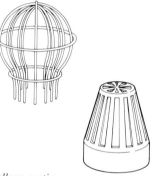

Balloon gratings

Soakaways

A soakaway is simply a pit – typically about 2m deep and 1.2m across – through which water can percolate into the ground. Soakaways may be constructed from pre-cast concrete rings, or be lined with bricks topped off by a concrete slab, or simply be filled with rubble and covered by one or two layers of polyethylene sheet. In most cases the top of the soaka-way will be at least 0.3m below ground-level, so there'll be no obvious sign of where it is.

home. Look carefully at the outlet where the gutter meets the down-pipe – some birds seem to find this an attractive nest site (and it's also a favourite spot for tennis balls to lodge).

After scraping out the worst of the muck, flush the gutters with water – a hosepipe is easier than carrying buckets of water up the ladder – to

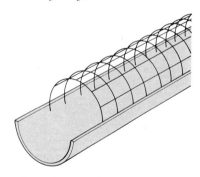

Wire or plastic mesh cover for guttering

Maintaining your rainwater system

Keeping your gutters clean

Regular cleaning of your gutters can be an unpleasant job, but it's essential. You can use a trowel to remove the debris, but it's worthwhile making a scraper of a shape and size which suits the guttering on your

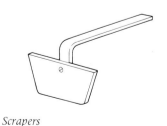

Scrapers

Leaks in plastic guttering

Leaks and overflows from gutters and downpipes should not be ignored, because of the risks of damp penetrating the walls of the house.

Leaking joints in plastic guttering usually mean that the guttering has been disturbed – by a ladder bumping into it, for example. Unless the rubber seals have been damaged, the problem can usually be solved by cleaning the affected area and reassembling the joint. If there's any doubt about the condition of the existing components, replace them: new couplings cost only a few pounds.

Leaks in cast-iron guttering

Minor leaks can be cured by cleaning the affected area and applying bitumastic paint – a thick, dark, waterproof paint – or a proprietary mastic compound. Where the leak is caused by the gutters rusting through, perforated zinc sheet and car body filler can be used to make a temporary repair, but eventually the rusty guttering will have to be replaced.

To replace a length of cast-iron gutter, or to renew a leaky joint, the first step is to remove the small nuts and bolts that hold the joints together. This is likely to be difficult, as they're usually firmly rusted in. If penetrating oil fails to budge them, saw them off with a hacksaw.

If you have to replace part of the guttering, take a sample of the old gutter to the builders' merchants to make sure that you get a good match. Cut the new gutter to length if necessary, and drill a hole for the bolt at the join. Paint the new section thoroughly before you fit it, finishing the inside with a coat of bitumastic paint.

Scrape away old putty or sealing compound from the remaining old guttering and replace it with a proprietary mastic. Line up the holes and put in new nuts and bolts.

Leaking downpipes

Cracks in downpipes can be sealed temporarily using mastic and waterproof adhesive tape, or somewhat more permanently using a polyester resin plumbing repair compound. For a truly permanent repair, however, the offending section of pipe should be replaced.

Plastic downpipes may have push-together connectors, which are easy to separate, or solvent-welded couplings, which are permanent. If the connectors won't pull apart, cut the pipe with a hacksaw. To make a guide for a straight cut, wrap a sheet of paper around the pipe and bring the edges into line where the paper overlaps. You can use either push-on or solvent-welded couplings for the new piece of pipe.

Blocked downpipes

Straight downpipes can generally be cleared by pushing a long stick through them. If the pipe has a bend in it, you may have to undo at least one of the joints and reseal it when the blockage has been dealt with.

Sagging gutters

Unless the guttering itself is broken, sagging gutters will be caused by failure of one or more of the supporting brackets. If the gutter brackets are of the type which fit on the top surface of the rafters, they'll have been fitted before the slates or tiles. It's rarely worth removing slates or tiles to replace these: choose new brackets which fit on the sides of the rafters or, if necessary, the type which are driven into the masonry below the eaves of the roof.

Adjustable gutter bracket fixed to masonry

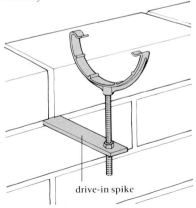

drive-in spike

Silted-up soakaways

If water fails to drain through a gulley at the base of a downpipe, and the gulley itself is clear, it's likely that the soakaway has silted up. Clearly, the first step to a cure is finding the soakaway. This can be difficult: there is rarely any evidence of the location of soakaways at ground-level. The plans of the house (which should be available for inspection at your local Department of Building Control) may indicate where the soakaways are, but this can usually be taken only as a rough guide.

Tracking down a soakaway is largely a matter of trial and error. Dig out around the gulley to expose the underground outlet pipe, so you can see which way it runs. Follow that line until you're 3m from the walls of the house, and dig again. With luck, you'll uncover the soakaway. If not and all you reveal is the continuing pipe, move out a further $1\frac{1}{2}$m or so and try again.

If the soakaway is lined with brick or concrete sections, you can simply dig out the accumulated silt. If it's an unlined pit filled with rubble, it may be better to abandon it, dig out a new one (not less than three metres from the house) and rerun the pipe from the gulley.

Painting cast-iron systems

Cast-iron rainwater systems must be painted regularly to keep rust at bay. Remove any flaking or blistered old paint, and rub down to bare metal where evidence of rust is found. Prime immediately with a metal or universal primer, then finish with oil-based undercoat and gloss. Paint the inside of cast-iron gutters with bitumastic paint.

Replacing cast-iron gutters with plastic

If you have cast-iron gutters which are in poor condition, the idea of gutters which require no maintenance other than cleaning may have considerable appeal. You can replace iron gutters and downpipes with plastic in whole or part.

Although plastic gutters are commonly grey, they're also available in black, brown and – to a limited extent – white. Special couplings make it possible to connect plastic and cast-iron gutters.

Don't use the old gutter brackets when replacing cast iron with plastic. If you can't easily remove the old brackets, saw them off. To make sure that new gutters are laid in a straight line, stretch a string along the eaves, checking the fall with a spirit level. When the new guttering is in place, check again.

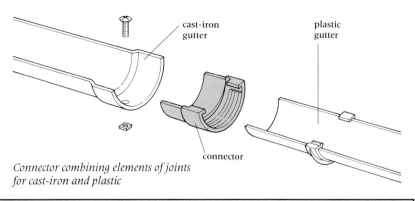

Connector combining elements of joints for cast-iron and plastic

---

For safety, use a ladder long enough to extend three rungs above the guttering; a stand-off improves support and prevents the guttering from bearing your weight

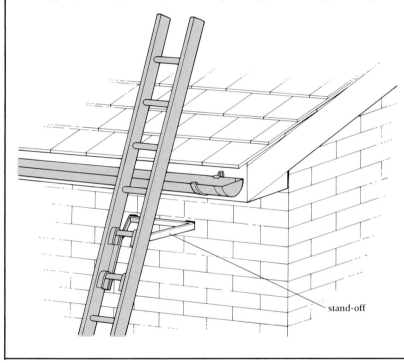

Working safely on your guttering

Even simply cleaning out your gutters means working on a ladder some distance above the ground. An extension ladder which will reach about three rungs above the eaves, used in combination with a stand-off which keeps the ladder clear of the guttering, makes the job much easier and safer. Always make sure that the feet of the ladder are firmly planted, and use a rope to hoist heavy materials aloft – this is much safer than trying to carry them up the ladder. Keep other people away from your working area, though it's sensible to have someone within earshot in case of difficulties or accidents.

If you have a large job to do – such as replacing a cast-iron system with plastic – consider hiring a platform tower.

12 Drains

About a hundred years ago, inadequate drains were held to be responsible for all manner of ills. Although the Victorians may have exaggerated the role of drains in some respects, the result was that high standards of domestic drainage were established. The design and construction of drains is now controlled by the Building Regulations.

Provided that they have been properly built, drains shouldn't need frequent maintenance – it's worthwhile checking them once a year, though. When drains do need attention, the work is made more difficult by the unpleasant nature of what they contain and by their being buried underground, although the various forms of access provided are usually adequate.

This chapter is about drains which are connected to sewers, cesspools or septic tanks. These drains usually carry only foul water – the waste from sinks, baths, basins and wcs. Rainwater is normally directed to soakaways where it is reabsorbed into the ground. See Rainwater Removal chapter, p. 111. If any rainwater from your house is directed into the sewer, your water bills will include an extra charge.

Inspecting your drains

An annual inspection of your drains should be only mildly unpleasant if the system is working properly. It can be combined with your annual inspection of the household plumbing. It's a good idea to flush through sinks, baths and wcs with hot water, washing soda and disinfectant – see Plumbing, p. 93. This will also help to keep the drains clear, and is a good moment to lift the inspection covers.

At the inspection chamber:
- remove any debris which might block the drains – sticks and stones, for example
- check that the masonry inside the inspection chamber is sound
- wash down the walls of the chamber with a hosepipe – confirm that the water drains away quickly
- make sure that the cover is sound – steel covers can corrode rapidly when hot, steamy waste is discharged into the drains – by a washing machine, for example
- if the inspection chamber has a fresh air inlet – a metal box with a grille and a hinged flap – make sure it's working. If it's not, remove it and seal up the hole – see page 116
- if the inspection chamber has an interceptor trap, make sure that the stopper in the rodding arm is firmly in place – see page 116
- rake out the groove in the inspection cover surround and replace the cover.

Outside the house:
Check for other signs of potential trouble:
- unpleasant smells
- neighbours with drainage problems
- large trees in the vicinity of underground drains

If your house drains into a cesspool, you must have it emptied regularly. Just how regularly depends on how large it is and how quickly you fill it.

If you have a septic tank, it will need to be emptied about once a year.

How drains are built

The basic rules governing the layout of drainage systems are that access should be available to all parts of the underground pipework, and that the contents should flow without hindrance. Drains are therefore laid in straight lines, with sufficient gradient or 'fall' to ensure that they are self-cleansing. For older drains made of glazed ceramic pipes, the fall is likely to be about 1 in 40. For smoother modern drain pipes, made of PVC or pitch fibre, a fall of around 1 in 60 is satisfactory.

Branch drains must connect to the main drain in the direction of flow, and inspection chambers or rodding points must be provided at connections, changes of direction or gradient and at intervals in long runs.

In a typical house with a two-pipe waste system the drains from the soil pipe and the trapped gulley under the waste pipe come together in an inspection chamber at the back of the house. The house in the drawing has a second inspection chamber where the drain turns a corner, and a third before it joins the public sewer.

The second drawing shows a house with a single stack system which shares a communal drain with other homes. Inspection cham-

Drains – symptoms, faults and remedies

Symptom	Fault	Remedy	*see page*
Foul water 'backing up' in inspection chamber	• Blocked drains	• Flush through with hot water and caustic soda	118
		• Clear blockage with drain rods	118
		• Call in a professional drain clearing service	118
Suspicious damp patches of soil	• Leaking drains	• Get professional advice, then:	
		• Dig up old drains and replace them, or	
		• Call in a professional drain service	118
Nasty smells	• Air vent not working	• Remove and seal up hole	116
	• Leaking drains	• Call in a professional drain service	118

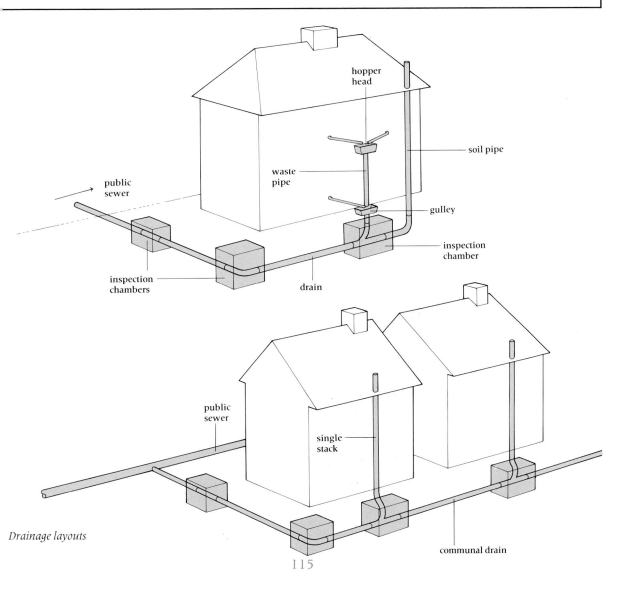

Drainage layouts

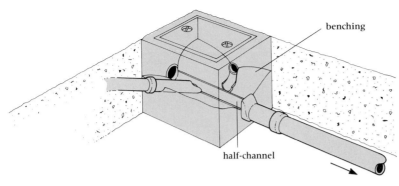

Inspection chamber with branch drains

bers have been provided where each stack meets the communal drain.

Inspection chambers

Inspection chambers may be built of brick, prefabricated concrete sections or plastic. The drain runs through a half-channel at the bottom of the chamber, with concrete 'benching' built up on either side. Branch pipes entering the chamber should be 'swept' – angled – in the direction of flow.

Brick inspection chambers may have been rendered on the inside, to make them waterproof. This is now frowned on, since if the render cracks and falls off the fragments can block the drains. Instead, if rendering is required to waterproof the brickwork, it should be applied to the outside, before the earth is replaced around the inspection chamber.

Inspection chambers in older homes may also have **interceptor traps**. These incorporate a **rodding**

arm with a **stopper** so that rods can be inserted to clear the drain, bypassing the trap. Interceptor traps were intended to prevent any sewer gases – or even rats – coming up the drains. In practice, they cause more trouble than they prevent, because the traps block much more easily than straight pipes. Sometimes the blockage is caused by the stopper coming adrift from the rodding arm – it should have a chain to prevent it falling into the trap.

An inspection chamber with an interceptor trap may well also have a ventilator (see drawing). This should have a hinged flap behind the grille, so that air can get in, but no gases can get out. In reality they serve little purpose, and can be removed and the hole sealed up.

Inspection chambers have cast iron or pressed steel covers with a downward-facing lip which fits in a groove around the top of the chamber. If an inspection chamber is

within a building, the cover should be sealed with grease and screwed down.

Rodding points

In some circumstances, it may be sufficient to have a rodding point, which affords limited access, rather than an inspection chamber at a junction or bend in the drains.

Tracing your drains

It's not always obvious where individual drains from a house enter the underground drainage system. To find out, lift the inspection covers and get someone to flush each WC, or fill and discharge each sink or bath in turn. Make a simple plan for future reference.

If there is still some doubt, add dye to the water – food colouring, for example – but take care not to stain plastic sinks and baths.

Cesspools

Some houses for which there is no access to a public sewer have drains which discharge into cesspools. A cesspool is simply an underground vessel for the temporary storage of sewage, and has to be emptied regularly.

Cesspools may be built of brick – carefully waterproofed to prevent sewage getting out and water getting in – pre-cast concrete sections or fibreglass. Since the mid 1960s, when the Building Regulations came into force, the minimum volume required for cesspools has been 18 cubic metres (4000 gallons). This should be sufficient for a family of four for about two months. But older cesspools may be smaller, in some cases as little as 2.25 cubic metres (500 gallons).

Many local councils operate cesspool emptying services, or can put you in touch with a suitable contractor. Even if the service is run by the local authority, you will usually have to pay for it, and it will be up to you to arrange visits of the necessary frequency.

Inspection chamber with interceptor trap and vent

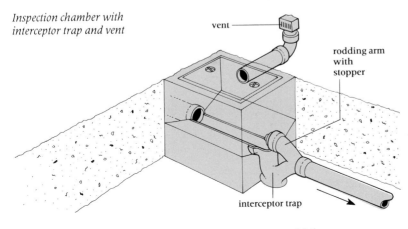

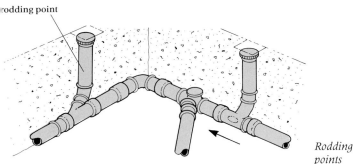

Rodding points

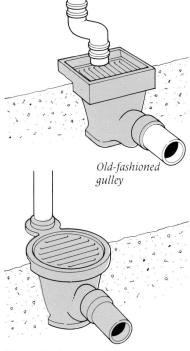

Old-fashioned gulley

Modern back-inlet gulley

If a cesspool fills up, sewage will 'back up' in the drains and the cesspool will overflow. Pouring more water into the system will only make matters worse – the only solution is to get the cesspool emptied as quickly as possible.

If a cesspool seems to need emptying either more often or less often than it should, or if there are suspicious smells, it could be leaking. This is illegal, and a serious health risk, so it should be investigated and corrected without delay.

In a house with a cesspool, it clearly makes sense to minimise your consumption of water. Take showers rather than baths, and don't run the taps unnecessarily. It's likely to be worthwhile installing modern dual-flush WC cisterns.

Septic tanks

Septic tanks are much more sophisticated than cesspools. A septic tank is essentially a small sewage treatment plant which separates out the solid and liquid parts of the sewage, making the liquid part harmless so it can be discharged into a ditch or through a soakaway.

Most septic tank installations consist of two underground vessels: the septic tank itself and a filter bed. The septic tank separates out the solid and liquid wastes, and the filter bed purifies the liquid. The solids collect as a sludge which has to be removed regularly – once a year is usually sufficient. In some installations the filter bed may not be necessary because the half-treated sewage can be discharged through land drains.

Septic tanks work by allowing bacteria to break down the sewage. It's

important not to use too much disinfectant or detergent in the house, since this will inhibit the action of the bacteria and could clog up the tank.

Problems with drains

Overflowing gulleys

These are usually caused by grilles being blocked by leaves or other debris, or by solids accumulating in the trap. Either way, you should be able to clear the blockage by hand. If that fails to cure the problem, then the blockage must be further down the system (see Blocked Drains).

Gulleys where the waste pipe discharges above the grille tend to become blocked more easily than modern back- or side-inlet gulleys, so it's worthwhile fitting an extra grille.

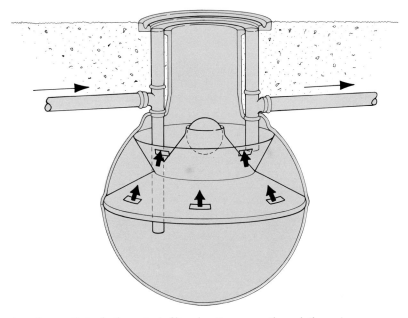

A modern septic tank: the water is filtered as it passes up through the various chambers of the tank, and the sludge collects in the bottom, to be emptied about once a year

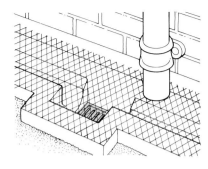

A grille will prevent leaves blocking a gulley

Blocked drains

If the drains are blocked, waste water will accumulate in the upstream parts of the system. This may mean that sinks or WCs fail to clear, or water overflows from an inspection chamber or rodding point.

Removing the covers will reveal which section of pipe is blocked. If the water is draining away slowly, it may be possible to clear it by flushing through with hot water or with a special drain-clearing solution containing caustic soda. If the pipe is completely blocked, however, adding more water is only likely to make matters worse.

Blocked drains can generally be cleared by **rodding**. Drain rods are flexible canes which can be screwed together to reach down the drains. There are a variety of end fittings to

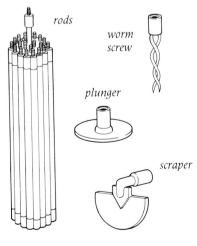

Drain rods and fittings

break up or push through blockages. Sets of drain rods can be hired, and they'll come with a selection of end fittings.

Start by joining a couple of rods and attach a wormscrew fitting to the business end. Rodding has to be done in the direction of flow of the drains, so the rods have to be inserted at the point where the waste has accumulated. If there's an interceptor trap at this point, remove the stopper and insert the rods into the rodding arm. Otherwise push the rods into the end of the blocked pipe, screwing on more rods as you go. Use a twisting action, *always turning clockwise*. This is very important, since turning anti-clockwise may unscrew the rods and leave them in the drains. When you reach the blockage, try to push it through to the next access point and remove it.

Extract the rods, remove the wormscrew and replace it with a plunger disc or brush. Use this to clean the pipe thoroughly. Disinfect everything when you've finished and flush the drains with plenty of water.

Leaking drains

Drains can leak because:

- they weren't constructed properly in the first place
- they've been disturbed by other construction work
- they've been displaced by large tree roots.

The evidence of a leak may be quite difficult to spot. Patches of ground which seem to stay moist even in long dry spells may indicate leaking drains, particularly if there's also an unpleasant smell. Drains which have been disturbed by building work or tree roots are likely to be partially blocked as well as leaky, and you may see soil at inspection points downstream of the problem.

For serious disturbances, or to cure a drain which has collapsed, there's no practical alternative to digging up the pipe and replacing it.

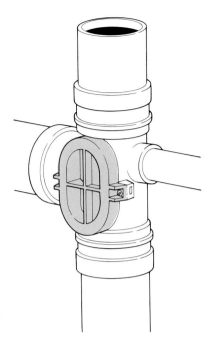

Rodding point in a single stack drainage system

Getting professional help

Professional drainage firms are listed in Yellow Pages under Drain, Sewer and Pipe Cleaning Services, and in the Business Directory of Registered Plumbers, published by the Institute of Plumbing and available in larger public libraries and Citizens Advice Bureaux. Professional drainage firms can investigate drainage problems by putting a small TV camera down the pipe to examine it from the inside. They will also clean drains using high-pressure water jets and can seal small leaks by injecting sealants. But drainage work can be expensive, particularly if you've had to call the firm in an emergency. Make sure you get an itemised quote before the work commences.

If there are large trees near your home and you're worried about the effect their roots might have on your drains, your local authority Department of Building Control should be able to offer advice.

Part Three
PRESERVING YOUR ASSETS

13 Householders' legal rights and responsibilities

Owning a house and the land it stands on doesn't give you the right to do as you please. The concept of the ownership of land is not all-encompassing: you have the right to exclusive use of the land for the purpose of a dwelling, but other people may still have a right of access over it, for example, or to extract minerals beneath it. The house itself will be subject to planning law, to the Building Regulations and may be listed as a building of architectural or historic interest. Your neighbours also have rights which have to be reconciled with your own. All in all, there's a vast range of laws and regulations which confer rights and responsibilities on house-holders, whether owner-occupiers, lease-holders or tenants.

When you carry out maintenance work on your home you need to ensure that you comply with the law. This can mean simply checking with the local authority whether planning permission or listed building consent is required, and obtaining approval under the Building Regulations. But you also need to be aware of the law governing party walls, boundaries and leaseholds. Finally, it's important to know what your rights are if tools or machines you buy or hire aren't up to scratch, or if builders or other professionals you employ don't do a satisfactory job.

Permissions

For further information see also Home Improvements · chapter, p.131.

Do I need planning permisson for all types of maintenance work to my home?
No. You can carry out a substantial number of alterations to your property as long as they are internal changes which do not affect the exterior or alter the existing use of the building. For instance, removing a partition between a front and rear room does not need planning permission. But converting a house into flats does. Generally, planning permission is required for any action which can be called a 'development'. So to be on the safe side you should submit the plans for any proposed changes to the local authority.

I have just moved into an old house. I want to modernise the kitchen. Are there any Building regulations to comply with?
Yes. Building Regulations are detailed standards laid down to ensure that buildings are weather-tight, structurally sound and so on, and comply with modern standards, that is the building works themselves must be reasonably durable, with a moderate life expectancy and un-likely to cause injury to the occu-pants or to passers by. You can obtain consent under the Building Regu-lations from the local authority. Most authorities issue guidance notes about what you need to do. A number of Building Regulations could apply in this case: electric cookers need a separate electricity circuit; a central heating boiler needs an air supply and a flue; even a lar-der needs a certain amount of venti-lation, according to its size. the cold water supply must come from a ris-ing main; it cannot be mixed with the hot supply through some mixer taps (only those which keep the two streams separate). So you must con-tact your local authority to check the necessary details.

I live in a Grade II listed building. Are there any restrictions regarding alterations that I want to make?
A listed building is one that the Department of the Environment (DoE) considers as being of specific architectural or historic importance. The DoE exercises stringent control over alterations to listed buildings which they transmit to all local auth-orities by list. You must obtain per-mission from the local authority for any alterations that is likely to affect the character of the building. This means any changes to the outside of a Grade II building, such as adding a window or porch. You will also need to get permission for any interior construction work.

You apply to the local authority Department of Planning and Build-ing Control. You may have to have both planning permission and listed building consent. If listed building consent is refused, you can ulti-mately appeal to the Secretary of State for the Environment.

Neighbours

As a general rule, if you are having trouble with your neighbours it is always wise to contact them in person to try to resolve your differences. But if this fails, the following should give you a step-by-step approach to dealing with the most common problems.

Our neighbours have been renovating their house for several weeks now. The noise from the builders starts at 7 a.m. and goes on until 8 p.m. Is there anything I can do to make the builders reduce the amount of noise they make?

Common law says that the occupiers of one property are not allowed to use it in such a way as to interfere with the other people's reasonable enjoyment of their home. If your neighbours' behaviour generally interferes with the enjoyment of your home, then it is a 'nuisance'. Whether the work constitutes a 'nuisance' depends on how it's being carried out, the methods used, and the steps taken to keep any annoyance to neighbours to a minimum. If the noise is intolerable and will continue for several months, this may well be 'nuisance'. You should approach your neighbour to see whether the builders can work more reasonable hours. If this is not possible, you can contact the local authority Environmental Health Department, which can help to stop the nuisance under the Control of Pollution Act 1974. If this does not achieve a solution, you should consult a solicitor. Your ultimate remedy is to obtain an injunction and your solicitor will help you with this.

My neighbour has been sandblasting his home for the last few days. The dust from this comes into my house and I can't hang any washing out or even sit in the garden. is there anything I can do?

Again, if your neighbours unlawfully interfere with your enjoyment of your property, it is a nuisance. If the sand-blasting is to continue for a long period of time, it's going to be very annoying. And it's going to be a 'nuisance'. But if it is to continue for only a few days, this may not be considered enough of a nuisance for the local authority to take action.

The local authority Environmental Health Department should be informed. They should come out and inspect your property to assess the situation. They can take your neighbour to court if necessary.

I have just moved into a very run-down property. The garden is like a jungle and my neighbours keep pestering me to remove some branches from bushes and trees that are overhanging their garden. They say that if I don't they'll lop off the branches themselves. Can they do this?

Yes, if the trees and bushes overhang the boundary of your property they are trespassing on your neighbours' property. So your neighbours are legally entitled to lop off the branches that cross the boundary. The branches themselves remain your property, so your neighbours should put them back in your garden rather than dispose of them. But your neighbours must not lop off any branches that do not overhang their garden. If they do, you too can claim for trespass.

My neighbours' new extension blocks out the light into my dining-room. I have lived here for 25 years and now I have to switch on the light in my dining-room in the daytime. Is there anything I can do?

The law gives no automatic right to daylight. But if you have enjoyed light for 20 years, you have acquired a right to it by the common law. Your neighbours are not allowed to block it out altogether, which is what has

happened. You should contact your neighbours and explain that the extension has blocked out the light into your dining-room. If your neighbours are not prepared to do anything about this, you can take them to court. However, it will be up to you to prove that you have enjoyed a certain level of light for at least 20 uninterrupted years and that the room is now unfit for normal use. If the court decides that you do have a right to light, your neighbours may well be ordered to demolish the extension.

Insurance

I have just extended my home by converting the loft into a bedroom. Do I need to inform my building insurance company?

Yes. You are under a legal duty to disclose all material facts that might affect your insurance cover. If you fail to do so, you may invalidate the policy, and the insurance company may well refuse to pay on a future claim. Obviously, if the value of your home has increased, then your insurance cover is affected and the premium that you pay will be increased too.

You also have to be careful about causing subsidence. This is because claims for subsidence are generally excluded if the subsidence is caused by structural alteration or repair or by faulty workmanship. It is therefore essential to let your insurers know that structural alterations have taken place and have been done to a reasonable standard. You may need to provide the insurance company with a surveyor's report showing that the work is of a reasonable standard.

I live in a top-floor flat. I have just converted the loft into another room. Will this affect my insurance cover?

Yes. You should advise your landlord or management company. It is usual for you to pay for the insurance of your flat in the service charge. The conversion of the loft increases the value of your flat and therefore affects the insurance cover. Thus, the insurers must be informed.

A few weeks ago I noticed that one of the walls in the kitchen of my house had developed a crack. The crack seems to be getting wider, so I called in a surveyor. He says that the house is suffering from subsidence and that repairing it by underpinning may cost £30,000. Can I claim this on my buildings insurance?

Your house buildings insurance policy should contain a clause about what will happen if your house is subject to subsidence. Basically, provided that you can prove that the subsidence has occurred only during the time that you have lived there, your insurance should cover the repair bill.

If the clause of the subsidence occurred before you bought the house, your claim will not be covered in full by your insurers.

There should also be a clause covering any costs you incur because you have to move out while the work is in progress. Check your insurance policy very carefully, and get in touch with your insurers as soon as possible.

If I have builders in my house, am I responsible if they are injured while at work?

Yes. Your buildings insurance policy should detail what will happen if anyone is injured for whatever reason while at your property. This is known as 'third-party liability'. If you are about to have extensive work carried out, it is wise to check your policy to make sure that you have adequate cover.

You can also arrange to have temporary cover for the period that the builders are at your home. Again, discuss this with your insurers as soon as possible.

Boundaries

I need to carry out repairs to the brickwork and paint the guttering on the side of my house. To do this I need to use the passageway down the side of the house. This passageway belongs to my neighbours, and they won't allow me to use it. Can I force them to give me access so that I can get on with the work?

No, you don't have an automatic right to go on to your neighbours' property. To use the passage without their permission may amount to a trespass. They can refuse permission for any reason whatsoever, and the courts will not intervene. If you can't come to some sort of amicable arrangement, don't despair. The deeds to your property may specify that you hve a right to enter the next-door property for specific purposes. Take a look at your deeds and check this point. The deeds wills probably be kept at the building society, which will send you a copy (you will have to pay for it). Also, the solicitor who did the original conveyance may have a copy.

Alternatively, the common law provides that if you and the previous owners of your property have regularly gone on to the neighbouring passageway to do these repairs for the last 20 years or more, you may have acquired a right to carry on what is an historical habit. It is important that the work was done without your neighbours' consent. You should check into what used to happen by asking other neighbours or previous owners.

If either of these applies, send your neighbour a copy of the deeds or the details of the repairs made in the past. If you can't reach an agreement with your neighbour, get a solicitor to write a letter setting out the legal position.

I have just returned from holiday to find that the old fence which used to separate my garden from my neighbours' has been removed and a new one erected in its place. The old fence was certainly in a very bad state of repair, and if it had not been pulled down, was in grave danger of falling down. The problem is that the new fence seems to be some six inches further into my garden than it should be. Although there are no flowerbeds which show the position of the original boundary, there is a strip of earth where no grass grows. I think this is because the old fence followed the line of that strip. What should I do?

You should approach your neighbours and discuss the problem with them. It may be that the workmen employed by your neighbours have innocently place the fence in the wrong place. If not, and if your neighbours refuse to move the fence, you much check the deeds of your property. There is usually a plan attached to the deeds which will show who owns the boundary and its correct position. If the deeds do not have a map, you should try to produce evidence that the fence was in the old position for a continuous period of 12 years. If you can do so, the bare strip of land is yours. This is set out in the common law. If you haven't lived at your property for that long, you should try to obtain a written statement from the previous owners and other neighbours. If your next-door neighbours still refuse to move the fence, you should consult a solicitor, who will advise you of the next step to take.

The wall which separates my property from my neighbours' belongs to them. It is in a terrible state of repair and looks as if it will fall down in the slightest storm. I have many valuable plants along that side of the garden, some of which depend on the wall for shelter. I also have a greenhouse that would be crushed if the wall falls down.

Can I insist that my neighbours repair it?

If you and your next-door neighbours live on a modern estate or in newly built houses, there is a good chance that the deeds make the owners of the wall responsible for doing all the necessary work to keep it in proper repair. However, there is no general rule that requires the owner of a wall or fence to take positive steps to keep it in good repair, and if there is nothing in the deeds requiring your neighbours to maintain it as a dividing wall between the properties, or to keep it in good repair, your neighbours may decide to remove it altogether. As long as they cause no damage to your plants and trees in the process, you can't do anything about it. But check your deeds, because the common law provides that if you can show that for at least 20 years your neighbours and the previous owners of the property maintained and repaired the wall on a regular basis, your current neighbours may be obliged to carry on doing so. If the wall did fall down through disrepair and caused the damage you fear, you would be entitled to claim damages as compensation from your neighbours. You will have to prove the value of your plants and greenhouse, so you should keep any receipts that you have.

Hiring and buying services and equipment

I recently bought a new electric drill. When I bought it I told the manager of the tool section in the store that I needed a drill that could drill through masonry and concrete. He advised me that a particular model would be ideal. But when I came to use it I discovered that it won't in fact drill through masonry or concrete. Can I take it back and complain?

Yes. You should go back to the shop immediately and return the drill. The Sale of Goods Act 1979 provides that goods must be fit for their purpose. You told the department manager exactly what you needed the drill for, and you relied on his advice to buy the drill. The fact that the drill is not suitable for masonry work means that it is not fit for its purpose. The store is in breach of its contract with you and you are entitled to a full refund of your money.

I am in the process of renovating my house. I employed a local plumber to supply and plumb in a new bathroom suite. He finished the work on time and I was very pleased with the result. I paid him in full and in cash. But two days later the hot water tap on the bath started to drip and I discovered that the basin overflow had never been connected up. A day after that, the shower door came off its hinges. Is there anything I can do?

The plumber was under a duty to fit the suite with reasonable skill and care and to use materials that were of merchantable quality. He was obliged to do this by virtue of the Supply of Goods and Services Act 1982. The fact that you are experiencing numerous problems with the suite is clear evidence that the work was not carried out with reasonable skill and care. Also, the failure of the shower door indicates that the product is not of merchantable quality. You should ask the plumber to come back and put right all the faults, without charging you any extra. If he won't do the work, or he attempts to do it and cannot do it to a satisfactory standard, you are entitled to employ another plumber to do the job and get the original plumber to reimburse you. If he won't pay, then provided the remedial work has cost £500 or less, you can take out a claim using the small claims procedure in the county court (£500 is the maximum amount you can claim in the county court; the figure will rise to £1000 in July 1991; if the work currently costs £500 or more you should seek help from a solicitor).

After knocking down an old outhouse at my home I decided to hire a small van to take away the rubbish. I 'phoned a local hire company and agreed to hire a 1300cc van that I could collect the following day. When I arrived at the depot I was told that someone else had taken my van and all that was left was an 1800cc van for which I would have to pay the extra rate. Surely this is not right.

No. You arranged to hire a 1300cc van and the company agreed to supply you with a 1300cc van. If the company cannot provide what you hired, it is in breach of the contract. You can insist that the company lets you hire the larger van at the lower van's price. Alternatively, if the larger van is too big for your property, you can hire a smaller van from another company and look to the original firm for any additional cost. But you must make sure that you let the original company know exactly what you intend to do.

I recently renovated my oak-beamed study. This meant that I had to buy expensive authentic beams to replace the old ones. I have just discovered that they are riddled with woodworm. I went back to the company from which I bought the beams to find that the place was boarded up and was no longer trading. What can I do now?

If you paid for the beams in cash, you should contact the Trading Standards Department of your local authority to find out who is the official receiver. You will then have to register with the receiver as an unsecured creditor. This means that you will take second place to all secured creditors, such as the employees of the company, the Inland Revenue and other companies to whom the liquidated company owes money. At the end of the day you may receive some money back, but you must be prepared for the fact that you may get nothing at all.

If you paid by credit card and the beams cost more than £100, you will be protected by Section 75 of the Consumer Credit Act 1974. This provides that the credit card company is equally liable with the supplier of the goods if the goods are not of merchantable quality. You must therefore contact your credit card company as soon as possible. You should simply state when the contract was made, how much you paid, the name of the company and what is wrong with the beams.

I am currently building an extension to the front of my house. I intend to do other building work in the future and have therefore bought a cement mixer under a hire-purchase agreement. Today the mixer broke down and will not work at all. What should I do?

You should contact the hire-purchase company as soon as possible. Your contract is with the hire-purchase company, and under the Supply of Goods (Implied Terms) Act 1973 the company must make sure that the mixer is of merchantable quality. Since the cement mixer belongs to the hire-purchase company until your last payment is made, you may be able to reject the mixer and get your money back. You cannot demand a replacement mixer, because your right is to receive a refund. However, there is no reason why you should not try to negotiate with the hire-purchase company for a replacement mixer.

I asked a local builder to build a conservatory on the rear of my house. He said he would start the job four weeks after I asked him to. It is now three months since the date of the order and he still hasn't turned up. I paid him a £200 deposit but I've got nothing in writing to prove this. How can I get him to come and do the work?

Hopefully, the builder has just over-committed himself and he does intend to do the work. But even if you did not agree a specific date for the work to commence, the builder must still start and finish the work within a reasonable time. In your case, four weeks was the tentative arrangement, so the builder is eight weeks late. This is unreasonable if he has all the materials ready and simply hasn't got around to your job.

However, if he is waiting for some materials or parts to arrive, then the delay is not his fault and eight weeks may be reasonable. In any event, what you should now do is write to the builder and make 'time of the essence of the contract'. This is your common law remedy. You must use these exact words and give him a definite date for the work to start. If you don't use these words you will not incorporate time of the essence into the contract. There is a contract simply by virtue of the fact that you asked the builder to do the work and he agreed to do it. If he doesn't start by this date, you will no longer be bound by the contract and you can treat it as being at an end. You will then be entitled to recover your deposit. If he will not give you the deposit, you may have to issue a summons using the small claims procedure in the county court. The fact that you do not have a receipt for the £200 does complicate your case. It makes it more difficult for you to *prove* that you had a contract with the builder and paid him money up front. But this does not mean that your claim will not succeed.

Last month I employed a painter to redecorate my living-room. When he arrived he did not cover the suite or the carpet. When he'd finished the job and went to leave, I checked the room and to my horror there was paint all over the carpet and suite. When I asked him what had happened he just shrugged and said it was nothing to do with him. What is my position?

You are protected by the Supply of Goods and Services Act 1982. The painter must carry out the work with reasonable skill and care. It is quite clear that he did not do the work to a reasonable standard. However, you cannot demand that the painter pays for the cost of a new suite or new carpets, as you are under a duty to mitigate (cut) your losses. Thus, you should get the suite and carpet professionally cleaned. You can then look to the painter for this cost. If the cleaning does not remedy the problem and you have to buy a new suite and carpet, you can also claim this cost from the painter. But if the items were several years old at the time of the damage, you have to take this into account when making your claim. In other words, you cannot claim the cost of a brand new suite if the suite you have lost is seven years old, say. You have to take into account the fact that you had had several years' use out of the items before they were damaged. Your legal adviser will help you to assess a reasonable sum to claim.

A friend of mine recently attempted to repair my gas central heating system. He is not a qualified engineer but he does enjoy d-i-y. Unfortunately, the whole system went haywire soon after he had finished the work. It bangs and clanks and there was even smoke coming from the motor. I had to call in a proper engineer, who says that the system has been extensively damaged by someone meddling with it. It is going to be very expensive to repair. Is my friend liable for this cost?

You should approach your friend and ask if he is prepared to pay anything towards the repair costs. If he isn't, then there is little that you can do. While professionals are legally obliged to exercise reasonable skill and care while carrying out work, there is no such obligation on laymen. They are only expected to have the standard of skill and care of an ordinary layman. You allowed your friend to tinker with the system knowing full well that he was not qualified to do so. So it is now difficult to argue that he was negligent.

With regard to companies and self-employed people who install, repair or service gas appliances, from the end of March 1991 they must be registered with a new body called the Council of Registered Gas Installers (CORGI). Under the new scheme no one will be registered unless they can show that they understand safety procedures and have reached a level of professional competence. If they are not registered with this body, the Health and Safety Executive will have the power to prosecute them under the new Gas Safety (Installation and Use) (Amendment) Regulations 1990.

I had double glazing installed eight years ago. Last week, after a rainstorm, I noticed a puddle of water beneath two of the windows. Rainwater must be leaking in. Do I have any redress against the company that installed the windows?
You will be able to approach the company to remedy these problems only if you have a guarantee. This is because under the Limitation Act 1980 you have only six years from the date that the contract was broken in which to bring an action for breach of contract. In your case the contract was broken eight years ago when the work was carried out badly, so you have exceeded this limit by two years. The only way that you will have any redress against the company is if you were given a guarantee with the contract and the period of the guarantee has not expired. But you will need to show

that the windows are faulty and have not been misused.

I employed a firm of builders to knock down an interior wall and extend the lounge. They started the work on time and all seemed well. But last week they left and have never returned. Although the extension is built, they haven't plastered the walls or redecorated. The house is full of dust and debris and their dust-sheets are still in place. What, if anything, can I do?
You should write to the firm, keeping a copy of the letter, stating that 'time is of the essense' and that the builders must return to finish the work within seven days. It is important to keep copies of all letters that you write in this regard because they may be used as evidence if the matter proceeds to court. If the builders fail to return within seven days, you will be entitled to treat the contract as terminated. You can then employ another firm to finish the job. You will have to pay for this, but then you can recover the cost from the original firm. If the original firm pursues you for the cost of the work that it *has* done, you will have to pay, unless the standard of the work is so appalling that the company cannot reasonably expect payment.

Duties

As a result of a severe storm, several of the tiles on the roof of my cottage have become dislodged. The builder cannot come to repair the roof until next month because he is so busy. What will my legal situation be if a tile falls on someone as they come to my house?
The Occupiers' Liability Act 1957 states that a householder must take care that his home is safe for visitors. If someone is injured as a result of your premises being faulty, you can be sued for damages for negligence. It is not enough simply to warn

people that the tiles are loose, unless the warning is sufficiently detailed to enable a visitor to be reasonably safe. In other words, it should warn people that the tiles are loose and clearly explain how they can enter your property safely. You must attempt to make a safe route to your house. If this is not possible, see if the builder or someone he recommends can come and do a temporary repair. You should check your insurance details carefully to make sure that you are adequately covered for any injuries to third parties. You can increase your cover on a temporary basis for the period until the repair is finished.

I am in the process of carrying out extensive work on my house. I have nowhere to store the building materials and have therefore left them in the front garden. Yesterday, one of my neighbours came to complain that his son had fallen off a pile of bricks while playing in my garden and had cut and grazed his arm. He is threatening to sue me for damages. Can he do this?
Yes, he can. The Occupiers' Liability Act 1984 states that you owe people *other* than visitors, a duty to take such care as is reasonable in all the circumstances. If the child has suffered any injuries, however slight, the common law gives the father the right to claim compensation in the form of damages. But for the claim to succeed the father must show that you owed the boy a duty of care. Technically, the boy was trespassing when he was injured. However, the courts have decided that if you knew that it was likely that children would play in your garden, you owed them a duty of care. If this is the case, you will be liable to pay compensation.

The ornamental lantern at the end of my drive has been rusting for some time. I was waiting for a replacement to arrive when the old one fell off and hit a man

who was walking past. He had to be taken to hospital suffering from a cut forehead. I have just received a letter from his solicitor saying that I am liable for damages and threatening to take me to court. It wasn't my fault, surely?

Yes, it was. The common law deems it to be your responsibility to take care not to injure members of the public if your property adjoins a road. If you knew or ought reasonably to have known that there was a danger that the lantern might fall and cause damage, you will be liable for negligence if someone is injured. You should contact your solicitor straight away to see whether the amount of damages the man is claiming is reasonable. You will certainly have to pay the injured person some, if not all of the amount he is claiming.

My old chimneystack blew down and fell on to my neighbours' greenhouse. The greenhouse was extensively damaged, and my neighbours want to claim from me the cost of buying a new one. In my opinion the damage was an act of God and no one's fault. How can I be responsible for damage caused by wind?

Once again, the common law provides that you are responsible, not because of the wind but because you failed to take reasonable care of your property. You are under a duty to prevent damage to people and property on adjoining premises. Thus, if the chimneystack was old and dangerous and you were aware of this, you ought reasonably to have done something about it to prevent damage in high winds.

You are also liable if you use your own premises negligently: for instance, if you fail to secure your ladder adequately while working on your house and it falls on to your neighbours' premises, causing damage. It is always wise to keep your

property in a good state of general repair.

Two workmen had to dig a trench in my garden to fix the drains. They left the trench open when they finished work for the day. Last night I had a barbecue party, and one of the guests fell into the trench, tearing her dress and twisting her ankle. Am I liable for the cost of repairing the dress and any claim for damages arising from the injuries she suffered?

Under the Occupiers' Liability Act 1957 you were under a duty to take reasonable care that visitors to your premises would be reasonably safe. But in this case you should have let your guests know that an independent contractor was responsible for the trench remaining uncovered. The guest can sue just the contractor, because the trench was left in an unsafe condition with no warnings or a cover, or she can sue both of you because you allowed the workmen to leave the trench in an unsafe condition, knowing full well that you were going to have a party that night.

I want to replace the wooden fence at the bottom of my garden with a wire one. The fence separates my property from a neighbour's. When I told my neighbour what I was going to do he said that I would have to put up another wooden fence because of a 'restrictive covenant'. Is he right?

He may well be. It is common that where a number of houses are built on an estate, the developer imposed restrictive covenants on subsequent purchasers. The idea behind this is to keep a degree of unity in the appearance of the estate, thereby ensuring that the houses keep their value. If you live on an estate-type development you should check your deeds. Details of any restrictive covenants will be specified in them.

National House Building Council

I have just moved into a brand-new house. I am absolutely disgusted at the state it is in. There are cracks galore in the walls some of the stairs are loose and the floor is sagging in several places. What should I do?

Almost all new houses are sold with the benefit of the National House Building Council (NHBC) guarantee. It is therefore likely that the builder who built your home is a member of the NHBC. This means that you would have received a Buildmark Certificate when you bought the house. Under this agreement, the builder undertakes to put right in the first two years defects which result from his failure to comply with the NHBC's minimum standards of workmanship. Minor defects are not included in the guarantee, and wear and tear and neglect are expressly excluded. You should have received a booklet outlining these standards; if not, contact the NHBC and ask for one. But it seems clear that the standard of workmanship on your house is totally unreasonable. You must get in touch with the builder and tell him of the problems. If you have difficulties with the builder, the NHBC will intervene and act as a conciliatory body. Keep the NHBC informed as matters progress.

I have just moved into a house which is five years old. When I started to redecorate I noticed that the walls are all out of line, and I cannot hang wallpaper. Do I have a claim against the builder?

If your house was built by a builder who was a member of the NHBC scheme, after the first two years (during which period the builder himself must correct certain defects; see. preceding question) the NHBC undertakes to make good any major defects in the load-bearing structure. Such defects include those that

THE WHICH? BOOK OF HOME MAINTENANCE

entail major repairs or complete or partial rebuilding. You should get a builder to inspect your home and prepare a report setting out the exact faults. You should then contact the NHBC and advise it of the problems. If the faults are that bad and you had a survey carried out before you bought the house, you may also have a claim against the surveyor for negligence if he failed to notice the defects.

Leaseholds

Unlike houses, which are nowadays mostly owner-occupied, flats are nearly all owned in blocks and let out. The owner retains the freehold and gives other people leases of the flats.

It is normal to buy a flat on a long lease, for instance a term of 99 years or however many years of that lease remain. In this case you are the leaseholder of the flat. You can sell it just like a house while the lease lasts. But you still have to pay rent, called ground rent, which is a low amount, and probably a service charge to cover the costs of maintaining the whole building; and you have other obligations too. The freeholder has certain responsibilities, such as maintaining the structure of the block – he is in fact the landlord.

Sometimes flats are let out for short periods to tenants: they do not buy their flats but just pay rent for them.

I own a leasehold flat under a 99-year lease. I have noticed that the external walls are badly in need of repointing, and internally some replastering work is needed, especially in the bathroom. Is the landlord responsible for carrying out the necessary work?
Responsibility for repair and maintenance will be detailed in your lease. Almost always in the case of flats the landlord is responsible for maintaining the structure and common parts, such as halls and stair-

ways, and he is usually responsible for the exterior as well. You will normally be liable for internal repairs and decorations. In your case, the landlord will be responsible for the repointing and you will be responsible for the replastering.

If a long lease of a flat says nothing at all about repairs, or makes the flat owner responsible for all repairs, the lease is probably defective, and you should consult a solicitor with a view to applying to court to have it rectified under the Landlord and Tenant Act 1987.

I live in a leasehold flat which is one of four in a Victorian house. My flat is at the top of the house, and no one except myself and people visiting me uses the landing and stairs between my flat and the flat below. The wooden landing is in a poor state, and dry rot has been found. Am I responsible for commissioning the appropriate treatment and paying for it?
You should look at your lease, especially the clause that describes your flat. You will probably find that the stairs are not included in the lease as part of your flat, in which case they are likely to be one of the 'common parts' (which should be described elsewhere in the lease) – whether or not anyone but you and your guests actually use them. If they are included in the common parts, check the section of the lease listing the landlord's duties (covenants) to see what his responsibility is. Assuming he is responsible for maintaining and repairing the common parts (he should be – consult a solicitor if he is not), then it is up to him to arrange the necessary treatment. Indeed, if he fails to do so and anyone is injured as a result, he will be liable to pay the injured person compensation under the Defective Premises Act 1972.

However, the landlord may well have no responsibility if you do not *tell* him about the stairs. And in any

case the work must be paid for (along with any other repairs and maintenance undertaken by the landlord or his agent) by you and the other leaseholders by way of a service charge. You will have to pay a share of the total cost, calculated on a basis which should be laid down in your lease. The lease may allow the landlord to require you to pay some or all of your share in advance, or by stages while the work is being done. If the lease does not do so, then you need not pay until the work is finished. If you have already been contributing to a 'reserve fund', that should cover the cost, or part of it.

My landlord intends to paint the outside of the block of flats in which I live. It was only done five years ago and in my view the block doesn't need repainting yet. If he goes ahead with it, how can I make sure that we don't end up being charged an excessive amount for the work in future service charges?
Look at the terms of your lease, which will probably specify the frequency with which such work should be done. If the landlord is in fact doing this work when it is not necessary, you will be able to rely on the rights given you by the Landlord and Tenant Acts 1985 and 1987. Under these Acts, service charges must be 'reasonable' in two respects:

- reasonably incurred – that is, not repainting the exterior unnecessarily early, and
- for work carried out to a reasonable standard.

The landlord should consult you before the work is done. If he fails to do so, even if the expenditure is reasonable, you will not be liable to pay more than around £50 (less if the block has more than 20 flats). He should have obtained two estimates for the work, one from a contractor with whom he has no connection, and then have given each leaseholder the details at least one month before the work started. If he does not consult you and the work goes ahead, you should seek legal advice about applying to the county court for a 'declaration' that all or part of the service charge is unreasonable.

If you are quite sure that the work is wholly unnecessary, you could simply refuse to pay towards it, knowing that the landlord could not successfully sue you. But it is always essential to get legal advice before withholding rent or service charge money.

The window frames of my flat are rotten. Under the terms of my lease it is the landlord's responsibility to carry out the necessary remedial work. Although he is aware of the situation, he doesn't appear to be willing to take any action. Is there anything I can do?

As long as your lease states that the landlord should repair the window frames and you can prove that he knows about the problem (write to him, keeping a copy of the letter), you can sue him. You will need to see a solicitor or go to a law centre about this. Take a copy of your lease with you. You will be able to seek an order that the landlord does what the lease requires him to do. If he breaks a court order, he is punishable for contempt of court and can even be imprisoned. You can also seek damages for landlords' 'breach of covenant'. Damages could include:

- compensation for damage to property resulting from the breach: for instance, if your carpet is damaged by damp
- reasonable costs of alternative accommodation if you have to move out of your flat
- compensation for any serious discomfort, distress and inconvenience you can prove you have suffered because of the breach.

If the landlord fails to do the work, you can also claim the cost of getting it done by someone else. You should get estimates from two or three firms to show the court.

If my landlord fails to carry out essential repairs that are his responsibility, can I get the work done myself and pay for it by withholding the ground rent?

As a general rule you cannot withhold any sums properly due under your lease. However, there is an exception which permits deduction from rent of the costs of repairs which the landlord should have done and has not. You cannot withhold service charge money in the same way: you must pay your share of any costs properly incurred by your landlord (although you *can* withhold what is *unreasonably* demanded of you, as has been discussed earlier). Withholding ground rent alone will cover only minor repairs, unless a number of leaseholders act together.

First of all, see someone qualified to give legal advice, taking along a copy of your lease, because you must be sure of your legal position. Then:

- make sure you have notified your landlord *in writing* of the repairs that need doing, and that you have a copy of the letter you wrote (keep copies of *all* your letters)
- get two or three estimates from reputable firms
- write to the landlord again, pointing out that he is in breach of his obligations and warning him that if he does not do the work within a specified time (a fortnight, say), you will get it done yourself and deduct the cost from the rent
- if nothing happens, go ahead using the firm that gave the most reasonable estimate. Get a receipt
- work out how much rent you will withhold and write to the landlord explaining what you intend to do.

All this is to cover yourself if the landlord sues you. Remember that you can deduct only the cost of a *repair* in this way, not compensation for damage done, for example by damp: you have to sue him for that.

I have been unhappy for a long time about the management of the block of flats where I live. The exterior is a mess, the stairs are badly lit and dirty, there are slates missing from the roof and I'm sure I can smell damp in my flat. The flats are managed by an agent. He is never in when I 'phone and does not reply to letters. When I have managed to get to see him, he has made promises which have not been kept. Basically, I think he is incompetent, and he has never done anything to maintain the flats. What can I do about this situation?

The first thing to do is to get together with your fellow flat owners. You all have a common grievance, and should share the cost of sorting it out. You might like to consider setting up a proper tenants' association: you can require the landlord to recognise your association if it represents 60 per cent of you (get legal advice if he refuses). A recognised association will increase your bargaining power.

However, in your case it sounds as if you really need to get rid of the agent. There is a legal procedure for doing this, under the Landlord and Tenant Act 1987, and you should seek legal advice about it. Take along a copy of the lease and a list of the problems you have had.

You first need to serve formal notice on the landlord, detailing all the failures to maintain the flats, and notifying him of your intention to apply for a court order replacing his agent with an approved 'manager' if the maintenance and repairs are not brought up to scratch within a specified time. If, after this, the work is still not done, you then apply for the court order. The court will decide who the manager should be, how he should be paid and what his role will be.

I live in a flat and have to contribute towards the maintenance of a communal garden and other facilities. Do I have the right to see how the service charge is fixed?

Yes, you do. You have the right to receive a written statement of the costs which are reflected by the service charge. You should ask your landlord for a copy of the accounts. If there are more than four flats in your block, it should be certified by an independent qualified accountant. If you have any doubts about the accounts, you can insist on seeing invoices for the costs listed. If your landlord fails to provide a written statement, or refuses to let you see invoices, he is guilty of a criminal offence under the Landlord and Tenant Act 1985.

14 Home improvements

Few people would claim that their homes couldn't be improved in some way. Possible improvements range from relatively simple measures to improve comfort and convenience or reduce the burden of maintenance, to large-scale conversions and extensions.

When considering home improvements weigh up these four factors:

- the cost, and how you can finance it
- the extent to which the improvement will make your home better for you to live in
- the potential increase in the value of your home should you decide to sell it
- the effect on home maintenance

The ideal home improvement would cost less than it would add to the value of the house, would make it more comfortable or convenient to live in and would reduce the amount of maintenance required. Unfortunately it's rarely possible to achieve all these simultaneously – more often, the decision whether to opt for a particular home improvement involves balancing the potential advantages against some disadvantages.

Until 1988, interest payments for loans to finance home improvements could be offset against income tax, in the same way as mortgages and other loans for the purchase of property. This is no longer the case, however, and even if you arrange for the loan to be added to an existing mortgage you will only get tax relief on the amount advanced for the original purchase.

Improvements which don't involve building on

Cavity-wall insulation

Cavity-wall insulation involves drilling holes in the masonry and injecting insulating material into the spaces within cavity walls. Up to one third of the heat in a house escapes through the walls, so cavity-wall insulation can reduce your heating bills substantially. Although it's unlikely to increase the value of your home much, cavity-wall insulation will pay for itself in about six years.

Three types of material are used: polystyrene beads or granules, blown mineral fibre and urea-formaldehyde (UF) foam. Employ only a specialist installer. For UF foam, the contractor should be registered with the British Standards Institution and be prepared to guarantee that the work will comply with BS5618. For other materials, ensure that the product to be used is approved by the British Board of Agrément. In all cases, make sure that the installer is prepared to give you a long-term guarantee, and that this can be transferred to future owners.

A guarantee is important: cavity-wall insulation can occasionally encourage penetrating damp because the insulating material bridges the gap between the 'leaves' of masonry in the walls.

UF foam gives off formaldehyde fumes while it's curing; if you think that you or anyone else in the house is likely to be susceptible, choose one of the other materials.

Rot-proof 'timber'

Wooden fascias, barge boards and exterior cladding require disciplined maintenance to keep rot at bay. A number of firms now offer extruded UPVC sections as an alternative to timber in these applications. UPVC is a type of plastic; it needs no painting and can't rot, so maintenance is virtually eliminated.

Even UPVC won't last for ever, though, and because these products haven't been in widespread use for as long as the installers claim they should last, there's still some doubt over their reliability in the long term.

As well as products to replace timber forming part of the house, UPVC fencing is now available.

Installing central heating

Installing central heating, particularly with a gas-powered boiler, is a home improvement which meets all the criteria laid down at the beginning of this chapter: it adds considerably to comfort and convenience, the cost will generally be recouped in full by the corresponding increase in the value of the house, and it usually means that the burden of maintenance will be reduced in comparison to 'traditional' heating arrangements.

Designing a central heating system from scratch is quite complicated.

Potential home improvements compared

	For	Against
Cavity-wall insulation	• Will pay for itself in reduced heating bills	• Very little effect on value of house • Can encourage damp
Exterior woodwork replaced with upvc	• Greatly reduced maintenance	• Very little effect on value of house
Add conservatory	• Improvements in comfort and convenience	• Modest impact on value of house
Install central heating	• Big improvements in comfort and convenience • May recoup most or all of cost in increased value of home	
New fitted kitchen	• Big improvement in convenience	• Relatively little impact on house value
New garage	• Should recoup all of cost by increasing value of house	• A new building to maintain
Replacement double-glazed windows	• Some improvement in comfort • Big reduction in maintenance	• Cannot recover cost by savings in energy • Can *reduce* value of house if unsympathetic to overall style
Loft conversion	• Extra living space without increasing overall size of house	• Likely to recoup no more than half of cost in increased house value
Add extra bedroom	• Increased living space • May recoup most or all of cost by increasing value of house	• Likely to recoup less (may even *reduce* value of house) if materials and style inappropriate to existing structure
Add extra room downstairs	• Increased living space	• Less impact on house value than adding extra bedroom

Even if you're not inclined to take on the whole job yourself, some knowledge of system design will be very helpful in assessing quotations you receive from prospective installers. For more information, see *The Which? Book of Plumbing and Central Heating* – details on p. 144.

Re-fitting your kitchen or bathroom

Re-planning your kitchen and installing new appliances may make life a good deal easier, though it's unlikely to add much to the market value of the house.

Much the same is true for bathrooms, though the cost should be substantially less than for re-fitting the kitchen.

Replacement windows and doors

In the past, the energy-saving potential of replacement double-glazing was sometimes greatly exaggerated. In fact, in most cases it would take something like 100 years for the likely savings in energy to repay the original cost of installation.

But there can be a substantial benefit because aluminium and upvc window frames eliminate almost all the maintenance associated with traditional wooden window frames. Aluminium frames are generally fitted in a hardwood surround. This requires some maintenance, though a coat of preservative stain every couple of years will usually be sufficient. upvc frames generally fit directly into the masonry, so no timber is involved.

Installing replacement windows does not guarantee an increase in the value of the house. New windows in styles which are not sympathetic to the general appearance of a house tend to stand out like sore thumbs, and will reduce rather than enhance its value. You should also beware of replacing traditional opening casement windows with fixed replacement windows, thereby cutting off a potential means of escape from a fire.

Loft conversions

If your loft space is suitable, a conversion can be a very successful way to gain extra living space without increasing the overall size of the house. The conversion needs to be carefully planned and soundly constructed to ensure that it will add to the value of the house.

A 'full' conversion, meeting all the requirements of the Building Regulations, won't be cheap, though it's likely to be less costly than building on the same volume of space in the form of a ground-floor extension.

Improvements involving building on

An obvious way of increasing your living space is to build on to your existing house. What you build will depend on what extra space you need – bedrooms, a utility room, a play room, a study or perhaps a conservatory.

The golden rule with all extensions is that the style, the materials used and the method of construction should blend in with the existing house. Ideally, an extension should look as though it's always been there. If you stick to this rule, you increase your chances of recouping most or all of the cost of building the extension through the increase in the value of the house.

Conservatories

Many types, styles and sizes of prefabricated conservatories are available. Most conservatories do not qualify as 'habitable rooms', and are therefore outside the scope of the Building Regulations.

The main building work usually consists of providing a suitable foundation: often just a concrete slab. When comparing quotes, make sure it's clear whether or not the foundation is included in the price.

Aluminium- and upvc-framed conservatories should involve little maintenance. Timber-framed conservatories, on the other hand, require regular attention to keep them in good condition.

Garages

A garage is a valuable asset to a house. If you have the space to build one, you should be able to recoup all the cost through the corresponding increase in the market value of the house.

The disadvantage is that the garage is a new building to maintain, though this may be offset by a reduction in the maintenance required on the car itself. You may also be able to get a reduction in your car insurance premium: insurance companies usually increase premiums for cars which are kept outdoors overnight.

Ground-floor extensions

A ground-floor extension can be a big contribution to easing the pressure on your existing living space. Carefully planned, it can increase the value of the house to cover most of the building costs, though ground floor extensions tend to be less effective in this respect than extra bedrooms.

Extra bedrooms

Because houses tend to be classified by the number of bedrooms they have, adding extra bedrooms can increase the market value of a house substantially. However, take care that the house doesn't become 'top heavy', with too many bedrooms for the living space available on the ground-floor.

Planning permission

Whether you need to get planning permission for a home improvement or extension depends on the scale of the work and the extent to which it affects the external appearance of the house.

Except in the case of buildings which are 'listed' because of their architectural importance, work which is confined to the inside of the house does not need planning permission. Nor does external maintenance and repair – such as repointing the brickwork – which doesn't change the external appearance.

You can also enlarge a house to a limited extent without planning consent. This is known as 'permitted development' and allows you to build an extension of not more than 70 cubic metres (50 cubic metres in Scotland) or 15 per cent of the original volume of a detached or semi-detached house (up to a maximum of 115 cubic metres), or up to 50 cubic metres or 10 per cent for a terraced house. The volume of the original house is worked out from the external dimensions, including the roof, as it stood on 1st July 1948 or as it was built, if it was after that date. The new building must be no higher than the original roof, and any part within two metres of a site boundary must be no more than four metres high. It must not project beyond the original building line on any side facing a road and the area covered should not exceed 50 per cent of the available ground. These rules apply to extensions attached to the house and also to detached garages within 5 metres of the house. The new building must be an extension of the existing living space – if it is to be occupied as a separate dwelling (by an elderly relative, for example) it will need planning consent even though it meets the requirements for permitted development in other respects.

There are a number of other rules for permitted developments relating to sheds, greenhouses, porches, storage tanks for central heating oils, hardstandings, gates, fences and walls.

The best advice is to consult your local authority Department of Planning and Building Control if you're contemplating any additional building work, even where you think it should qualify as a permitted development. Where planning permission is required, it must be obtained before the work starts, and the local authority can insist that you demolish buildings which exceed the limits for permitted development where consent has not been granted.

Applying for planning consent

Your local authority Department of Planning and Building Control will tell you what details they need of any proposed development. The normal requirement is for a detailed drawing showing the construction of the new building, with before and after exterior views and a small site plan.

You will have to enclose a fee with your application. Fees are based on a scale which reflects the likely cost of the work.

If your home is a listed building, you will also have to apply for listed building consent, even for work which would normally be allowed as permitted development.

In England and Wales, the local authority will send notices to your neighbours informing them that they have received your application. In Scotland, you have to do this yourself. Either way, it will usually pay you to keep your neighbours

fully informed of what you intend to do.

Building Regulations approval

Any new building work has to be approved under the Building Regulations (or Building By-laws in Inner London). You have to make a separate application for approval under the Building Regulations, accompanied by suitable drawings and a fee. If the intended work is approved, the Department of Building Control will send an inspector to look at the progress of the building work once it is under way, and for a final inspection when it is complete.

Financing home improvements

If you're building on to your home, and particularly when you expect the extension to add significantly to the value of the house, it may make sense to increase the amount of your mortgage. Most lenders will want to satisfy themselves that you've obtained a number of quotes for the work, and that the building will be of a high standard.

Otherwise, you should find it easy to borrow the necessary funds from another source – a bank or finance

company, for example – as a loan secured on your home. However, this might be unwise where the work is unlikely to increase the market value of the house. In these circumstances, an unsecured personal loan would be a better bet.

Grants are available for some types of home improvement work. You can get an **intermediate grant** to help meet the cost of putting 'standard amenities' in a house which doesn't have them. The standard amenities are an inside WC, a bath or shower, a kitchen sink, a hand washbasin and hot and cold water supplies to these, as appropriate. **Repair grants** may be available for pre-1919 homes which need extensive structural repairs – routine maintenance doesn't qualify. **Improvement grants** may be available for homes built before 1961, for putting in a damp-proof course, electrical work, repointing, making the front door water-tight and for taking out a fireplace or chimney breast.

Intermediate grants are mandatory, whereas repair and improvement grants are available for the disabled and in housing action areas and general improvement areas. For details of grants in your area, contact your local authority Department of Planning and Building Control.

Useful addresses

A number of organisations are referred to throughout this book, as potential sources of information and specialist advice, as a first step to finding a qualified tradesman or to help you resolve disputes. Other organisations are not mentioned specifically elsewhere, but may be useful to you in particular circumstances.

Architects Registration Council
of the UK
73 Hallam Street
London W1N 6EE
Tel: 071-580 5861

Architects and Surveyors Institute
15 St Mary Street
Chippenham
Wiltshire SN15 3JN
Tel: 0249 444505

Association of British Manufacturers
of Mineral Insulating Fibres
39 High Street
Redbourn
Hertfordshire AL3 7LW
Tel: 058285 4624

British Board of Agrément
PO Box 195
Bucknalls Lane
Garston
Watford
Hertfordshire WD2 7NG
Tel: 0923 670844

British Cement Association
Wexham Springs
Slough SL3 6PL
Tel: 0753 662727

British Institute of Architectural
Technicians
397 City Road
London EC1V 1NE
Tel: 071-278 2206

British Ready Mixed Concrete
Association
1 Bramber Court
2 Bramber Road
London W14 9PB
Tel: 071-381 6582

British Security Industry
Association Ltd
Security House
Barbourne Road
Worcester WR1 1RS
Tel: 0905 21464

British Standards Institution
2 Park Street
London W1A 2BS
Tel: 071-629 9000

British Wood Preserving and Damp-
proofing Association
6 The Office Village
4 Romford Road
London E15 4EA
Tel: 081-519 2588

Building Centre
131 West Nile Street
Glasgow G1 2RX
Tel: 041-333 9701

Building Centre
26 Store Street
London WC1E 7BT
Tel: 071-637 1022

Building Employers Confederation
82 New Cavendish Street
London W1M 8AD
Tel: 071-580 5588

Building Research Establishment
Bucknalls Lane
Garston
Watford
Hertfordshire WD2 7JR
Tel: 0923 894040

Cavity Foam Bureau
PO Box 79
Oldbury
Warley
West Midlands B69 4PW
Tel: 021-544 4949

Chartered Institute of Arbitrators
International Arbitration Centre
75 Cannon Street
London EC4N 5BH
Tel: 071-236 8761

Chartered Institute of Building
Englemere
Kings Ride
Ascot
Berkshire SL5 8BJ
Tel: 0344 423355

Chartered Institution of Building
Services Engineers
Delta House
222 Balham High Street
London SW12 9BS
Tel: 081-675 5211

Council of Registered Gas Installers
PO Box 15
Basingstoke
Hampshire RG24 0WZ
Tel: 0256 819810

Draught Proofing Advisory
Association Ltd
PO Box 12
Haslemere
Surrey GU27 3AN
Tel: 0428 54011

Electrical Contractors' Association
ESCA House
34 Palace Court
London W2 4HY
Tel: 071-229 1266

Electrical Contractors' Association of
Scotland
Bush House
Bush Estate
Midlothian EH26 0SB
Tel: 031-445 5577

External Wall Insulation Association
PO Box 12
Haslemere
Surrey GU27 3AN
Tel: 0428 54011

Federation of Master Builders
14–15 Great James Street
London WC1N 3DB
Tel: 071-403 7177

Glass and Glazing Federation
44–48 Borough High Street
London SE1 1XB
Tel: 071-403 7177

Guarantee Protection Trust
PO Box 77
27 London Road
High Wycombe
Buckinghamshire HP11 1BW
Tel: 0494 447049

Guild of Master Craftsmen
166 High Street
Lewes
East Sussex BN7 1XU
Tel: 0273 478449

Guild of Surveyors
Rear of 61 Queens Road
Oldham
Lancashire OL8 2BA
Tel: 061-627 2389

Heating and Ventilating Contractors'
  Association
ESCA House
34 Palace Court
London W2 4JG
Tel: 071-229 2488

Incorporated Association of Architects
  and Surveyors
Jubilee House
Billing Brook Road
Weston Favell
Northampton NN3 4NW
Tel: 0604 404121

Institute of Building Control
21 High Street
Ewell
Epsom
Surrey KT17 1SB
Tel: 081-393 6860

Institute of Plumbing
64 Station Road
Hornchurch
Essex RM12 6NB
Tel: 040424 72791

Institute of Wood Science
Stocking Lane
Hughenden Valley
High Wycombe
Buckinghamshire HP14 4NU
Tel: 0240 245374

Institution of Electrical Engineers
Savoy Place
London WC2R 0BL
Tel: 071-240 1871

Institution of Structural Engineers
11 Upper Belgrave Street
London SW1X 8BH
Tel: 071-235 4535

Mastic Asphalt Council and
  Employers Federation
Lesley House
6–8 Broadway
Bexley Heath
Kent DA6 7LE
Tel: 081-298 0411

National Association of Loft Insulation
  Contractors
PO Box 12
Haslemere
Surrey GU27 3AN
Tel: 0428 54011

National Association of Plumbing,
  Heating and Mechanical Services
  Contractors
Ensign House
Ensign Business Centre
Westwood Way
Coventry CV4 8JA
Tel: 0203 470626

National Cavity Insulation Association
PO Box 12
Haslemere
Surrey GU27 3AN
Tel: 0428 54011

National Federation of Roofing
  Contractors
24 Weymouth Street
London W1N 3FA
Tel: 071-436 0387

National Home Improvement Council
125 Kennington Road
London SE11 6SF
Tel: 071-582 7790

National House-Building Council
Chiltern Avenue
Amersham
Buckinghamshire HP6 5AP
Tel: 0494 434477

National Inspection Council for
  Electrical Installation Contracting
Vintage House
36–37 Albert Embankment
London SE1 7UJ
Tel: 071-582 7746

National Supervisory Council for
  Intruder Alarms Ltd
Queensgate House
14 Cookham Road
Maidenhead
Berks SL6 8AJ
Tel: 0628 37512

Office of Fair Trading
Chancery House
Chancery Lane
London WC2A 1SP
Tel: 071-242 2858

Royal Incorporation of Architects in
  Scotland
15 Rutland Square
Edinburgh EH1 2BE
Tel: 031-229 7205

Royal Institute of British Architects
66 Portland Place
London W1N 4AD
Tel: 071-580 5533

Royal Institution of Chartered
  Surveyors
12 Great George Street
London SW1P 3AD
Tel: 071-222 7000

Royal Institution of Chartered
  Surveyors
9 Manor Place
Edinburgh EH3 7DN
Tel: 031-225 7078

Royal Society of Ulster Architects
2 Mount Charles
Belfast BT7 1NZ
Tel: 0232 323760

Royal Town Planning Institute
26 Portland Place
London W1N 4BE
Tel: 071-636 9107

Royal Town Planning Institute
15 Rutland Square
Edinburgh EH1 2BE
Tel: 031-337 3423

Scottish Building Employers
  Federation
13 Woodside Crescent
Glasgow G3 7UP
Tel: 041-332 7144

Scottish and Northern Ireland
  Plumbing Employers' Federation
2 Walker Street
Edinburgh EH3 7LB
Tel: 031-225 2255

Society for the Protection of Ancient
  Buildings
37 Spital Square
London E1 6DY
Tel: 071-377 1644

Society of Architects in Wales
75a Llandennis Road
Rhyd-y-penau
Cardiff CF2 6EE
Tel: 0222 762215

Society of Surveying Technicians
Drayton House
30 Gordon Street
London WC1H 0BH
Tel: 071-388 8008

Thatching Advisory Service
29 Nine Mile Ride
Finchampstead
Berkshire RG11 4QD
Tel: 0734 732361

Women and Manual Trades
52–54 Featherstone Street
London EC1Y 8RT
Tel: 071-251 9192

Building materials

This section gives a guide to the basic building materials mentioned in the book. It explains what's available and the quantities and sizes in which various materials are normally supplied, and offers a few simple guidelines to help you work out how much you need.

Timber

Softwood for general constructional work in buildings is usually either Baltic redwood or Scots pine (*pinus sylvestris*), or Baltic whitewood or European spruce (*picea abies*). The redwood is slightly heavier and more durable. For joinery – doors and windows – hemlock or Douglas fir may be used. Hemlock has properties very similar to ordinary redwood, but Douglas fir (also known as Oregon pine and Columbian pine) is stronger and more resistant to rot, and is a good choice for softwood exterior doors, for example. Western red cedar is a softwood with very good durability used for shingles and weather-boarding.

Timber is sold in metric sizes, but these are based on the old Imperial sizes. Standard lengths are 1.5m, 1.8m, 2.1m, corresponding approximately to the old lengths of 5ft, 6ft and 7ft.

Sawn timber is sold in actual sizes, but for most purposes you will need planed timber. This is sold by the size of the sawn timber before planing, so that planed timber of nominal size 22 by 50mm, say, will actually be about 18 by 44mm, and you must allow for this when ordering.

Hardwoods are considerably more expensive than softwoods, but stronger and more resistant to fungal attack and hence to rot.

Bricks

Types of brick are named after the clays used, the manufacturing processes and the places where they are or were traditionally made.

Bricks are classified according to use, as **commons**, **facing bricks** or **engineering bricks**. Common bricks are suitable for general work, especially where appearance is not important such as where the bricks are to be plastered or rendered. Facing bricks are specially prepared or selected to give an attractive appearance. Engineering bricks are used where special strength or low water absorption are required. Within these classificiations bricks are further divided by quality as **internal**, **ordinary** or **special**. Internal quality are suitable only for indoor use, ordinary quality for normal exposure in the external face of a building and special quality bricks for conditions of extreme exposure.

The standard size is 215 by 102.5 by 65mm, to give a nominal size with 10mm of mortar close to the old Imperial size of 9 by $4^1/_2$ by 3 inches. A number of 'standard special' bricks are also available – **closers**, **squints** and **bullnoses**, for example – for use at corners and copings. Soft, sandy bricks known as **rubbers** and **cutters** are also available and are designed to be easy to shape for arches and decorative effects.

If you need new bricks to match existing brickwork, the best way is undoubtedly to take one of the old bricks with you (more if they vary a good deal) when you go to order the new ones. Even so, you need to take care: most bricks change their appearance over time as a result of weathering. The plans of your house held by your local authority Department of Building Control may include a specification for the bricks used.

Bricks are normally supplied in packs of 390, strapped to a pallet for ease of transportation. A pack like this weighs about a tonne, so it's very difficult to move about. Make sure you have a suitable number of bricks delivered.

Building blocks

Building blocks are made from concrete, Dense blocks contain gravel or limestone as an aggregate – see Cement, below. Lightweight blocks contain clinker, pulverised fuel ash, expanded clay or foamed slag.

The standard with and height are 448 and 219mm, equivalent to two bricks wide and three bricks high. Thicknesses range from 64 to over 200mm. Dense blocks weighs between about 14 and 45kg each, depending on thickness; lightweight blocks are about half the weight of dense blocks of the same size. Lightweight blocks offer much better thermal insulation and have generally superseded the dense blocks.

Cement

Portland cement is the basis for most types of mortar, render and concrete. Four grades are commonly available: **ordinary** Portland cement for general work, **rapid-hardening** cement for when time is of the essence, **low-heat** cement for large masses of concrete and **sulphate-resisting** cement for use where a high proportion of sulphates are likely to be present in the soil. Ordinary Portland cement will be suitable for most maintenance jobs.

For mortar and render, cement is mixed with sharp sand in proportions of one part cement to two to four parts of sand. Mix the dry ingredients thoroughly and add only enough water to make a workable mixture – if you make the mixture too wet it won't stay put. For bricklaying, plasticisers are available to make the mixture easier to work.

For concrete, the cement is mixed with sand and an aggregate such as gravel or crushed stones, in proportions of roughly 1:2:4 – see

Working Out How Much To Buy, below. Small quantities of concrete can be mixed by hand, but it's a laborious process and you may prefer to hire a cement mixer. Cement is usually supplied in 50kg bags, though d-i-y shops and stores usually offer smaller quantities. You can store unused cement for a short time, keeping it clear of the ground and as dry as possible. But concrete has a great affinity for water and the chances are that after a period of storage cement will be rock-hard.

For large quantities, buy the concrete ready-mixed. Potential suppliers will be listed in Yellow Page under Concrete, Ready-mixed. Ready-mixed concrete is supplied in cubic metres, each cubic metre weighing over two tonnes. So try to arrange for the wet concrete to be discharged as close as possible to the point of use. If you have to barrow it, put down planks to prevent the barrow sinking in soft ground and to make it easy to get up or down steps.

Sand and gravel

Materials such as sand and gravel are normally supplied in cubic metres. D-i-y shops and stores usually offer bags of smaller quantities – 25 or 38kg for example – but on a £ per kg comparison this is usually an expensive way to buy them.

A cubic metre of sand or loose gravel weighs about 1.5 tonnes. If you have sand delivered and store it on the drive, say, keep it well covered: it's a magnet for cats and dogs.

Working out how much to buy

Working out how much of the individual ingredients you need to produce a given volume of mortar or concrete can be tricky. The volume of the mixture will be much less than the sum of the volumes of the separate materials, because in the mixture the finer materials fill the spaces between the particles of the coarse materials.

Beware when converting cubic yards to cubic metres (or vice versa). A metre is longer than a yard, and in cubic measure the difference is about 30 per cent: one cubic metre is 1.31 cubic yards.

For mortar or render, the volume of the mixture will be roughly equal to the volume of the sand used, and you'll need ten 50kg bags of cement for each cubic metre of sand in a typical 1:3 mixture.

For concrete, the volume of the mixture will be roughly equal to the volume of the aggregate used, and you'll need $7^1/_2$ 50kg bags of cement and $^1/_2$ a cubic metre of sand for each cubic metre of aggregate in a typical 1:2:4 mix.

Roofing slates and tiles

As with bricks, these are available in a wide range of types and styles, and the best way to make sure you buy the right ones is to take an old one with you.

Roofing felts

These consist of felts impregnated with bitumen, usually coated on one side with sand or mineral chippings. Three types are available:

Type 1	Fibre base	$0.9-3.6 \text{ kg}/m^2$
Type 2	Asbestos base	
		$0.7-3.6 \text{ kg}/m^2$
Type 3	Glass fibre base	
		$1.8-3.2 \text{ kg}/m^2$

Types 2 and 3 should be used when fire resistant is important.

Roofing felts are supplied in rolls 4.6 or 9.3m long and 910mm wide.

Glass

Sheet glass is readily available in sizes up to 2m long and 1.2m wide, and thicknesses up to 10mm. 4mm glass is the usual choice for ordinary windows, 6mm glass for larger ones.

Toughened glass is produced by heat-treating the glass after cutting to size. Laminated glass incorporates a layer of flexible plastic which prevents penetration and holds the fragments together if it gets broken. Toughened or laminated glass should be used in vulnerable applications such as the lower panels of glazed doors.

As well as being fragile, sheet glass has edges which are extremely sharp – take the greatest care when handling it.

Plaster and plasterboard

Plaster has traditionally been supplied in 50kg bags, though some manufacturers are now using easier-to-handle 35kg and 40kg bags. Plaster doesn't keep for long, so buy only as much as you intend to use right away. As a rough guide, 50kg of undercoat plaster and 25kg of finishing plaster would cover about 10sq m of wall.

Plasterboard is generally supplied as sheets 2.4m long and 1.2m wide (slightly smaller than the old 8ft by 4ft sheets), and in thicknesses of 9.5 or 12.5mm. The sheets weigh between 20 and 35kg each. Square-edged board is also available in smaller sheets 1.8m long and 900mm wide.

Plasterboard is very easily damaged, especially at the corners, and the size of the sheets means it won't fit in any but the very largest of estate cars. Carrying it on a roof rack is almost certain to damage it, too.

Index

Other Books from Consumers' Association

The Which? Book of Plumbing and Central Heating £10.95

Whether you consider yourself a rank amateur or an experienced home plumber, you'll find *The Which? Book of Plumbing and Central Heating* a mine of information on all aspects of domestic plumbing.

It explains what you need in your tool kit, the various pipes and fittings you'll be handling and the four main water systems in your home. The techniques for the various plumbing tasks throughout your home are demonstrated in step-by-step diagrams and the book takes you through all the stages of planning and installing your own central heating system.

The Which? Book of of Do-it-Yourself £14.95

Whatever your level of skill you'll find this book a useful and practical source of reference. For the beginner there are clear, easy-to-follow instructions for a wide range of jobs. Those with more experience will be able to extend their skills and tackle more ambitious jobs with confidence by following the procedures described here. Illustrated with step-by-step drawings, the book covers decorating, plumbing, building, home security, roofs, electricity and maintenance.

The Which? Guide to Planning and Conservation £8.95

Information both for householders seeking planning permission for home improvements and for residents wishing to preserve the area in which they live from unwanted developments.

The Gardening from Which? Guide to Gardening without Chemicals £12.95

From choosing trouble-free plants and controlling pests, diseases and weeds to attracting natural predators, there are hundreds of easy and practical ways for you to get the most out of your garden without resorting to chemicals. The tried and tested advice in this book covers reorganising your garden to minimise problems; stopping slugs and snails from feasting on your plants; avoiding blackspots and mildew on your roses; preventing maggots from ruining your apples and much more. Fully illustrated with colour photographs and line drawings throughout.

The Gardening from Which? Guide to Successful Propagation £11.95

Drawing on the expertise of leading specialists from all over Britain, this guide contains a wealth of sound advice – much of which has never before been revealed to the amateur gardener. Using step-by-step diagrams and colour photographs, the correct propagation methods are explained for over 1,000 different plants, including trees and shrubs, rock plants, heathers, herbs, pond plants, fruit and vegetables.

These are just a few of the books published by Consumers' Association. For a complete list or to order any of the above, please write to Consumers' Association, Gascoyne Way, Hertford X, SG14 1LH. Cheques/postal orders should be made payable to Consumers' Association.

Prices are correct at the time of going to press and postage and packing are free.